To John —

Christmas '81

Love, Topsy

Showing Off in America

From
Conspicuous Consumption
to
Parody Display

BY JOHN BROOKS

Showing Off in America

An Atlantic Monthly Press Book
LITTLE, BROWN AND COMPANY   Boston / Toronto

Library of Congress Cataloging in Publication Data

Brooks, John, 1920–
  Showing off in America.

  "An Atlantic Monthly Press Book."
  1. Social classes — United States.   2. Social Status.   3. Consumers — United States.   4. United
States — Social life and customs — 1971–   I. Title.
HN90.S6B76   305.%'0973   81-1984
                                AACR2
ISBN 0-316-10967-3

A portion of this book appeared in *The New Yorker* in considerably different
form under the title "A Friendly Product," and other portions have
appeared in *The Atlantic*.

ATLANTIC-LITTLE, BROWN BOOKS
ARE PUBLISHED BY
LITTLE, BROWN AND COMPANY
IN ASSOCIATION WITH
THE ATLANTIC MONTHLY PRESS

Designed by Janis Capone

*Published simultaneously in Canada
by Little, Brown & Company (Canada) Limited*

PRINTED IN THE UNITED STATES OF AMERICA

To Peter Davison

Contents

Showing Off in America

Fighting with Property

A more or less random sampling of recent events and situations in modern America, each of them trivial in itself, suggests a pervasive madness — subtler than the great madnesses of, say, war or inflation, but not necessarily less important — to be at large in our society.

A young professor of neurobiology, for example, black, neatly bearded, wearing an open collar and a gold chain, is depicted in a whiskey advertisement printed in a quality magazine, surrounded by a mass of electronic equipment of indeterminate function. His home, we are told, is Cambridge, Massachusetts; his age is thirty-two; his hobbies are jungle exploration, film making, and archery. His latest accomplishment: "While continuing neurobiological research in the South American jungle, he discovered a little-known Bush Afro-American tribe. . . . " And his Scotch: Dewar's White Label, which is, of course, the product being advertised. But to whom, exactly, is the fact that such a person prefers Dewar's White Label expected to commend that brand? Neurobiologists? Blacks? Bearded men, or women who admire them? Wearers of gold chains? Residents of Cambridge? Jungle explorers, film makers, archers, thirty-two-year-olds?

Again: in 1978, at a peak of airline rate-cutting, American Airlines offered a full-fare flight about which it clearly stated that the advantage to the customer over a much cheaper "super-saver" flight was — not that the seats were wider, not that the plane was faster or the service better, not that the food or drink was better or more plentiful, but solely and simply that "your neighbors on the flight will be full-fare customers," not super-saver customers. The same year, Letitia Baldridge in *The Amy Vanderbilt Complete Book of Etiquette* told her readers that at bachelor dinners preceding weddings there is "no longer any need to smash champagne glasses" after the toasts (no explanation of why the necessity had previously existed, or of why or how it had passed); and Abigail Van Buren — "Dear Abby" to newspaper readers — reassured a worried correspondent that it should not be considered "cheap" to deliver Christmas cards by hand in order to save postage.

Yet again: at about the same time, watch manufacturers were competing to produce the world's thinnest watch; the apparent winner being Concord Watch Corporation, a Swiss concern, with its Delirium I, thickness one-sixteenth of an inch, or about the same as that of a dime, price (much of it presumably for the thinness), $4,400. Readers of a popular best-seller were being told that an important route to office power was the wearing of Gucci loafers, while as for a competing brand — visibly different, but not intrinsically inferior — the author was sneering with just a trace of irony, and indeed with an unmistakable trace of hysteria, "Florsheim shoes! The ultimate foot put-down, along with people who wear anklet socks." And around New York and other large cities, people were lining up at the doorways of "discos" to test their social rank by finding out whether or not they would be admitted to watch transvestites, drug abusers, homosexuals, sado-masochists, and heterosexuals dance and cavort — the sole arbiter of each petitioner's social fate being the disco doorman, of no discernible social status himself except what flowed from his position, who made his decisions on the basis of personal acquaintance, dress, or sheer whim, the preferred form of dress (apart from transvestism) generally being either blue jeans or traditional formal wear, and the least preferred being conventional business clothes.

And at well-to-do beach resorts near New York, a professional person picking up driftwood for the fireplace on a winter beach was treated by his peers, if any of them caught him at it, with patronizing kindness, which they tried to temper by saying, "It makes such pretty colors when it burns, doesn't it?" But in view of the fact that the peers were making no attempt to pick up wood themselves, it was clear that for them the prospective beauty of the colors was a lesser consideration beside the loss of self-esteem they would suffer if they were to lean over and do it, too.

Finally, at a higher level of madness, or desperation, so many men had had and were having synthetic wig fibers implanted in their intrinsically bald scalps, quite often at the cost of subsequent bleeding, sores, itching, and infection sometimes requiring surgery, that the situation was coming to be considered a public-health problem. And — to show that the madness was exportable, even to distant and nominally contrasting cultures —

Komsomolskaya Pravda, the Communist youth organ of Russia, reported on a young man in Moscow who thought he had defeated the absence of Western-style jeans in his country at that time by going to great pains to have a Western-style pair made specially for him by hand — only to be crushed when the friend he had been trying to impress commented only, "Where is the label?"

What, we may well ask, accounted and accounts for such odd behavior?

The answer, surely, is that the explanation lies in the set of phenomena and motivations first systematically described and analyzed in 1899 by Thorstein Veblen in his book *The Theory of the Leisure Class*. Although Veblen since then has been honored by the growth of a school of American academic social thought that traces all contemporary comment on and criticism of American institutions to him, his name even today is little known outside the academies. Although *The Theory of the Leisure Class* caused a great stir in academic circles on its publication, and has continued to interest social theorists ever since then, by the time of Veblen's death in 1929, a generation after its first publication, it had sold only about twenty thousand copies and was, for the moment, hardly selling at all.

Veblen's popular reputation and his book's sales have had their ups and downs since then, with the downs predominating. Yet curiously enough, his ideas are widely known where his book and even name are not. Probably millions of Americans find it all but second nature to accept the notions of "conspicuous consumption" and "conspicuous waste" — Veblen's most accessible ideas — who cannot identify Thorstein Veblen. His great discovery, that snobbery and social pretense play not a peripheral but a central, even dominant, role in shaping the life of a socially democratic society as opposed to a traditional autocratic one, has found its way into the national psyche. Another curiosity: even in the academic realm, although his theory and its ramifications have been analyzed, dissected, criticized, and reinterpreted to a fare-thee-well, seldom if ever have his categorical comments on specific American phenomena like clothing styles, eating and drinking habits, preferences of taste, lawns, sporting events, and the like been measured against current American customs and attitudes as to the same things, with an eye to discovering what has changed since 1899 and why.

In the later eighteen-nineties, when he was writing *The Theory of the Leisure Class*, Veblen, aged about forty, was working as a low-ranking faculty member at the University of Chicago — the first real job he had ever held in a life of desultory study at various well-established institutions of learning. He was a lazy, unkempt, shambling man with more apparent interest in women students than in academic promotion. On top of that, at Chicago he had to contend with various adverse forces, chief among them the prevailing prejudice against sons of immigrants (he had grown up in Wisconsin and Minnesota in a household in which Norwegian, his father's native tongue, was the first language); a similarly prevailing and even fiercer prejudice against anyone suspected, as he was, of socialist leanings; and his own natural indolence and distaste for dealing with students. His firsthand knowledge of his intended subject, the American leisure class — which he defined as the "propertied non-industrial class," that is, those who by reason of wealth need not work with their hands — was scanty and acquired from a distance. At home in the Middle West, he had seen almost nothing of that class until he had married into it; at Johns Hopkins in Baltimore, where he had studied for a few months in the year 1880 –1881, he had been quartered with a family of impoverished mid-South gentlefolk, who had initiated him (at a landlord-boarder remove) into the distinctive manners of well-bred *nouveaux pauvres;* and at Yale, where he had spent two and a half years getting a Ph.D. in philosophy and political economy, he had had a look at the manners and customs of the gilded youth of the Northeast. That was it: a skimpy course of field research, indeed. On the other hand, like those later students of leisure-class manners, F. Scott Fitzgerald, John O'Hara, and John P. Marquand, he was avid for information; his nose was resolutely, if sardonically, pressed to the window of the rich.

And at Chicago, where he finally got a teaching job in 1891, he was lucky in his scholarly contacts, one in particular. The already renowned anthropologist Franz Boas was then serving as curator of the Field Museum in Chicago. Boas a few years earlier had done extensive studies of the Indians of the Pacific Northwest, and there had observed the Kwakiutl Indian potlatch, which, as almost any schoolchild knows now, was a socially competitive feast the point of which was for the host to show off his wealth and thus enhance his status by giving away lavish presents to all his guests. Sometimes the potlatch host threw caution to the winds and went a step farther. To underline beyond cavil his boundless wealth, he might publicly destroy some of his property — say, by making a bonfire of some of the family's best blankets. Reciprocation of such hospitality was considered mandatory in

Kwakiutl society, and thus the potlatch could be used as a social weapon. To destroy a poorer social rival once and for all, one need only invite him to a potlatch; when he could not afford to give one himself and perpetrate an equally lavish orgy of distribution and destruction, he would instantly drop off everyone's invitation list. Veblen knew all about Boas's findings and conclusions, which had been published in the 1895 *Report of the United States National Museum,* and elsewhere. "Possession of wealth is considered honorable," Boas wrote of the Kwakiutl. ". . . Formerly, feats of bravery counted as well as distribution of property, but nowadays, as the Indians say, 'rivals fight with property only.' " The rivalry, Boas went on, finds "its strongest expression in the destruction of property," and if a rival "is not able to destroy an equal amount . . . without much delay, his name is 'broken.' " Finally — and for Veblen, crucially —Boas insisted that the apparently ridiculous and uneconomic institution of the potlatch "is founded on psychical causes as active in our civilized society as among the barbarian natives of British Columbia." In other words, potlatches, or their equivalent, were being held in Chicago and elsewhere in the United States at that very moment. Possibly, indeed, leisure-class life in America in the eighteen-nineties was a kind of never-ending potlatch.

That idea was all Veblen needed to shake him out of his natural lethargy and send him on his way. Reading Boas on the Kwakiutl, and putting it together with what he had seen of American life in his time, he seems to have experienced a sort of revelation. Veblen never gave Boas credit as a source for his *Theory* (for that matter, he never gave anyone else any credit, either). But there can be no doubt that the genesis, the first strand of the intricate web he would weave, was Boas. After Boas's account of the Kwakiutl, the most familiar and memorable concepts that Veblen handed down to us — those of "conspicuous consumption" and "conspicuous waste" — needed only to be given their names.

The key distinction of Veblen — the one to which we will have to refer constantly in testing his ideas against current American practice — was between what he called the "peaceable savage" and what he called the "predatory barbarian." Those very phrases are purest Veblen, with their overtones of jocular pedantry, and also of the rolling cadences of the Norse sagas that Veblen's father had drummed into his head in his childhood. The whole spiky, difficult, ironic, curiously poetic, and unique personality of the man is expressed in them in cameo form. According to Veblen's suspect anthropology — he was a far better sociologist, even bardic poet, than anthropologist — the peaceable savage represents the earliest stage in the evolution of society, which moves on progressively from peaceable savagery through a series of outright barbarian stages and eventually reaches its current "peaceable barbarian" stage — one in which barbarian tendencies no longer take the form of military heroism, priestly mumbo jumbo, or chattel slavery, but (as with the Kwakiutl and the Gilded Age millionaires) find ample outlet in invidious display of money and property. Meanwhile, traces of the peaceable-savage temperament survive, and are in constant conflict and tension with the dominant predatory-barbarian tendencies.

Let us pin down what Veblen meant by "peaceable savage" and "predatory barbarian." Indeed, we had better, because it is not what the dictionary says they mean.

Having largely invented an entire anthropology of his own — one conspicuously absent from other books on the subject, past and present — he felt free to make the words mean what he thought they should mean. As he conceived himself, and has persuaded so many others to conceive him, he was a man apart, not to be impeded by anthropological orthodoxy or dictionary meanings.

"Predatory barbarism" presents only minor problems of this kind. The predatory barbarian, we have no trouble grasping, is the hunter dragging home the prey; the club-wielding caveman subduing his mate; the Visigoth hordes sweeping down on Rome; Saint George slaying the dragon, or Saint Joan inspiring the troops with the magic of faith; or the robber baron through force, fraud, and chicanery trampling his economic rivals and pillaging the property of others. Also, at another level, the femme fatale reducing strong men to jelly; the con man fattening on the less sophisticated predatory impulses of others; the loan shark or slumlord fattening on the human needs of others; the snob or social climber of either sex living for a succession of small advantages over others; the practical joker, the one-upman, the ambulance-chasing lawyer, the petty cheater at games, the parent who habitually boasts of an offspring's exploits in classroom or at play. The predatory barbarian's key trait is summed up in Veblen's beloved word *invidious*. He lives to weigh himself in the balance against others, and find the others wanting. Veblen believed that the predatory barbarian was the central figure of American society in his time, and it is safe to say that if he were alive now he would say the same about *our* society.

The "peaceable savage" is another matter. Dictionaries treat *barbarian* and *savage* as synonyms, but Veblen does not. In his lexicon, they are opposites. His peaceable savage is a person without a predatory bone in his body. In his heyday, he lives in a society in which forms of employment are not rigidly differentiated or ranked in a hierarchy of esteem, in which class distinctions are vague and unimportant, and in which everybody who is anybody does handwork, thus ruling out the existence of an honored leisure class. Private ownership exists, but it isn't considered very important, because nobody owns much property. The peaceable savage is poor, sedentary, and diligent. He will work — indeed, the "instinct of workmanship" is strong in him — but only for the work's sake, never for manipulation, never to gain advantage. He lacks any desire for wealth, fame, or power over others. His chief pleasures are in workmanship, amiable conversation, and idle curiosity about the world around him. If by chance he should be confronted with a predatory attempt to take advantage of him by force or fraud, he faces the challenge, Veblen tells us, with "a certain amiable inefficiency."

Veblen believed that evidences of peaceable savagery survive in our essentially predatory-barbarian modern culture. (One can't help suspecting that his peaceable savage is a self-portrait as he liked to think of himself, which wasn't necessarily as he was.) He believed that an understanding of the tension in our culture between the two contrasting approaches to life is the key to understanding it. In our own time, the best part of a century after Veblen, we have all seen an occasional pure example of peaceable savagery — say, the moony schoolboy who, forced against his will by the school rules to take part in baseball, becomes the despair of his barbarian peers by sitting at his place in the outfield beatifically picking dandelions, while they ferociously go about the quest of honor, power, and possibly the love of women. Later in life, our beatific friend will doubtless catch the contagion of barbarism to one extent or another, or he may have to adopt it to survive; but for the moment, he is a peaceable savage. It is expressive of society's values that when he crops up, he is usually called a born loser. Thus he is discouraged almost out of existence in his pure form. Veblen dredged up some primitive peoples, the Andamans of India and the Todas of Saharan Africa, as examples of peaceable savages, but he was ready to admit that the evidence for the existence of pure peaceable savagery lies as much in psychology as in anthropology. The peaceable savage is a dream. But he was Veblen's dream, his ideal vision of human life, his lost Edenian to contrast with the people of Outer Darkness that he found around him.*

There can be no doubt that Veblen found, in turn-of-the-century America, staggering evidence of the quest for reputability through display. Fifth Avenue in New York City, the nation's leisure-class showcase, had over the previous two decades become a row of fantastic palaces almost palpably snubbing each other. Their displays of wealth, splendor, and waste — the baroque details of which have been adequately chronicled elsewhere, and need only be touched on here — perfectly fulfilled the Veblenian requirement of being readily translatable into cash figures by the people they were chiefly intended to impress and humiliate. Fifth Avenue was by common

---

*Veblen's theory and key concepts — conspicuous consumption, conspicuous waste, pecuniary decency, pecuniary emulation, industrial exemption, and others — are briefly summarized in Appendix A, page 277.

consent the official national showcase for explicit displays of private wealth, lightly disguised as family residences. For example, the steel tycoon Henry Clay Frick, looking for the first time at the new Vanderbilt mansion on the block between Fifty-first and Fifty-second streets, had a pecuniary rather than an aesthetic reaction. He instantly calculated that the upkeep would cost $300,000 a year. "That would be six per cent on five millions . . . say a thousand dollars a day," he mused, not bothering to mention the architecture. The Vanderbilt mansion, then, had precisely accomplished its purpose — rather than being considered a work of art or a potentially pleasant place to live or to visit, it was, to Frick, a publicly displayed bank account of enviable proportions.

So it was with private railway cars and yachts. The principal feature of William H. Vanderbilt's car, the *Vanderbilt,* was — as the proud owner was careful to let the world know — that it had cost more than the car of the rival railroad man Leland Stanford. J. Pierpont Morgan's third yacht, launched in 1898 while Veblen in Chicago was scribbling away, was three hundred and two feet long — longer, of course, than anyone else's yacht; but even more to Veblen's point was Morgan's comment that anyone who needed to ask the cost of a yacht couldn't afford it. In a few lordly words, Morgan thus drew a circle around those entitled to have yachts, and it was a circle that excluded almost everyone but himself. His remark has perhaps never been surpassed as a succinct statement of predatory invidiousness.

As to the parties of the rich — the literal counterparts of the Indian potlatches — there were tales, repeated in the newspapers, of dinners on horseback; of banquets for pet dogs; of hundred-dollar bills folded into guests' dinner napkins; of a hostess who attracted attention by seating a chimpanzee at her table; of centerpieces in which lightly clad living maidens swam in glass tanks, or emerged from huge pies; of parties at which cigars were ceremoniously lighted with flaming banknotes of large denominations. What came to be accepted as the paradigmatic party of the Gilded Age was the fancy-dress ball given in New York in February, 1897, by Mr. and Mrs. Bradley Martin; for it, at a cost that the host and hostess were glad to estimate publicly as three hundred and seventy thousand dollars, the interior of the Waldorf-Astoria Hotel was converted for an evening into a plausible replica of Versailles. August Belmont came in a suit of gold-inlaid armor valued at ten thousand dollars. The host, in a particularly nice piece of invidiousness, came as Louis XV, the king celebrated for having said, *"Après moi, le déluge."*

And so on. What surely struck Veblen as he read about such doings — so distant from his farm childhood, and even from his sheltered academic lair at the Rocke-feller-supported University of Chicago — was the absence of shame, of tasteful understatement, of noblesse oblige. Those traits — survivals of "peaceable savagery," as he thought of them — had been periodically observable in leisure-class behavior throughout past history, and had been notably present in his own country, particularly in New England and the South, until quite recently. Now they seemed to have been forced offstage entirely in a total triumph of predatory invidiousness. Taking as his reference point an extreme and inevitably transient moment in history, one of those moments of group madness that seem to crop up at intervals, he tried to evolve a theory of social behavior that would be good for all times. Such an enterprise seems on its face to be doomed to failure.

And indeed, in some respects American social changes over four-fifths of a century have made *The Theory of the Leisure Class* obsolete, even ludicrously so. In particular, there have been two crucial changes.

First, the attitude of other classes toward those most vigorously engaged in competitive display — Veblen's "leisure class" — has undergone a radical change. As John Kenneth Galbraith remarked in an essay on Veblen, his was "a time when gentlemen still believed they were gentlemen, and . . . that it was wealth that made the difference. And, by and large, the rest of the population still agreed." That is, others took the leisure class at its own assessment, and both admired and envied its proofs of its status, however bizarre. This is emphatically no longer the case.

True enough, the qualification "by and large," in reference to general acceptance of the leisure class's view of itself in Veblen's time, is necessary and important. There had been among the American yeomanry a certain surly disdain of the pretensions of the rich and the well-bred long before Veblen — certainly since the opening of the West, where the surly disdain chiefly flourished. It found its most eloquent expression in the works of Mark Twain. However, this disdain was directed mainly not at the rich but at the well-bred. Mark Twain had a raucous horselaugh for the refined manners and locutions of the Brahmin poets and intellectuals of Boston, but for most of his life he was much gentler with the more characteristic kind of American rich, the lowbrow kind, and indeed he was pathetically eager to become one of them. Veblen's unrestrained ridicule of the robber barons' vulgar mansions and bejeweled wives was so shocking in its time because it was a social desecration, a guffaw in the middle of a church service. *The Theory of the Leisure Class* for the first time gave Americans general license to laugh at their economic superiors.

They have been doing so in increasing numbers and with increasing volume ever since. Today, lower-class irony about competitive display of the rich is more or less taken for granted. The new millionaire who collects Andy Warhols and raises or buys a monstrous pile on the Long Island dunes — complete with a swimming pool within a few hundred feet of the reasonably swimmable Atlantic Ocean — *expects* to be mocked by the local yeomanry, and, in an economic expression of that mockery, to be outrageously overcharged by them for such services as plumbing, carpentry, and lawn mowing. He does not care. It is those closer to him on the socioeconomic scale, the rival but lesser millionaires down the dune or across the lane, that he seeks to impress. The same applies to the lesser exponent of "pecuniary decency" (decency, in Veblen's personal dictionary, meaning conventionality) in some less exalted purlieu, such as Peoria. The impact of competitive display no longer crosses class lines, or crosses them much less readily than formerly. And, as will be argued presently, irony has now come to figure prominently in display aimed at members of one's own class.

The second great change follows from the first: the "leisure class" as Veblen saw and described it — a national ruling class consisting of winners in the national money game, its numbers running only into the hundreds or thousands, its superiority generally unquestioned, its most extravagant posturings generally held in respect or awe — vanished like a dissipating cloud.

Veblen defined his "leisure class" as those who enjoyed "industrial exemption" — freedom from what we now call blue-collar work. In his time, such people were comparatively few. Now they are a national majority. Leisure itself no longer belongs to the "leisure class." The leading industrialist of today, the lineal descendant of Veblen's leisure-class member, heads such a large and complex organization, which he would not head in the first place unless he had an unusual taste for unremitting work, that he may work at his job ten or twelve hours a day and have almost no leisure time at all, although he maintains the facilities for lavish leisure for the family's benefit and for display; while the hand-working member of a strong union may have short hours, long vacations, and ample time for leisure, although his display takes the modest form of fancy lawn-mowing equipment, fancy automobiles, and perhaps a motor boat. Literally speaking, his has become the nearest thing to an American leisure class.

In the new American structure there seem to be an almost infinite number of "classes," constantly merging and disintegrating and reforming. Membership in these classes — perhaps more accurately called cliques — is based partly on money, but to a far greater extent than in Veblen's time it is based on other factors such as education combined with predilection. Examples of such "classes" might be middle-level suburban corporate executives, factory workers, hippies, Vietnam war protestors, or environmentalists. Russell Lynes in *Snobs,* an astute little book published in 1950, distinguished eight new kinds of snob that he believed had superseded the old social snob: intellectual; regional (Virginia in the South, Boston in the Northeast, San Francisco in the West); moral (either religious or antireligious); sensual ("being able to wrest more pleasure from the flesh than anyone else"); emotional ("I feel more deeply than any one else"); occupational; political; and finally, "reverse" (one who tries too hard not to be a snob). Each of Lynes's categories of snob was, of course, engaged in the characteristic act of snobbery, competitive display; but in each case it was a form of display that, unlike the kind Veblen described, did not require the possession or expenditure of huge sums of money. Display had become a game anyone could play. The leisure class, defined as Veblen defined it, had become nobody and everybody.

These great social changes came about gradually. The fin-de-siècle class lines and attitudes that Veblen built his theory upon were beginning to crack by the time of the First World War, partly because of public revulsion against the excesses of the rich as reflected in various pieces of reform legislation, and particularly as a result of the introduction of an income tax in 1913. It was in the nineteen-twenties that new lineaments of competitive display began to appear clearly. The annual automobile model change, introduced in that decade by General Motors, was a Veblenian development beyond Veblen's 1899 dreams — but with a difference. It was competitive display institutionalized; but the very point of it — to sell more cars and thus make more profit for the manufacturers — was that the display should be available not to hundreds but to millions. (Display of the eighteen-nineties kind was also still available in the automobile business; the Italian manufacturer Ettore Bugatti in 1927 made one model of which just eleven specimens were produced, for sale, so the maker decreed, only to kings.) Other signs and portents of the twenties signaled a trend toward the democratization of competitive display. The expression "keeping up with the Joneses," which was in currency at that time (the comic strip with that name dated from about 1910), expressed the idea of competitive display in connection with one of the commonest of all American names, and the name most commonly used to stand for anybody and everybody. The mythic conspicuous consumer of the twenties, Jay Gatsby in F. Scott Fitzgerald's famous novel, would not have qualified for Veblen's leisure class; the means of his making his pile (a bootlegging ring) and his class and ethnic identification (lower class, possibly Jewish) would not have qualified him for "decency" in the eighteen-nineties, but did in the nineteen-twenties. The parties that constituted Gatsby's instrument of display were attended not by fellow industrialists and not predominantly by fellow millionaires, but by actors, directors, producers, sports figures — the emerging class based on talent and aptitude for self-promotion that was just then coming to be called "celebrities." Hangers-on of no talent or accomplishment, if passably amiable and respectful of their betters, were tolerated and even encouraged as guests, to serve as a claque for the stars. In direct contrast to the potlatch system, Gatsby's guests were not required or expected to return his hospitality; it was assumed that they would lose no face, and would be invited back, on the strength of nothing more than remaining civil and interesting. The arena for large-scale competitive display thus had changed from the old Society to the new and more democratic Café Society, the exploits of which were democratically disseminated in the expanding news media, recently augmented by radio. Reporters for those media came at intervals to Gatsby's mansion just to ask him if he had anything new to tell them.

The nineteen-thirties saw a setback for the progressive democratization of competitive display. In a time of dire national depression, all but a few of the surviving rich came to feel that straightforward display was temporarily in bad taste, and either gave it up or replaced it with counterdisplay; while almost everyone else was in such straits that economic survival tended to force competitive display off the stage entirely. Among a few of the rich and near-rich, fund-raising parties for unionists or for fighters for the Spanish Republic marked the birth of "radical chic" — as Tom Wolfe would later call it — which would then lie doggo for three decades before surfacing again. Display often took the form of conspicuously appearing to love the common man more than one's neighbor did. A nominal act of altruism — "peaceable savagery" in the language that we may call Veblenian — became in substance an act of predatory invidiousness.

The Second World War, along with its preliminaries and aftermath, effectively froze American social change (including change in the role of display) throughout the nineteen-forties, although high wages for manual work in war plants created an enormous group of people who for the first time had discretionary income, and thus became eligible for competitive display. This group would have a large role in determining the course of such display in the postwar world.

In the nineteen-fifties — or rather, the period from 1950 to 1965, since in this case the next major change in the national social texture came in the middle of a decade rather than at the beginning of one — the democratized version of old-fashioned, Veblenian competitive display, based firmly on conspicuous consumption and waste of money, reached its apogee. By common consent of economists, the automobile industry had become the engine of the national economy, and the annual model change the engine of the automobile industry. Upward social mobility, made possible by a rapidly enlarging national economic pie and an increasingly broad distribution of the slices, had reached unprecedented heights. "Status seeking" had become a national preoccupation, as certified by the instant huge success of Vance Packard's *The Status Seekers* when it was published in 1959. Masses of Americans, including many who had previously disdained such activities and attitudes, had come to feel that "trading up" from last year's Ford to this year's Mercury or Oldsmobile, or from last year's three-hole Buick to this year's four-holer, was essential to their personal and social well-being, and that failure to take the upward step meant loss of esteem in one's own eyes and in those of others.

As these automobile status seekers had their prophet in Mr. Packard (or more fundamentally in Veblen, of whom they were probably unaware), the more refined and intellectual strivers upward who continued to disdain the automobile pecking order had *their* prophet in Stephen Potter, an Englishman who earlier in the decade had explained to them how personal and social advantage are gained in nonpecuniary ways through "gamesmanship" — a series of "ploys" calculated to make the gamesman "one up" on the opposition. Predatory invidiousness, for the many rather than the few, was riding high.

And then came a strange development. With the arrival of a recession at the end of the nineteen-fifties, not just manufacturers of automobiles and other goods, but leaders of national government, too, came to believe that predatory invidiousness was essential to the national economic welfare. A "buy now" campaign, personally led by President Eisenhower, urged any and all Americans to buy new cars and other expensive objects immediately, whether they needed them or not — and implicitly, whether the objects were any good or not — in order to bring about economic recovery. ("You auto buy now" became the repulsive slogan of this philosophy.) This was to say that competitive display was now patriotic. Veblen had never dreamed of such a thing. He had never spoken of the national economic effects of his leisure class's conspicuous spending, one way or the other. And indeed, such effects were certainly minute in 1899, because the leisure class had so few members. Builders, architects, caterers, and tradesmen benefited from the wasteful spending of the rich, but the public did not. Such economic effects, good or bad, as the robber barons had came from their work-time rather than their leisure-time activities. But now, with conspicuous display become the habit of millions, it was being urged on everybody as a national duty, without regard to whether the display goods they bought were useful and beautiful, or hideous and shoddy.

This went too far; it was like saying that wars should be encouraged because they buttress the economy and hold down population. A reactive correction came beginning in about 1965, with the rise of environmentalism and the rebirth of the consumer movement. The automobile junkyard and the throwaway bottle, talismans of the period just past, began to be called into question as symbols of the good life in America. At the end of the sixties and on into the seventies, unprecedented inflation made indiscriminate consumer spending appear as at best a mixed blessing for the national economic welfare. The oil shortages that began with the OPEC boycott in 1973 made fuel-guzzling display automobiles and lavish dwellings seem downright subversive. While these things were happening — and partly as a result of them — straightforward Veblenian display did not disappear, but it became muted. The more complex display system of the present began to take shape.

Veblen lives. The whiskey advertisement showing the young neurobiologist illustrates "emulation" at its ultimate development — display that seeks not just to copy others but to be copied. American Airlines' offering for a higher price a seat entitling the holder to sit beside others paying the higher price is an almost laughably bald expression of unveiled invidiousness. Miss Baldridge's advice that champagne glasses "no longer . . . need" to be smashed at bachelor parties is a transparent hint that to smash them may be more esoterically fashionable now than ever before. To smash them now would be not only conspicuous waste but also what Veblen called "veneration of the archaic," an impeccable predatory trait. When "Dear Abby" publicly advises a reader that saving stamps by hand-delivering Christmas cards is OK, she implies that the question of what is "cheap" and what isn't is one of broad general interest, which along with other forms of saving must be submitted to her decision as to their qualification for pecuniary decency. The disco doorman as social arbiter suggests that, in bizarrely changed form, the same social anxiety that drove the robber barons to conspicuous display still exists. The painful and perhaps dangerous practice of having wig fibers implanted in one's scalp suggests that the amount of pain and danger some will endure to achieve "decency" has become not less but greater over the years. The gentry's condescension toward the wood-picker on the resort beach shows how vividly Veblen's "industrial exemption" still lives. The watch that is expensive because it is thin, the popular author's comparison between acceptable Gucci loafers and unacceptable Florsheim ones, and the Russian woman's complaint about the absence of a label on her friend's jeans are so obviously Veblenian in their overtones as to require no comment.

What we note if we look closely at some (though not all) of these examples is the introduction, faint and muted, of a note of irony. Various forces, among them education and the social sophistication that it tends to bring with it, have given rise to a need to laugh at display. Mark Twain's horselaugh has found its way into the fabric of display itself, and given display a new form.

2

Showing Off with Style

Fighting with property eventually gets to be a bore and an embarrassment. A Kwakiutl host burning up blankets, or an American lady seating a chimpanzee at her fine table, is an act that won't run for long; impressive when first presented, on repetition it soon appears silly, and therefore becomes counterproductive as a status-raiser. Veblen argued that fashions in dress, originally so breathtakingly comme il faut that they look beautiful although they aren't, eventually give rise to "aesthetic nausea," thereby leading to a need for new fashions. Similarly, acts of direct competitive display of money and property, such as turn-of-the-century Americans were so prone to, eventually lead to aesthetic depression, vomiting, itching, restlessness, and, worst of all, contempt. If a guest now were to find a chimp at a rich hostess's table, the guest would think, "Oh, my God, Althea is too much," and make a mental note not to go there again. If someone now were to put up a small house with a huge facade painted in trompe l'oeil to look like an antebellum mansion, the neighbors would say, "Pathetic! The Allisons obviously can't afford a big house; why don't they admit it?" In both cases, the competitive display would have failed of its purpose, because the response of others would be feelings not of inferiority, as planned, but of superiority.

More intricate games are needed.

Parody display, the new and rising form of American competitive boasting, is an offshoot of literary parody — surely among the literary modes best adapted to the spirit of our times. Freud and his followers have taught us the importance in our psychic makeup of ambivalence, or mixed feelings. The literary parodist believes that the work he chooses to parody is ridiculous, otherwise he would not want to parody it; but he also thinks it is in some way marvelous, otherwise he would not bother with it. Only the most celebrated writers get parodied. Literary parody is half obeisance, half ridicule. Its essence is ambivalence.

The same is true of parody in life rather than in literature — Action Parody, we may call it. Action Parody is ambivalent in its attitude toward the state of being relatively rich or powerful. It pays tribute to that state by making much of it, but at the same time it is careful to make clear that it is partly kidding. The latter statement may not be entirely sincere — showing off wealth and power may still be the real point of the exercise — but it has to be there to take the curse off. At least on the surface, parody display is showing off wit and irony as much as, and usually more than, showing off wealth and power.*

---

*For a more detailed discussion of parody as the term is used here, see Appendix B, page 285.

The New York City art world is dedicated to constant change in artistic style because of its generally worshipful view of the idea of a constantly advancing "avant-garde." Dedication to this idea gives rise in the art world to a rough but alarmingly precise equivalent of the annual model change in the automotive industry. Moreover, the art world is dominated economically by a small group of collectors who are generally people of fashion, or consider themselves as such, and is dominated culturally by a few museums and galleries, heavily beholden to and dependent upon that same group. As a result, it is a world close to the world of fashion. And fashion is by its nature largely a matter of competitive display. Therefore in the art world we may expect to find a laboratory of the newest styles and variations of competitive display.

And so we do. In the nineteen-fifties, when the Abstract Expressionist (also called Action Painting) movement was first coming to fame, the spatters and smears of paint that were characteristic of that movement tended to look to the uninitiated like designs for home decoration. For example, some of the canvases of Jackson Pollock, the most famous and later the highest-priced artist of the school, were frequently compared to the designs on commercially sold linoleum. But the intention — and, in the view of leading insider-arbiters like art critics and collectors, the achieved intention — of Pollock's works was anything but to divert or soothe momentarily the eye of the artistically uninformed and insensitive masses, as decorated linoleum was supposed to do. Rather, Pollock was perceived by the initiated as trying to express states of being in a new way — to achieve high art. The priests and acolytes of that art reserved their greatest scorn and contempt for those who missed the point and compared

Pollock's canvases to linoleum. Concomitantly, the word *decorative* came to be the worst anathema a critic or collector could lay on the work of an Abstract Expressionist artist. *Decorative* in avant-garde art circles came to be a word with many of the overtones that *bankrupt* had and has in the business world.

Yet by the later nineteen-seventies, numerous annual model changes later, the prevailing attitude had undergone a polar reversal. Now Abstract Expressionism had been relegated to the past; it had joined the Old Masters and Post-Impressionists, fossil objects to be preserved in museums and traded at enormous prices among millionaires, but emphatically not part of the living present (even though its second most celebrated exponent, Willem de Kooning, was still living and working). As for *decorative,* it was now a word of warm praise for the work of new young artists. The attitude of twenty years earlier that had made *decorative* a term of opprobrium was now looked upon patronizingly as the attitude of aesthetic primitives lacking in modern sophistication.

In both the fifties and the seventies, art-scene people who used the word *decorative* were showing off their knowledge and ability to discriminate and appreciate. That is, both groups were engaged in competitive display and emulation. Yet the meaning in one case was precisely the opposite of the meaning in the other. The nineteen-seventies view was a parody of the nineteen-fifties one. The new people of the art world pride themselves, along with their sensitivity to the latest trends and styles and ideas, on their sophistication and self-awareness. Not wholly without justification. They know, for example, that straightforward, irony-free display has come in their circles to be considered "square" — another favorite anathema of theirs — and consequently counterproductive of status. Therefore, to make display palatable to the new taste, they leaven it with a dash of irony. Their use of *decorative* with a value precisely opposite to the one they used to give it is display, all right; but somewhere in the back of their minds they know, and appreciate, that a word used to mean the opposite of what it recently meant is as silly as a conversation in Lewis Carroll.

Next, a couple of phenomena at Harvard University, an institution frequently in the national vanguard as regards cultural style. Enrique Hank Lopez, a recent commentator on the Harvard scene, tells the following story:

> There have been several colorful clerics around Harvard, but few as memorable as Brother Blue, an imaginative, articulate black clergyman who preaches brotherly love in a singular fashion, mixing scripture with Shakespeare in his own inimitable way. Always dressed in bright-blue clothes, with spangles and ribbons that suggest a medieval court jester, he recites soliloquies from "Hamlet," "Henry V," or "Romeo and Juliet" with the sonorous splendor of a seasoned English actor, then suddenly switches to black-dialect interpretations of the same lines.
>
> Shortly after the historic blizzard of 1978, Brother Blue stood on a huge mound of snow in Harvard Square and held a crowd of 500 spectators spellbound with a stunning rendition of "Hamlet." After delivering [a *Hamlet*] soliloquy in a resonant conventional English voice, he paused a moment, smiled at the expectant crowd with a ghetto impishness, then proceeded to talk about "poor old Ham."
>
> "That dude had himself a problem," he said. "The minute his ol' papa died, his mama starts messin' around with his uncle. That's right man, his

daddy's very own brother. Couldn't hardly wait to
hop 'tween those sheets that Brother Bill called in-
cest-you-us. Now you know that anything that
sounds like *that* has got to be bad, real bad. But not
that kinda bad, brother, I mean *bad* bad. So poor ol'
Ham . . ."

American blacks have always shown a particular gift
for social parody. Brother Blue projects that gift into one
of the nation's most elevated intellectual and social mi-
lieus (and one especially blatant about intellectual competitive display) at a time when sophistication is at large
in the land to an extent that it never has been before. His
parody has unusual scope. Cleverly using the scene following a huge snowstorm as a dramatic backdrop, he first
takes off Cambridge high culture (with admiration and
respect, like a true parodist) in his impeccably cultured
recitation of Shakespeare. The unmistakable implication
is: if a black-ghetto product like me can pull this off and
sound plausibly like a Harvard professor or drama student, what's so special about them? And then Brother
Blue shows that there is another string to his bow. With
an abrupt but elaborately artful transition, he switches to
a parody, equally loving and at the same time equally
ironic, of black street language and thought. Brother
Blue's message is that, when you stop to think about it,
Harvard high culture and black culture are equally to be
both admired and ridiculed. He is a parodist of display at
both extremes of the social scale, and his popularity with
students shows how closely he is attuned to the spirit of
his time.

Still at Harvard, we read in the newspapers in 1979,
a decade after self-styled radical students there tore up
part of the campus and took over a building in Harvard

Yard in violent protest against the way the university was being run, there was an "equally angry" demonstration. This time, the demonstrators were students, faculty, local alumni, and members of the university administration, all united in opposition to the presence on the campus of a United Artists crew engaged in making a movie about the 1969 demonstration. Students complained that they were being denied access to the places where the crew was working; students and faculty alike complained that the film makers were polluting the Harvard earth and the Harvard air with plastic artificial snow; a professor tried to knock over one of the crew's cameras, and finally the Harvard administration formally asked the crew to leave the Yard.

Was this merely cultured distaste for the crass ways of the mass entertainment media, or was it a form of parody? Surely it was some of each. An element of irony in a Harvard demonstration in which faculty, students, alumni, and administration were on the same side could hardly escape the notice of anyone who knew anything about the events of 1969. Moreover, an element of irony in a Harvard demonstration against the making of a movie about a Harvard demonstration could hardly escape the notice of anyone, including a Harvard student, alumnus, alumna, or faculty member. Parody — apparently part conscious, part unconscious — seemed to be becoming a way of life on the banks of the Charles River.

In the late nineteen-seventies, a new home-furnishing style made its appearance in certain urban centers noted for their sophistication. Called High-Tech, it was rooted in the use of industrial and institutional equipment in the home. In a High-Tech apartment, all the pipes and support posts are exposed, sometimes as the product of effort as long, loving, and expensive as used to go into concealing them. Fine old hardwood or wide-board pine floors are scrupulously covered with, let's say, the plate used on the decks of destroyers. "Furniture is upholstered with movers' pads, closets are appointed with dry-cleaners' rotating racks, the refrigerator is a hospital blood bank's, bookcases are commercial steel shelving, chests of drawers are stacked swimming-pool baskets, lighting is from factory lamps, and the dining-room table is a restaurant booth," *The New Yorker* explained patiently. The place ends up looking like a nightmarish collage of a factory, attack vessel, emergency room, moving van, cheap restaurant, third-rate resort hotel, et cetera. "We can think of no more fashionable gift than the Rubbermaid commercial twenty-two-gallon cylindrical trash bin with a push-and-swing lid," *The New Yorker* commented. A book by Joan Kron and Suzanne Slesin, entitled *High Tech: The Industrial Style Source Book for the Home*, which immediately became a bible of the movement, warned the reader that many items essential to the new home-furnishing aesthetic would be hard to buy, because the purveyors of industrial and institutional equipment were still used to selling their goods only wholesale. The authors suggested that the would-be buyer of a hospital sink imply to the seller that it is wanted "for a doctor's office you are building," rather than for a powder room; while dealing with restaurant-supply houses, the buyer might "say you are opening a small motel or coffee shop or buying for your club."

(Within a year after that was written, American enterprise had successfully adapted to the problem. Commercial outlets realized that they had discovered a new market, and home-furnishing shops had sprung up specializing in High-Tech and nothing else. Young couples furnishing their first apartments found it less often necessary to pretend to be motel operators or dentists' contractors in order to feather their nests à la mode.)

High-Tech is high-grade parody display. After generations during which the direction of design influence ran from the industrial toward the domestic — corporations installing art collections in their hallways, their executives eliminating desks and other traditional accouterments of commerce from their offices in favor of homelike furnishings and decoration — a reversal of the flow was the most dramatic possible way of attracting attention, at whatever cost in domestic comfort and grace. Moreover, it is clear that the parody is conscious. Those who furnish their places in High-Tech style are well aware of, and exultant about, doing something witty and ironic. They flaunt commercial and industrial objects to prove that they don't have to be serious about such matters. What they may not be so conscious of, if they are conscious of it at all, is High-Tech's relationship to Veblen. As we are instructed by him, "industrial exemption," that sine qua non of leisure-class status, categorically requires members of that class to eschew all styles, objects, and habits of mind that suggest useful work. Furnishings that suggest that and nothing else might be considered a deliberate send-up of Veblen, but for the probability that most of those who adopt such furnishings have barely heard of him.

The pervasiveness of parody display in our time is unmistakable. Pop Art and its satellite movements — despite the heated denials by some of the artists — appear to be rooted in parody of American popular culture.

There are movies now, some of them highly successful, that are parodies of other movies that are themselves parodies. One gets invitations to benefit cocktail parties for mildly liberal political candidates at which the "hosts," as listed on the invitation, are industrial heirs or heiresses, Hollywood agents, famous authors and producers, and big-time real-estate operators. That is, the rich and famous are displaying their status by begging money from the relatively poor and obscure. The studied simplicity of modern architecture of the "less is more" school by implication ridicules the ornateness of earlier buildings. The contemporary International style makes a point of exhibiting the functional and structural elements that were so carefully concealed in earlier buildings, just as High-Tech home decoration does. (Veblen, by the way, must be given credit for anticipating these changes. In *The Theory of the Leisure Class* he wrote, "the endless variety of fronts presented by the better class of tenements and apartment houses in our cities is an endless variety of architectural distress and of suggestions of expensive discomfort. Considered as objects of beauty, the dead walls of the sides and back of these structures, left untouched by the hands of the artist, are commonly the best feature of the building.")

A compulsion of the well-to-do to try to be artists themselves is a key feature of the new tendency to show off style rather than naked wealth. The turn-of-the-century robber barons and their wives probably did not dare, and in any case did not aspire, to attempt creative or artistic flights of their own, beyond competent musical performance of standard works by the wives. To them, artists were lower-class people whose useful role was to produce objects that could serve as currency for competitive display. One need not aspire to emulate a mere employee in a mint. Now we find the wives of rich and prominent men turning up, if not as suburban real-estate agents, then as artists who by whatever means are accorded wall space and even solo shows by well-known art dealers. At a more modest level of pretension, we find a good-sized national vogue among the well-to-do for macramé work, pottery making, or the hand manufacture of harpsichords. (Kits elaborately prepared by enterprising manufacturers simplify the conversion of persons with time and money to burn into hand craftsmen.) It is as if the rich and prominent were saying, "If I am rich and prominent, I must be smart. Now I will show you how smart I am."

Irony is rampant in the world of display. Even death itself does not escape the contagion. Once it was honored in America by direct display of the purest Veblenian kind. A flourishing industry catered to mourners with silk armbands, samplers depicting burial places, expensive posthumous portraits, and even specially designed mourning jewelry (a macabre opportunity for a little vicarious consumption by women). Now mourning hardly exists in any formal sense — almost the sole exceptions are the funerals of admired public figures like John Kennedy — and death itself is treated with degrees of irony proportionate to the fashion aspirations of the survivors. A funeral at which there are no jokes, and even putdowns, at the expense of the departed one are thought to lack something. As Martha V. Pike, history curator at The Museums at Stony Brook, New York, shrewdly points out, in the nineteenth century sex was a taboo topic for serious conversation and death a favored one, while now the exact reverse is the case.

To an extent, parody display is the boasting of the educated. It can be executed by the uneducated if they are dedicated and clever enough, but generally speaking it is practiced by college graduates and (perhaps more to the point) those who spend their lives associating with college graduates. But here is something to be noted: although parody display on the surface is display of style rather than money, in an indirect way it is old-fashioned display of money — the money that went for those college educations. Parody displayers who would rather be caught naked in Times Square than boast about their money seldom think of the matter that way.

But these generalizations must be quickly qualified. The examples of parody display that I have cited all take place in rather rarefied atmospheres; the art world, Harvard, the literary scene, the realm of fashionable urban home decoration. Conversely, we may find parody display in the mean streets of urban ghettos and working-class neighborhoods, not only flourishing but exercising a remarkable upward influence. The astonishingly successful 1978 movie *Saturday Night Fever,* which is loaded with parody display, is very insistent on the skimpy education and working-class, upward-striving status of its characters; that film's influence on the more privileged of our society is shown by the apparent fact that it almost singlehandedly created a nationwide fad for disco dancing.

Parody is the cutting edge at the top and bottom of American display, its twin knives slicing toward the solid middle. Despite these inroads, that middle remains resistant and relatively intact. Display in that sector is still relatively straightforward, uncomplicated, unembarrassed, Veblenian. Thus in the chapters that follow, in which the notions of the social prophet Veblen will be measured against certain manners and customs of our own time, not everything will be parody display. Indeed, not everything will be display at all; display, while the central idea of Veblen's system, is by no means its whole.

Nor is the purpose here only to make mock, either along with our social parodists or at the expense of our naive conspicuous consumers. I would be disappointed if there were not occasions for laughter in what follows. But the point being made is a serious one. Parody, even though it is nominally based on the parodist's sense of superiority to his subject, does not necessarily or usually imply that the parodist feels invulnerable. We cannot help suspecting that the literary parodist, in making his literary subject appear ridiculous, is secretly telling us that he knows in his heart that he could not do as well as the one he ridicules, and is writing the parody partly to set himself in fantasy higher than he knows himself to be in fact. Similarly, the clever insouciance of the parodist of display may mask a painful social insecurity.

As for the dead-center displayers — those middle-class social heirs of the robber barons — their insecurity, and pain, lies right on the surface. For those who rely on bank loans, mortgages, and installment payments, competitive display (penthouses, summer homes, country clubs, sports cars) may and often does lead to disaster. It may drive the not-quite-rich to bankruptcy, divorce, social disgrace, and misery. It may keep the poor in poverty despite rising wages and benefits. We deal with desperate people engaged in desperate actions. Manners can be matters of life and death.

3

Playing Games

Looked at Veblen's way, all American society is a transaction between predatory barbarism and peaceable savagery. Because the transaction is largely unconscious
and morally uneasy rather than rational and fully conscious, the novitiate receives confusing signals. Students
at leadership-training institutions such as the leading
New England preparatory schools are constantly put in
ferociously competitive situations in academic, athletic,
and nonathletic extracurricular activities, and thus get by
implication the message that life is a contest and that
satisfaction in it is to be obtained by (in Veblen's words)
"clannishness, massiveness, ferocity, unscrupulousness, and tenacity of purpose." At the same time, they
absorb by explicit and constantly repeated precept a precisely opposite message: that good manners and good
sportsmanship come first, that the value of working and
playing is intrinsic rather than in winning, that generosity
and good manners for their own sakes are primary virtues.
One of those schools has for generations had this conflict enshrined in its motto, "Simplicity of Life,

Self-Reliance, Directness of Purpose." "Simplicity of
Life" — symbolically dramatized by the vows of personal poverty taken by the order of Episcopal monks who
ran the school until recently — counsels material ren-
unciation, a rejection of predatory barbarism in general
and conspicuous display in particular. The other two
parts of the motto, somewhat more subtly, counsel the
opposite. Woe betide the students who learn too well the
explicit lesson of peaceable savagery as opposed to the
implicit one of predatory barbarism. Such unfortunate response to the wrong signal has led to many disappointed
American lives and not a few cases of alcoholism, drug
addiction, and suicide.

In sports, both participant and spectator, the issue
comes to a head, because sports are the arena of "sportsmanship" and also of the most categorical form of predatory exploit that is legally available in "America, her
athletic democracy" (as Walt Whitman called it). Veblen
wrote that sports "afford an exercise for dexterity and for
the emulative ferocity and astuteness characteristic of
predatory life"; they are "essentially of the nature of invidious exploit" to such an extreme degree that continuing addiction to them to some extent "marks an arrested
development of [a] man's moral nature."(Christopher
Lasch has recently added a sort of footnote to this analysis, which Veblen might well have accepted. Veblen saw
sports in his time as very much of a leisure-class preoccupation, but according to Lasch, it had not always been
that way. The original aristocrats of the American republic, he says, had been essentially scholarly, ruminative,
and sedentary. Addiction to sports had been introduced
mainly by lower-class immigrants, and had, by Veblen's
time, gradually been taken over by the ruling leisure

class, because it suited that class's invidious purposes so well.) Veblen went on to argue that in addition to the opportunities sports gave for predatory exploit, they neatly satisfied the "requirement of substantial futility" so crucial to leisure-class activities as described in his system; and he saw the sporting temperament, at least in colleges and universities, as closely allied to the religious one, which he insisted was equally predatory.

Needless to say, not all of this will pass muster now. The cult of the Christian athlete that Veblen observed turned out to be a temporary phenomenon; it has barely survived this century's broad secularization of our whole culture. (See chapter 11.) Indeed, professional sports and organized religion now appear to be poles apart. The cult does survive, in residual form, in ritual media emphasis on the piety of a few sports superstars. We still want to think of our heroes as *perfect*. Meanwhile, a journeyman professional athlete who admits to praying is considered almost a freak. Dr. Thomas Tutko, a California psychologist who between 1968 and 1978 gave psychological tests to about one hundred thousand professional athletes, said recently, "The teams needed guys . . . with a mean streak. If you get nice, cleancut Christian types and expect them to go to church on Sunday morning, you put them in conflict when it comes time to be mean and retaliatory on the field." Veblen would argue that there was no conflict, since he saw organized religion ("devout observances," he derisively called it) as a prime predatory-invidious activity itself, designed chiefly to promote earthly rather than heavenly status. But since Veblen's time the Dr. Tutkos of life have tended to replace priests and bishops as our nominal moral arbiters; if Veblen were writing now, he might call attention to the invidious uses of psychology — the way, for example, that people use its half-understood jargon for competitive display — rather than of "devout observances." Again, the commercialization of sports since 1900 has in a sense put an end to what he called their "essential futility" in a time when amateurism was highly prized by the leisure class. If making money is still the main American measure of useful accomplishment — and to a marked extent it is — then star athletes earning more than a million dollars a year, as dozens now do, can hardly be called futile.

The fact remains, though, that for both the participant and the spectator, sports are as much an expression of the predatory temperament now as they were in Veblen's time. Probably more so. Their progressive professionalization and commercialization have tended to suppress the peaceable-savage elements — good sportsmanship, amateurism, innocent physical enjoyment — that are to some extent inherent in them. Tournament tennis, for example, has changed from an elite amateur cult sport to which ritual manners were essential (violation of them meant banishment), to a mass entertainment retailed by television, in which the bad manners and overt predatory activity of some players not only are usually tolerated but appear to add to those players' appeal to audiences, and therefore to their success and fame. Television commentators, not wishing to quarrel with success and fame, endorse such behavior by using the euphemism *colorful* to describe it, when *unacceptable* would formerly have been the word. (Not incidentally, when the spectators take up their own racquets and become participants, they tend to emulate the pros; thus amateur tennis manners have deteriorated, as I will maintain in more detail later on.)

The professionalization and commercialization of sports has moved their "emulative ferocity" well beyond the point where parody begins. In Veblen's time and for several decades thereafter, when the amateur spirit still generally reigned except in boxing and baseball (and when most professional ballplayers were so badly underpaid that they needed a peaceable-savage love of the game, memorably described by Ring Lardner, as motivation to keep them in it), the secret of sport's appeal was that it offered a neat paradigm of the larger national cultural tug-of-war between predatory invidiousness and peaceable savagery. To be admired, a sports performer was expected to bring into play every ounce of invidious skill and ferocity that he could muster — but subject usually to a strict code of "sportsmanlike" behavior. (There were exceptions. The great Ty Cobb was the meanest competitor ever to put a spike in a shortstop's kidneys.) An athlete who broke that code was often subject to very severe sanctions, including disgrace. Now the old balance has been tipped and the tug-of-war won by the predatory side. In an earlier time, Pete Rose would have been subject to general censure when, after the end of a record hitting streak, he complained that the pitcher who had been responsible for ending the streak had thrown him a curve on the crucial pitch, instead of "challenging" him with a fast ball. And the censure would have been logical; curve balls are within the rules of baseball, and by definition the opposing pitcher was supposed to be trying to get Rose out, not to help him continue his record streak. But in 1978, when the streak and its ending actually occurred, most of the public interest centered on how much of a salary increase Rose's exploit would entitle him to, and his sour grapes about the curve ball — a surely forgivable lapse, but also a regrettable one — was treated as par for the course, or even with outright approval.

Then, there is the question of women reporters and their access or lack of it to the locker rooms of professional athletes. Traditional male-chauvinist sports reporters and athletes argue that the macho mystery of sports heroes is violated when their naked bodies are exposed to the eyes of women reporters. Purists and traditionalists argue that no visitor of *either* sex should be allowed in the locker rooms — that the eyes and ears of reporters of both sexes should be trained on what happens on the field, not in the shower. Women reporters put their case on practical and professional grounds: the readers want locker-room gossip, they say, and if women are not allowed to go into the locker room along with the men and get it, then they are competitively disadvantaged. The fact that, in spite of male prejudices, the women reporters' premise is coming to be generally accepted — that is, that the sports public does want reports on gossip about money and feuds between players and coaches as much as it wants sports reporting — is a barometer of what has happened to sports in America. So, perhaps, is the sinking feeling one has on seeing and hearing Larry Czonka, the Herculean football line-smasher with the happily onomatopoetic name, on television plugging such an unheroic product as Roll-On deodorant. If Czonka is deodorized, we think, sport is denatured.

Lasch points out that the "radical critics" of American sport who appeared in the nineteen-sixties — Paul Hoch, Jack Scott, and Dave Meggyesy, among others — have all argued that the modern problem is that sports are taken too seriously: that they promote militarism, authoritarianism, racism, and sexism rather than innocent exercise, sportsmanship, and good fun, and thus serve as a "mirror reflection" of society at large and vicarious gratification for its frustrated members. He goes on to argue plausibly that this diagnosis is exactly wrong — that, rather, sports are not taken seriously *enough*, because they have been trivialized into easy entertainment and gossip about money and feuds. Doubtless this is true. But even though the old balance between the predatory and the peaceable has been seriously tipped, it still exists. On the one hand, we have the much-quoted apothegm of the football coach Vince Lombardi, "Winning isn't the most important thing, it's the only thing." On the other hand, there remains dimly in memory the quatrain of Grantland Rice, which was quoted widely in the nineteen-twenties and -thirties:

> *And when the One Great Scorer comes*
> *To write against your name,*
> *He writes not that you won or lost*
> *But how you played the game.*

The sentiments, if not the words, of this marvelously succinct statement of a code remain in the mind of the American sportsman, particularly the sports participant. If he does not expect that code to be observed by the athletes he watches in the stadium or on television, he knows that at least a semblance of it is expected of him when he himself is on the golf course, squash court, or tennis court. But the code must now not be stated so explicitly; it has come to be a matter for irony. A sportsman who would quote Rice now only in ironic derision may nevertheless pride himself on his personal adherence to the Rice code. American sportsmanship has moved into the area of parody display.

The friendly tennis game among amateur players of intermediate ability has sharply changed its character over the past generation. (A parallel change has taken place in the case of golf.) Formerly it was Veblenian: ferocious competitiveness in delicate tension with impeccable sportsmanship. One of the crucial characteristics of amateur as opposed to tournament tennis is that the players call their own lines, which is to say that they serve as umpires at the same time as they are in the role of competitors. This conflict of interest provides a test of sportsmanship. Any regular player has noted that the quality of line calling by players has deteriorated recently in the direction of the predatory. A generation ago, in all but the most disreputable games, consciously or semiconsciously miscalling a shot in one's own favor was considered beyond the pale. One simply did not do it — partly because of the fear of being caught, which would probably mean ostracism, but more because of the need of meeting one's own standard. Now that standard has eroded to the point where many well-regarded players give themselves the benefit of the doubt in any situation where the opponent (or spectators, if any) is not in a position to verify the call. The old habit of deliberately throwing a point to compensate for a point that has been won by luck (a bad bounce, say) has vanished, along with the white flannel pants of the players who used thus to display an excess of sportsmanship. (Indeed, any tennis coach today would describe that habit as the essence of folly, the sure mark of a "loser.") Moreover, the mood of the players can now be seen to change, in an invidious direction, in the course of a match, as the going gets hotter. In the first set, a player may applaud his opponent's exceptional exploit with the traditional accolade "Good shot." In the third set, though, when tempers are frayed and each point counts, he may greet the same circumstance with a muttered (or shouted) obscenity.

These changes, of course, have been influenced by the conduct of the professionals whom the amateur player watches when he can — evidence that the break between the sports spectator and the sports participant is less sharp than it is often said to be. The pros, an amateur tennis player's role models, have their lines called for them, by hired linesmen; nevertheless, many of them give sanction for amateurs' bad behavior in the matter of line calls by loudly protesting, gazing at the sky, cursing in foreign languages, ordering the offending linesman removed, and so on. In their postmatch interviews, they emphasize the practical, indeed the moral, necessity for ferocity and unscrupulousness in playing the game. "I just couldn't work myself into a mean enough mood to be able to win," a loser will report, ruefully. Evonne Goolagong, the most elegant stroke-maker among women players, is criticized by broadcasters, and presumably by fans, for lacking the "killer instinct"; poor Evonne, she is (or so it is supposed) too interested in the pleasure of shot-making and not enough in that of winning.* The point is emphasized by the television commercials advertising tennis equipment, in which the actors representing amateur players put on shows of ferocity and meanness suitable for representations of Genghis Khan. Actual amateur players are quick to take the hint.

*She apparently overcame this shortcoming in 1980, when she won the biggest tournament of them all, Wimbledon.

A symbolic incident that occurred in December, 1978, in a game of football — almost certainly the team sport most forthrightly conducive to predatory behavior — serves to dramatize the new mood of sports participants and fans alike. With less than two minutes to play in the Gator Bowl game in Jacksonville, Florida, Clemson College was leading Ohio State University by 17–15. At this point, an Ohio State forward pass was intercepted by Charlie Bauman, a Clemson linebacker, near the sideline in front of the Ohio State bench. The interception, since it would almost certainly enable Clemson to keep possession of the ball for the remaining time, virtually clinched the verdict for Clemson. Whereupon Woody Hayes, the sixty-five-year-old veteran coach of the Ohio State team — and a man long known for his outstanding record of his team's victories and for his tendency to temper tantrums when his team was losing — jumped off the bench, ran onto the field, and punched the Clemson player who had made the interception.

The punch did no damage, and not surprisingly: besides being an old man dressed in street clothes and wearing spectacles, Hayes was a heart patient, while Bauman was a huge, thoroughly conditioned college-age athlete protected by the masses of armor that football players ordinarily wear. The following morning, the Ohio State athletic director relieved Hayes of his duties as coach, thereby presumably affirming the university's commitment to peaceable-savage sportsmanship — or at least to the noncombatant status of college football coaches. But some of the subsequent public reactions suggested contrary attitudes toward the incident. Hayes's fellow coaches, while not defending his action, tended to close ranks with him. One belittled the punch as an "in-

discretion" that could be excused on account of "the
enormous pressure of coaching football today." Another
commented, "Sometimes you do some things that if you
have second thoughts, you wouldn't do." A third looked
upon Hayes's act as a "tragedy" such as is liable to "happen to all of us in our lives." To the former president of
the National Collegiate Athletic Association, the whole
thing was "really too bad." Some of those who called in to
radio station WBNS in Columbus, Ohio, where Ohio
State is situated, went even farther in their defense of
Hayes's unorthodox support of his team. John Bothe, an
announcer for the station, reported that while the majority
of callers had expressed the feeling that Hayes had dis-
graced the university, "a lot of people said he was com-
pletely right in punching out that guy." The guy had, after
all, caused the defeat of Ohio State.

The huge stir that the incident occasioned provided
an index to a national anxiety on the winning-versus-
sportsmanship issue. Meanwhile, the incident itself,
along with the reactions to it, provided a fine example of
the new national way of dealing with that anxiety. Russell
Baker wrote in *The New York Times* that it provided "a
rare moment of memorable comedy," in that it exposed
the "antique cant" that football coaches are in the business of building young men's characters, and football
fans in the business of admiring such activities. What
might be added to that analysis is the suggestion that the
comedy may not have been entirely unintentional on the
part of the various actors in it. Was retirement-age, ail-
ing, bespectacled Coach Hayes entirely serious in his
attempt to punish the offending linebacker? Granting that
he certainly did not think the matter over in advance, to
suggest that he was would be to insult his intelligence.

Was the opinion of callers to Station WBNS who said that Hayes had been "entirely right" to be taken quite at face value? More likely it was to be taken as the kind of contrary view, expressed for its shock value and its capacity to prolong discussion, that is routine in barroom dialectic. Hayes and his supporters, it is suggested, acted with just enough realization of what they were doing to enable the whole episode to qualify as parody display.

Perhaps nowhere on the contemporary scene is such display better exemplified than in what was first called "jogging" and later — in a characteristic invidious language change in some respects similar to the sudden anathematization of "Negro" and substitution of "black" — it became de rigueur to call "running." Several million Americans were participating in this sport by the later nineteen-seventies. According to *The Wall Street Journal,* the readers of which by that time had much reason to be interested in running, in 1979 there were more than six million *women* runners.

Running is in some ways classically Veblenian. It is highly conspicuous, since the characteristic arena for it is a public roadway or walkway, where fellow citizens are conveniently announcing their inferior status by indulging in less status-producing forms of movement as riding and walking. It is wasteful, in that the objective is clearly not to get from here to there, and it involves maximum, often indeed heroic, expenditure of energy for no measurable result. It is invidious: aficionados, not content with defending it on the ground that it helps prevent heart attacks, make a point of insisting (on shaky medical evidence) that other forms of violent exercise, such as squash or tennis, are relatively useless toward that goal.

Although theoretically free, in practice it has become conspicuously expensive, as an industry has emerged to supply esoteric pieces of equipment that few runners are brave or independent enough to feel that they can do without. The Adidas shoe, a glorified sneaker at fifty dollars or so a pair, suddenly became the outdoor equivalent of the Gucci loafer. A single company, Formfit Rogers, Inc., sold more than a million "running bras" at $12 to $15 each in the first half of 1979, when regular bras cost half as much. Overnight fortunes were made by alert promoters on warmup suits, cooldown suits, steady-state suits. Finally — exactly like such more classical forms of conspicuous display as corset wearing and hair implantation — running may be injurious to the participant. Doctors have reported a huge increase in shin-splint fractures and damaged muscles, hospitals in the vicinity of running Meccas an alarming increment of corpses in running costume.

On the other hand, in key ways running stands in sharp, even in pointed, contrast to run-of-the-mill forms of sport. Of these, the chief one is that, as practiced by most of its participants, it is not competitive. Unlike George Allen or Woody Hayes, the typical runner does not do it to win; he or she does it for self-realization, to achieve a certain state of mind and body. As with the taking of drugs that cause nausea and other unpleasant reactions before they produce euphoria, running produces pain and near exhaustion before it produces what runners call "the runner's high." Theoretically, then, in this respect running is the perfect anti-Veblenian form of exercise: that is, it looks down on invidious competition and all the "clannishness, massiveness, and ferocity" usually associated with such competition; it does not even have many of the elements of craft and exploit; it is, apparently, a peaceable-savage activity.

However, as Veblen noted, noncompetitive sports (riding to hounds and walking with a stick were the particular ones he cited), while theoretically peaceable-savage, tend in the long run to take on the invidiousness characteristic of predatory barbarism. In the case of running, this invidiousness comes in the attitudes of runners and the language they use to express them. Patti Hagan, a runner with a sense of irony, has called the language that some writers about running use about running "psycho-babble recyled as runner-babble." Miss Hagan cites Valerie Andrews, author of *The Psychic Power of Running:* "While we activate the archetypes of primal running man and the information code for genetic and evolutionary past as we run, at the same time we reach a transcendental state that may enable us to connect with other forms of consciousness flowing through the universe at large." And Joel Henning, author of *Holistic Running:* "We begin to run as a dinosaur or a lizard may have, for self-preservation," but when we get our second wind, "our limbic system is now engaged and we have recapitulated our evolution to the stage of, say, the puma. . . . Finally, we reach our highest, our truly human, level, at which thoughts and insights bring us to the edge of unique human awareness — what some might call a state of bliss." And Miss Andrews again: the runner at his peak "is like a miniature universe in the process of creation, spewing out dreams like stellar bodies whirling into psychic space." Let up hope it is only dreams that are being spewed out.

Miss Hagan does not herself go in for transcendental language about running. This is not to say that her attitude toward it may be described as calm and rational. About as much so, say, as that of the Crusaders toward the Holy Grail. Here is Miss Hagan in her book *The Road Runner's Guide to New York City,* on the "hazards" of running in Riverside Park:

> Unleashed muggers and rapists at all times of day and night; *always* risky for lone women runners (Riverside Drive route as well), group running recommended; some air pollution from Riverside Drive traffic and Henry Hudson Parkway; dogs off leash; harsh winter winds off the Hudson; kids on bicycles and Big Wheels; in summer, poison ivy lines narrow river path below 125th; occasional rats along river; isolated areas of woods and tall bushes along northern segment of Riverside Drive and river path.

Violent theft, rape, potential murder, poisonous air, possible dog bite; on top of that, for heaven's sake, poison ivy, rats, overhanging branches. Some might judge the hazards unacceptable. Not Hagan; Riverside Park is second, after Central Park, on her list of recommended running tracks in Manhattan.

Is she kidding? Yes and no, a nonrunner must conclude. Exhaustion, hypoglycemia, and oxygen deprivation may produce states of mind that give rise to such attitudes, but it seems evident that their comic effect is to some extent sought — that the writers about running, like the much more numerous talkers about running, are largely engaged in parody display.

4

Being a Sport

$O_{f\ all\ card}$ games, and probably of all games of any kind, poker is the one that most elegantly expresses in symbolic terms the conditions and atmosphere of competitive commercial life. The object, to begin with, is to get the other players' money; a poker game not for money, or for stakes so low that no player is at consequential risk, is no poker game at all. The thrill of winning money, and the chill of losing it, are the essence of the game.* (Lest the analogy be pushed too far, let it be noted that in poker the potential booty is a finite amount, the sum of all the players' available. money — that is, it is a zero-sum game — while by contrast, in competitive business, new technology and aggressive marketing often make it possible to expand markets and progressively fatten the pot, so that most or even all of the players can win.)

The qualities needed to win at poker are more or less those most useful in competitive commerce. Luck is a

*This is conspicuously untrue of the perenially popular parlor game Monopoly, which attempts to represent business dealings literally rather than symbolically, and is not a gambling game at all.

distinct factor, but not the major factor. It will be decisive among otherwise equal players, but between a lucky poor player and a less lucky good player, over a matter of hours (and five hours is probably the minimum for a decent poker session), the latter will win. The qualities needed for success are coolness, gall, calculated unpredictability, concentration, the ability to appraise character, a minimal skill at arithmetic, and, perhaps most of all, a passion to win — a quality that, however, not all players, even otherwise good ones, possess.

Poker, then, does not merely imitate the conditions of business competition — it refines, simplifies, exaggerates, parodies them. For example, in its formal structure it allows no room for the noninvidious objectives that mitigate the predatory character of business: producing a socially useful product or service, providing jobs, and so on. Poker gives rise to no product, service, or jobs. The name of the game is winning money by fair means or foul: lying, dissembling by word or gesture, intimidating, hypocritically trying to evoke sympathy are all part of the game. Surely one of its appeals is the fact that poker permits and even encourages forms of conduct that are unacceptable in ordinary society. Poker's code of acceptable conduct is very wide indeed. Cheating is dealt with severely — at the least, with permanent expulsion from the game. But practically nothing except false dealing, palming cards, and peeking at other players' hands is considered cheating.

By a paradox that is at the heart of the matter, this game of naked aggression is best played among friends, in an atmosphere of conviviality in which eating, nonalcoholic drinking, smoking, and conversation play a large role. (Those who venture to play in a game of strangers thereby become professionals, for whom the situation is entirely different; our subject here is amateur poker: that is, poker among friends.) There are several preconditions for a successful amateur poker game. One is that the players should be of at least approximately equal financial means. Another is that they should have strongly ambivalent feelings about each other — shared interests in life and genuine respect if not liking for each other, combined with an equally strong urge to get the upper hand. A shared trade or profession obviously helps fill this need. The stakes must be such that a player's potential loss over a session is significantly, but not catastrophically, more than he can afford. The possibility of being seriously hurt must be present. Sandwiches and beverages — including beer, but not spirits; games at which liquor is drunk usually turn nasty — must be provided either by the host of the evening in a game that rotates locations, or by general subscription of all players when the game is always in the same place. Cigars, the most aggressive (and it would be remiss not to add, phallic) form of tobacco product, will be heavily used; an incidental form of invidiousness that comes into play is the offering of cigars by one player to one or more, but not all, of the others. General conversation about nonpoker topics — jokes, trade gossip, public gossip, witticisms — is a key element in the equation. It is essential to the health of a good amateur poker game that such conversation take place before the game, between hands, and after the game. (Usually not *during* hands, when conversation may be interpreted as a slightly unethical attempt to distract a player's attention; one thus distracted is entitled to say peremptorily, "Deal the cards!") Such conviviality among antagonists is always present to one extent or another in competitive business dealings, including those of the most cutthroat sort.

The players in such a game engage in it for two apparently conflicting purposes — to take part in friendly conversation and exchanges of wit, and to hurt each other or be hurt. Peaceable savagery and predatory barbarism live in delicate balance. A game that achieves and maintains this balance may endure and flourish, on, say, a once-a-month basis, with more or less the same personnel, over twenty-five or thirty years, though in the majority of cases it declines and breaks up a good deal sooner than that, for reasons to be examined.

When such a game is in full flower, various definable poker-character types emerge, and they bear considerable resemblance to character types that appear in competitive business. There is, for example, the equable, conservative player who generally goes by the book, only occasionally taking a flamboyant risk (technically, "running a bluff") on which he expects to lose, solely for the purpose of avoiding a reputation for predictability, which would be damaging to both his effectiveness as a poker player and his reputation as an interesting fellow. His bluffs are analogous to well-calculated advertising appropriations, and he may be regarded as the careful small-town banker of the game. On balance, he is a winner; he would be regarded as a little too calculating, a little too efficiently predatory, but for the fact that he takes the curse off his penchant for success by being exceptionally goodnatured and by sedulously holding up his end in the evening's incidental banter. Sitting next to him, we may find the defensive player, concentrating on avoiding losses. If the game is "table stakes" — a form of play in which a player's loss on any given pot is limited to the amount of money that he places on the table in front of him at the start of each pot — he will prudently keep a moderate-sized sum thus at risk, and if he wins a good-sized pot he will "salt" most of his winnings (that is, put them in his pocket and thus out of contention, a practice that causes a degree of opprobrium in some games because it withdraws a portion of "the game's money" from circulation). However, the player who "salts" winnings, like the one-talent man in the biblical Parable of the Talents, pays a price for his thriftiness; a small initial stake deprives him of the possibility of betting aggressively when he draws a good hand or wishes to bluff, and he usually ends up a small loser. That is acceptable to him, because he does not really like poker much and does not really expect to win. He plays for the sake of the conviviality, and of feeling like a sport, and is willing to pay a modest price for it in losings. He may be compared to one in the larger society who lives comparatively happily on an income that is progressively, but not disastrously, reduced by inflation.

Here are some other poker-game types.

The Indulged Beginner, who is generally acknowledged to be a less skillful and resourceful player than the others, but who likes the idea of being in the game, especially for the image that it gives him of himself. The other players at first avoid taking undue advantage of him in hopes that his passion for the game will grow until he graduates to the status of a Pigeon, a poor player experienced enough to be considered fair game. (This strategy often backfires, and the beginner graduates instead into a consistent winner; that is, he follows the figure-of-fun-to-big-success pattern familiar in competitive business.)

The Complainer about Bad Luck, who is given to such sentences as "I just sat down and already I'm fifty dollars behind," and "I've been playing for two hours and I haven't won a pot yet." (I have known one such complainer who, in what I take to have been a Freudian slip, combined these into the inspired malapropism "I just sat down, and I haven't won a pot yet.") The complainer, like his obvious counterpart in business life, seldom wins, because he does not *expect* to win.

Perhaps the most vivid type, and one of the most common in friendly poker games because he loves poker so much that he seeks games out, is the Expert Loser. He is a student and connoisseur of the game, with a quick head for percentages in any given situation, and a store of inarguably wise maxims such as "The cards can't remember." In sum, his theoretical approach to the game is informed and rational; he should be a large and steady winner. But unfortunately for him, his temperament repeatedly betrays him at the crucial moment. He holds, for example, four cards to an inside straight in seven-card stud. His rational mind tells him precisely the odds against filling the straight on the last card, and emerging with the winning hand. Those odds, he knows, are overwhelming. But another side of his nature, either an insane belief in his luck or a self-destructive drive, leads him to ignore reason and pay to draw the last card anyhow. Having drawn and failed to fill the straight, he may then compound the error by trying to bluff the other players out with a large bet, a tactic that only occasionally will succeed. The Expert Loser, although theoretically by far the best player in the game, often ends up paying for it with his losses. Recent psychoanalytical analyses, in which he is called a "compulsive gambler," have described him as a masochist who plays primarily to enjoy the perverse satisfaction of losing. In our context, we know nothing of that. We perceive, rather, that he is a counterpart of such businessmen-speculators as Edwin Gilbert and Louis Wolfson.

Along with the various personality types, the successful friendly game develops and maintains certain marked characteristics. In the course of the game, interim winners, if asked how much they are ahead, tend to understate the figure. A winner who reports that he is currently "up" about twenty-five dollars is probably up twice that much; a player who says he is even is probably a bit ahead of the game. The purpose of this minor dissembling — which, incidentally, is not illegal or even subject to criticism — is to head off the hostility, and consequent targeting for attack, that goes naturally with being a big winner. (Of course, corporations similarly overreport or underreport their earnings or losses, according to convenience, through the use of accounting devices.) As for the interim loser, he tends to exaggerate his losses in the hope of gaining a measure of sympathy. But he must not show sympathy to himself; his goal above all is to remain cheerful and equable in the face of adversity, to take his losses in good part. He may be bleeding inwardly, thinking of the apologies and explanations he may subsequently have to make at home, or bitterly of the hours he has spent earning the money that has just gone down the drain; outwardly, he must be game and smiling. His only honorable escape from further losses is to declare himself "tapped out" (a "tap" being a bet equivalent to a player's total stake), and leave the session prematurely; he doesn't want to do that, though, because it would deprive him of the rest of the evening's conviviality as well as the chance to recoup. So he must bravely hide his bleeding heart. If he shows it — by whining, edginess, or even sullen silence — he will lose face. The poker ethic preserves, without shame or alteration, the stiff-upper-lip British Empire ethic that found such resounding expression in Kipling's "If": "If you can look on triumph and disaster / And treat those two impostors both the same / . . . You'll be a man, my son." Current business life seems to know no such ethic. Losers are free to whine or to sue — and they do.

In the postgame rituals, which play such an important part in the evening, final winnings and losings are reported fairly accurately. (If someone is lying then, it is immediately evident, since the winnings and losings of all the players must add up to zero.) It is incorrect for a winner to show sympathy for a loser, even if he feels it, because such a show might be construed as invidiously patronizing. The heavy loser, however, may be faced with the necessity of taking self-preservative measures as regards his life outside the game. Specifically, he must deceive or placate his wife. In particular, and for sufficient reason, the wives of Expert Losers — who both play and lose frequently — are prone to becoming angry or unhappy about their husbands' poker losses. To protect themselves, such players devise intricate systems of fiscal juggling and concealment, such as maintaining secret bank accounts, financed by poker winnings augmented by a portion of professional earnings, solely for the purpose of privately financing poker losses. Such accounts function as a cushion under the domestic economy, like a nation's central bank. The usual rule is that no one is eligible to enter a friendly poker session with a debt from the previous session still outstanding — that is, no pay, no play. Most players, however, prefer to give this taboo a wide berth by settling on the spot immediately after the losing game, rather than waiting until the last moment, when the group has reassembled for the next session. This can be done with a check on a special, secret account. By resorting to such central banking, a regular poker loser can contrive to bring home more *cash* from each game than he took to it, even after a heavy losing night. So far as his wife — the General Accounting Office — is concerned, he was a small winner again. Of course, the piper has to be paid eventually, and I have known regular losers who earn enormous sums professionally and whose families live on a relatively modest scale — as a result of poker losses. It does not seem too extravagant to suggest that great professional success is sometimes motivated by the need to minimize the domestic impact of such losses. I have never heard, by the way, of a marriage broken by a wife's discovery of the wrong checkbook, though I feel sure there are some.

This is probably the moment to speak of mixed-sex poker games. They do exist, and even flourish, but usually for unthreatening stakes, and usually they consist of fancy forms of poker like high-low games with wild cards, in which the element of luck is significantly increased. Individual women of special qualities occasionally are accepted into normally all-male games. This works no more than passably well. The problem of woman as an inhibitor of language used around the table has lessened in recent years to the vanishing point, but there remain the frailties, based on obsolescent but persistent codes, of the men: they are apt to spoil her fun by subtly giving her special consideration, and to parade their own sexual insecurity by showing particular chagrin when she wins and they lose. In addition, women, up to the present stage of society, are less natural poker players than men are. (On the other hand, there is good evidence that they are

more natural players of games of pure chance like roulette.) It is interesting that no woman has ever been a big-
time gambler or predator in competitive business; even
Hetty Green, financial genius that she was, was a basically ultraconservative investor. I have never known a
mixed poker game that played for serious stakes and en-
dured for any length of time.

Meanwhile, it is characteristic of those poker games
that do endure over a long period, with very few exceptions, that they suffer a gradual, progressive deteriora-
tion. One cause of this is simply economic: some of the
players prosper greatly in their business or professional
lives, while others prosper little if at all; the result is that
what began as a game among economic equals becomes
one among gross unequals. The sum of money that represents a significant but not catastrophic loss, once the
same for all of the players, may now be fifty dollars for
one and five hundred for others. One of the preconditions
for a successful game has thus been removed. The problem may be partly corrected by resort to the table-stakes
rule, which, as previously described, enables the poorer
players to compete — although at a marked disadvantage — for smaller stakes than the richer players compete for. (The role of table stakes is somewhat analogous
to that of the antitrust laws in business life, and with analogous results. Both aim to bring about fairness in competition between the lion and the lamb, and, of course,
neither succeeds.)

This functional change leads to a structural one.
Some of the original players, usually the now less pros-
perous ones, become disillusioned with the game or no
longer feel that they can afford their losses, and leave it.

(Or players may leave because their employers have transferred them to another city.) The replacements, in most cases, are players previously known to only one or two of the game's original players. They may share outside interests with those one or two, but not with the others. These added starters, because they are recruited from a pool of those who are "looking for a game," and because they were not part of the original mutually convivial group, are apt to be players with a bent of character and an attitude toward the game more predatory and less convivial than that of the originals. It happens more often than chance dictates that these added starters are lawyers.*

Thus the game is tipped off its necessary balance between rapaciousness and conviviality, and is tipped toward the former. This change is reflected in both the technical style of play and the social conduct of the game. As to the former, there are certain actions in poker (as, of course, there are in business) that are undeniably legal under the rules but are frowned upon in some games as too ruthless. One of these actions is betting heavily on a "sure thing." For example, in a game of five-card stud (in which each player is dealt five cards only, the first face down), a lucky player may hold a pair of kings, of which one is concealed; after the deal is complete, if no other player has a card as high as a king showing and there are no possible higher hands — flushes or straights — in sight, the one with the kings knows he has the pot won,

*Of whom Veblen wrote, "The lawyer is exclusively occupied with the details of predatory fraud, either in achieving or in checkmating chicanery" — unfairly, since nearly all lawyers are occupied with other things some of the time; but understandably, since Veblen's father and both of his grandfathers had been dispossessed of land through the agency of lawyers.

and no one else knows it. On the last round of betting, he may bet substantially, but not heavily; that is, when there is no element of chance he will not try to milk the last dollar out of the opposition. Of course, he expects the same merciful treatment himself when the conditions are reversed. In the same friendly game, it would be even more of a breach of decorum for the holder of a sure thing to "check-raise" — that is, to pass his opportunity to bet after the last card has been dealt, thereby inducing his opponents (if they are foolish or trustful enough) to make large bets against him, and then to crush them risklessly with an even larger raise. To do so would be roughly equivalent to attempting a hostile takover in business. Although check-raising is done routinely in professional poker among strangers, it generally isn't done in friendly games. The first check-raise of a sure winning hand that takes place in a friendly game often marks the beginning of its decline.

The social component of the decline consists of pro-gressively more rigid attention to the game itself and less talk and fewer jokes about other matters of mutual inter-est. For one thing, in the now tougher, more ruthless game, more concentrated attention is needed just to hold one's end up; for another, the players are no longer all friends outside the game, and they have fewer topics in common to talk about. Other intimations of conviviality gradually disappear: the original ante for each pot be-comes bigger, tending to drive away the financially weaker players, and the sandwiches are now ordered in from a delicatessen rather than personally provided by the host of the evening. Eventually, almost the sole point of the game is to win money — that is to say, it has be-come for practical purposes a professional game. The evolution from amateurism to professionalism is complete.

This evolution neatly recapitulates Veblen's evolution of society from peaceable savagery toward predatory barbarism. Moreover, Veblen insisted, and it would be hard to dispute, that a propensity to gamble is a "subsidiary trait of the barbarian [predatory] temperament." However, Veblen badly misunderstood the gambling propensity. He equated, or nearly equated, it with belief in luck; the only complicating factor that he noted was that, in betting on contests of strength or skill, the bettor believes that his bet in itself will in some nonrational way have an effect on the outcome of the contest. The bettor feels, according to Veblen, that the "substance and solicitude" that he displays in taking a personal risk on the outcome "cannot go for naught in the issue." Veblen describes the gambler's sense of luck as "an inarticulate or inchoate animism" closely related to the religious impulse.

But this is — and certainly was in Veblen's time, too — true only of the very stupidest of gamblers. A pure, uncomplicated belief in luck may motivate the person who spends all day pumping coins into a slot machine at Reno or Las Vegas; it may even motivate the more affluent, if not more sophisticated, casino roulette player who stubbornly plays one pet number or color over and over again, waiting for the lightning to strike. As for the belief that his bet itself has a positive effect on the outcome, that may well move the more naive sort of horse player. (If he would think about the matter, he would realize that the exact reverse is true. His bet, to one extent or another depending on its size, actually lowers the odds on his chosen horse when it is mathematically as-similated by the totalizer machine. The amount he will receive if his horse wins is less, not more, than it would theoretically have been if he had not made the bet. That is, his bet has actually had a negative effect on his chances, financially speaking.) It is a certainty that, over time, the players of slot machines or casino roulette will be losers, because the maker of the machines or the pro-prietor of the casino arranges the odds that way. The odds can be beaten in short bursts, but in the end, mathemat-ical law will assert itself.

And that is what Veblen — clearly no gambler; in-deed, it would have been profitable to have sat in a poker game with him — failed to understand. The serious gam-bler plays not slot machines or roulette, where luck, and predominantly bad luck, is in charge, but rather poker or one of its variants in which luck is only one factor. This is not to say that the serious gambler has no interest in luck; on the contrary, it fascinates and threatens him. His attitude toward it is well summed up in the song "Luck, Be a Lady Tonight," from the musical *Guys and Dolls,* in which luck is allegorically represented as a dangerous, irresistible femme fatale. The gambler knows that, if he is to be successful, he must warily keep luck at arm's length, embracing her only occasionally, casually, and as unemotionally as possible. In sum, the serious gam-bler who usually wins must be a calculating person of reason — one who categorically *dis*believes in luck.

It is ironical, in view of Veblen's misapprehension of gambling and the gambler, that the greatest of all gam-bling games, poker, so beautifully fits his system. Al-though he recognized poker as "the great American game," he does not appear to have recognized this fact —

as he surely would have if he had ever sat a few evenings in a good amateur game. He would, I think, have seen the slow decline of a poker game such as I have described as a process of cultural progression in which a nice tension between peaceable savagery and predatory barbarism — the tension that made the game work — gradually gives way to the outright triumph of the predatory. And it seems reasonable to suppose that he would have seen a parallel to contemporary processes in the real world of business — for example, in the book publishing industry, which a generation ago was a comparatively healthy "game" in which most of the players mixed the peaceable motive of putting good literature before the public with the predatory one of making a profit, but which, with the coming of new players (conglomerate bosses) and bigger antes (million-dollar book advances), has tended progressively to emphasize the latter motive at the expense of the former.

5

Getting Down with the Joneses

*T*he endlessly pursued debate about whether or not the United States is (or has become) a classless society is a bootless one. Of course, we have classes, including a ruling elite; it is just that, in contrast to all previous class societies, the membership in the various classes (including the ruling elite) is changing all the time. The illusion of classlessness is created by this fluidity. The next thing to note is that not all of the current strivings to cross class lines are in an upward direction. Many, although generally not the most successful, of these border assaults are attempts to get into classes below one's own.

This is not merely game-playing; it may be in deadly earnest. Ours is probably the first society so socially (if not politically) democratic that, in certain circumstances, substantial status attaches to those who lack status as traditionally measured. Harun al-Rashid, caliph of Baghdad, explored his city disguised as a commoner, and similar disguises have been adopted by aristocratic literary heroes over many centuries. Indeed, such imposture came to be a literary cliché, and was satirized by, for example, W. S. Gilbert in *The Mikado*. But the purpose of these acts of declassing was to provide amusement for the disguised aristocrat; he stood ready at any time, if danger or convenience required, to throw off the disguise and assert his rightful class power. When declassing occurs in the United States, it is undertaken not to toy with the populace but rather to become indistinguishable from it — most characteristically, in order to gain popularity or to avoid ridicule. For Americans, getting down with the Joneses is a serious matter.

Some fine examples are provided by the third generation of the ducal Rockefeller family. Early newsreels of Nelson show him speaking with what is generally known as a boarding-school accent (although in fact he did not go to a boarding school). Much later, in his time of political eminence, he still had an apparently intractable air of arrogant patronage, but so declassed was his accent that he managed to make it seem the arrogance of a particularly successful undertaker or taxi-fleet owner. The word *party*, for example, had been transformed from "pahty" to "purrty." Again, there came a time when Nelson Rockefeller's brother Laurance decided to invite his former classmates at the Lincoln School in New York City to Pocantico Hills, the family fiefdom in Westchester County, for a reunion luncheon. In the planning of this event, it was first proposed that, in order to avoid the least semblance of pretension or display, only hamburgers be served, accompanied by no alcoholic drinks, even beer. Fortunately for the spirit of the occasion, reason prevailed, and drinks were served, along with a respectable if not sumptuous lunch. But the declassing impulse had been there, and it had nearly prevailed. (Just possibly an impulse to thrift had been there, too.)

The United States military services in the Second World War were a unique social laboratory, in that they brought together involuntarily young men of all American classes for the first time since the modern fluidity between classes had come into being. As a result, the services became a natural environment for attempts at declassing to avoid demotic ridicule or ostracism. At the outset, traditional class lines were officially recognized by the authorities in their determination that, generally speaking, college graduates were officer material while others were not. (Let us note that the distinction was not exclusively, and perhaps not primarily, a matter of education. A college degree in those days still usually denoted, as it no longer does now, a certain amount of family affluence and social position.) Graduates of the better colleges, if willing and physically qualified, were often funneled directly into officer-training courses without serving any apprenticeship in the ranks. Thus their initial military environment, socially speaking, became a replica of the college environment they had come from. However, many college graduates from high-status families did not join such programs, either from choice or, more often, because they could not qualify on account of some minor but militarily crucial physical defect, such as myopia or color blindness.

Such a defective son of privilege became an involuntary Harun al-Rashid. Plunked down in a barracks in which he was entirely surrounded by colleagues whose previous lives had been less privileged and sheltered than his own, he felt isolated. The obbligato of intricate obscenity — based on monotonous repetition, but nevertheless capable of breaking occasionally into inspired originality — that was and is an essential part of barracks speech both amused and oppressed him. Above all, it made him feel like an outsider. So, perhaps even more, did his colleagues' sexual attitudes. His own sexual experience had been sharply limited by the monastically segregated educational arrangements then in vogue in leisure-class circles, and by its training in puritanical gallantry of boys toward girls. His colleagues, on the other hand, seemed to find locating and seducing complaisant young women no harder than putting on or taking off their own pants, and the detailed recounting of these effortless triumphs made up the bulk of their conversation. In this case, to his sense of isolation was added sharp envy. The lower classes, he was forced to conclude, were allowed to enjoy life more than the upper classes.

The conclusion led to an earnest and calculated attempt on the part of the well-born recruit to join the lower classes, principally by forcing himself to speak ungrammatically and to curse incessantly. Unless the well-born recruit happened to have an unusual gift for mimicry, this attempt was not usually successful. (In truth, all attempts to change class through speech patterns, regardless of whether they are attempts to change it upward or downward, are doomed to failure because they are so easily detectable by the authentic members of the class aspired to.) Even so, the well-bred young man in the barracks found his clumsy effort rewarded to a certain extent, because the authentic toughs, while detecting the fakery without trouble, nevertheless appreciated the attitude displayed in the effort itself. What it established clearly was the higher-class representative's recognition that, as far as life in the barracks was concerned, lower-class speech was a badge of superiority — in other words, that for the moment, lower was higher. In appreciation of this overt obeisance, the authentic toughs would begin to treat the impostor tough with condescending consideration, and even a measure of affection, instead of with the contempt and hostility they had shown him before he had begun trying to emulate them.

Of course, the status reversal of barracks life was transient. For example, if the former barracks mates of different initial classes happened to meet years later as civilians, the reversal would be found to have vanished entirely. The normal accouterments of civilian life, absent in the barracks — differences in clothes, household furnishings, public gathering places, and, particularly, wives — had reasserted themselves, putting the class hierarchy back in its former place. But the temporary reversal remained as one of the most striking features of social relations among American servicemen at that particular time.

Such attempts at declassing would not have been expected to occur to nearly such a marked extent, if at all, in the military in Veblen's time (and by all accounts it did not, in the Spanish-American war of 1898). The reason for the change is not hard to find. As has been noted, in that time the American "gentleman" (like the British one who served as his model) was still usually accepted by all classes at his self-appraisal. He considered himself better than others, and so did they. By the time of the Second World War, the others thought of him as better in no respect except that his family probably had more money than theirs had. Lip service was generally paid to this form of superiority in civilian life, partly because those with little money believed that proper obeisance to those with more of it would help them improve their own financial status. (It is notable even today that less affluent groups generally oppose tax reform that would close loopholes available only to the rich, evidently on the ground that they want the loopholes to be still available when they become rich themselves.) But in the artificially democratic society of the wartime barracks, where nobody was going to get rich anyhow and everybody knew it, such lip service was unnecessary.

The process of change has proceeded considerably farther over the years since then, so that what happened in the barracks appears now as a preview of what was to begin happening in a broader context later on. Americans now try to declass themselves quite often. Few self-respecting popular singers, white or black, dream of using anything but a black-to-mulatto accent. The sociologist Elliot Liebow, in researching a group of black "streetcorner men" in Washington, D.C., in the middle nineteensixties, found that he could "come close" to his subjects as to dress "with almost no effort at all," but that his essays in cursing and ungrammatical speech were so unsuccessful that he found himself remaining conspicuous in spite of all efforts to conform. However, he did find that through his assumed dress and speech he had "dulled some of the characteristics of my background" and "probably made myself more accessible" to the street men; moreover, he found that his effort to declass himself was as important for its effect on himself as it was for its effect on the street men. With the difference that his motive for the effort was primarily professional rather than social, Liebow recapitulated the experience of the wellbred young man in the wartime barracks — and with approximately the same results.

Russell Baker maintains that "being no brighter than anyone else is a social asset among Americans." It is, Baker points out, entirely acceptable to boast about one's incompetence in science, mathematics, poetry, or foreign languages. On the other hand, "to accuse an American of being unfit to drive [an automobile] is to invite a punch in the nose," "no American can bring himself to admit, even to himself, that he has no sense of humor," and "most Americans who lead monogamous sex lives would no sooner confess to it than they would admit to inadequate driving skill." It is no accident that the forms of accomplishment to be scorned or hidden, higher learning and language skill, are among those traditionally associated with an upper class, while those to be belligerently claimed — mechanical skill, joke-making ability, and promiscuous sexual prowess — are those associated with a working class. The huge and unprecedented phenomenon of blue jeans, which spread from the United States to the rest of the world in the nineteen-seventies (and which will be treated in more detail in chapter 19), was in its early phases largely a phenomenon of declassing. The person who for years has lived and worked in a high-status place (as conventionally regarded) like Boston, New York, or San Francisco, but who grew up in a lower-status place like Peoria, Illinois, or Des Moines, Iowa, will routinely announce himself or herself to strangers as being "from Peoria" or "from Des Moines."

Attempts at declassing to gain social acceptance are no less conspicuous display than similar attempts to raise one's class position. They are conspicuous display in the new mode, the flip side up.

6

Veblen's Cow

To get a sense of the place of lawns and lawn care in American life, an Easterner may dial toll-free on, say, a June morning to the east-of-the-Mississippi WATS number for Scott, the national purveyor of lawn seeds, fertilizers, and supplies.

A male voice, not sounding recorded, answers after the third ring, and says pleasantly, "We're sorry, but our lines are busy. Just hold on, and one of our consultants will be with you as soon as possible." Music begins — the bland, inoffensive music of elevators, airliner interiors, cocktail lounges, and other public places in every corner of the Union. Not knowing where it is coming from, you are wafted by the sound in your ear — the music of the States, if not of the spheres — to Lawnville, U.S.A. Five minutes, and three musical numbers, go by while you sit imagining yourself landing at Phoenix, or having a beer while waiting for boarding time at Tri-Cities. Then, abruptly, another male voice comes on, this one speaking in the mid-South accent that seems to be on the way to becoming a national vernacular, full of easygoing competence and willingness to oblige. "Scott's, can I help you?" You give your address, and ask for the name of your local Scott dealer. The answerer says that it will take a few moments to look it up. While the looking-up machinery, human or mechanical, is working, the answerer engages in knowledgeable yet comfortable weather-oriented conversation with you. "Nice weather you're having there on Long Island. Good after all the rain you had last week." "Yes," you reply, and then, realizing you are at what your interlocuter would call "a disadvantage," you ask, "Where are you?" "Out here in Ohio. Went down to fifty here last night." "We had a cool night here too." "Good for the grass." Ohio is appropriately reassuring. It would have been a shock to learn that your lawn consultant was in the Donner Pass, or in Death Valley.

Now he politely gives you the address of your local dealer, whom, as it happens, you know personally, although you had not known him as a Scott's dealer. "If there's anything more we can do, just call us again," the voice says.

Your local dealer does not have in stock the Scott's Lawn Manual, so the following morning, you call the toll-free number again. After your musical wait — during which you reflect with wonder that you can have this free trip, this short imaginary excursion out into green-lawned America, anytime you want it — another consultant, not the one of the previous day, comes on and promises to send a manual to your address. A couple of weeks later, it arrives, full of promises of turf-building, weed-killing, sentient automatic watering. You feel you have joined at last the mainstream of green-lawned America.

Veblen was fascinated by lawns, and put a closely packed page or two about them into *The Theory of the Leisure Class*. It was his notion that while a lawn "undoubtedly has an element of sensuous beauty," it appeals particularly, and for reasons not strictly aesthetic, to well-to-do people derived from the "dolicho-encephalic blond" stock of northern Europe. (Veblen held a number of more or less crackpot racial ideas, which he had picked up mostly from one of his colleagues at the University of Chicago. Interesting to note among the racial stocks that he treated most harshly was his own.)

The "dolicho blond," Veblen thought, had a particular affection for lawns because his ancestors had for centuries been a pastoral people living in a region with a humid climate favorable to their growth. Thus, "For the aesthetic purpose the lawn is a cow pasture." The cow historically (Veblen believed) served both to cut the lawn and to fertilize it, the functions later to be taken over first by hired hands, and later by homeowners themselves with the aid of equipment and preparations supplied by Scott and its competitors. However, according to Veblen, in his time "the vulgar suggestion of thrift, which is nearly inseparable from the cow, is a standing objection to the decorative use of this animal." Therefore, he insisted, recourse was had to "some more or less inadequate substitute," such as the deer or antelope, because of those beasts' "superior expensiveness or futility," which put them in conformity with Veblen's theories of pecuniary decency.

The point seems to be a bit strained. Even in Veblen's time, surely only a minority of leisure-class lawns were cropped by deer or antelope. (The first efficient hand-powered grass mower had been invented by Lewis Miller in 1855, and such mowers were cheap and plentiful at the turn of the century.) Going on to the keeping of public grounds, Veblen took note of the role of the hand mower and its operator: "The best that is done by skilled workmen under the supervision of a trained keeper is a more or less close imitation of a pasture, but the result invariably falls somewhat short of the artistic effect of grazing." In sum, a lawn is a pasture and a cow is its best keeper; all the rest is conspicuous display.

Anthony Trollope's industrious mother, Frances — that extraordinary pioneer among British observers of American ways, whose *Domestic Manners of the Americans* (1832) is given its special bite and hilarity by the author's incessant tone of screaming moral outrage — presents a vignette of early American lawn care that bears out Veblen's vision of the lost ideal. Speaking of a place near Cincinnati where she lived for a time, she writes, "We lived on terms of primeval intimacy with our cow, for if we lay down on our lawn she did not scruple to take a sniff at the book we were reading, but then she gave us her own sweet breath in return." At the other extreme on the matter stands H. L. Mencken. In an essay entitled "Professor Veblen" that was first published in 1919, when Veblen's reputation had recently passed one of its periodic peaks, Mencken set out to pulverize that reputation once and for all, and in the course of a torrent of invective, he singled out for special ridicule the passage on lawns in *The Theory of the Leisure Class*. "Why don't we employ cows to keep [our lawns] clipped, instead of importing Italians, Croatians, and blackamoors?" Mencken asked, ostensibly paraphrasing Veblen (who in the original had made no mention of Italians, Croatians, or "blackamoors"). Proceeding to Veblen's response to the question — that cows are eschewed because of their connotations of thrift and usefulness — Mencken replied, "Bosh! . . . Has the genial professor, pondering his great problems, ever taken a walk in the country? And has he, in the course of the walk, ever crossed a pasture inhabited by a cow (*Bos taurus*)? And has he, making that crossing, ever passed astern of the cow herself? And has he, thus passing astern, ever stepped carelessly, and —"

Passing astern of the remarkable insolence of the elegant urban Baltimorean Mencken in suggesting that he knew cows better than the farm boy Veblen, Mencken had a point; cow pats on lawns and in public parks do seem inconsistent not only with conspicuous display but also with simple comfort and amenity. The very notion presupposes a society more like the France of Louis XV than the America of the times when Veblen wrote or when Mencken wrote, and certainly in ludicrous contrast to the America of the nineteen-eighties. Moreover, it would seem that both Veblen and Mencken — fully in the tradition of intellectual disputants in all times and places — had their basic facts wrong. Cows were never the preferred lawn croppers. Sheep were, especially in England, home of the lawn, where in the landscaping of the traditional country estate there was a wall around the house for the specific purpose of preventing the lawn-mowing sheep from straying into the drawing room like berserk riderless Toros or Jacobsens. And the reason sheep were preferred goes directly to Mencken's point about cow pats — indeed, destroys it. Sheep leave pellets, which are not generally productive of human pratfalls, rather than pats, which are. But Veblen had a point, too, however excessive and therefore vulnerable his zeal in trying to prove it. Man-tended lawns were conspicuous display in Veblen's time, and so they are today.

Lawns are ancient, and to create them by one means or another in places where the necessary conditions exist — a relatively cool climate, and at least eighteen to twenty inches of rainfall per year — may well be a natural human urge. If we seldom find lawns in the Hebrew, Greek, and Roman classics of antiquity, it may be simply because the climatic prerequisites seldom existed in the places described. England, of course, is lawn heaven. The *Oxford Dictionary* dates the word *lawn* (from *laund*, or land) from 1674 as meaning "a stretch of untilled or grass-covered ground" and from 1733 as meaning "grass which is kept closely mown." (Shakespeare in *The Tempest*, written about 1611, has a scene that takes place on a "short grass'd green" which is called a "land," not a lawn.) Lawns became a primary feature of English country life during the eighteenth century, and a passion for them was brought by the English to America, some parts of which nevertheless will not support them without watering too troublesome even for the leisure class; hence Astroturf and other artificial ground covers to simulate grass.

The extent of the loathing for uncut grass that had developed in the United States by the early nineteen-thirties is vividly shown by the horror that was struck into American hearts when Herbert Hoover, campaigning for the presidency in 1932, said that his opponent's election would result in grass growing in the streets of our cities. The neuroses and invidiousnesses associated with maintaining a green and weed-free suburban lawn during the early postwar period, when the suburban home-owning explosion was taking place, became the subject of a subliterature of that period. A reasonable approximation of such a lawn came to be considered as much a requirement for decency as a body washed reasonably recently, clean and appropriate clothing, and short hair for men and boys. For a suburban homeowner to have a weedy or overgrown lawn carried a suggestion of depravity in other areas of life — of shiftlessness, alcoholism, atheism, or, worst of all, Communism. Possession of an expensive gasoline-driven mower, preferably in the form of a self-propelled vehicle, became a necessity to avoid loss of status. As time went on and mass suburban living moved on to a more mature phase, a certain relaxation of community standards as to lawn maintenance took place. Suburban homeowners in the nineteen-sixties and -seventies took to assigning complete responsibility for their lawns to lawn-care companies — the basic annual charge in the Northeast in 1979 was two cents per square foot, which comes to about eight hundred and seventy dollars an acre — or tending them themselves in a more negligent way. At the extreme of negligence, or relaxation, many of the rural communes that flourished around 1970 simply let their plots grow wild, and walked through waist-high grass and wild flowers. Much nearer the mainstream, *Forbes* magazine, which billed itself as "the capitalist tool," in 1979 printed prominently (and surely jocularly) a list of reasons submitted by a reader for *not* mowing one's lawn: mowing wastes fuel; it wastes human energy and time; cutting down grass removes air-purifying greenery; uncut lawns protect the water table by storing water; mowing destroys baby birds, butterflies, and bumblebees; mowing with power equipment causes more than fifty thousand accidents a year, some of which result in severed fingers, toes, and hands.

Nevertheless, most Americans went on mowing, or feeling guilty about not mowing, or feeling socially outclassed when neighbors mowed more than they did. In spite of the reaction against the lawn-tending excesses of the early suburban period of the nineteen-fifties — and the national tendency in recent years to move from straightforward display to parody display in other areas of life — the lawn remains a crucial arena for classical predatory invidiousness and its concomitant, anxiety. A focal point for that anxiety is a continuing and largely irrational fear of the most common of what are regarded as lawn weeds, crabgrass. This plant — *Digitaria sanguinalis* to a botanist, or a Mencken — was introduced into North America late in the nineteenth century by immigrants from central Europe. It is one of the fastest-growing of grasses, and one of the hardiest. In contrast to more honored grasses, it thrives in heat and drought, and attempts to eradicate it by hoeing are usually losing battles. A single plant is capable of producing up to ninety thousand seeds. Left uncut, it may grow taller than a man; when mowed, it spreads evenly and greenly, and the cuttings are pronounced by botanists to be excellent lawn fertilizer. It is a common thing during a blazing summer to see even a well-tended lawn, provided its gardener does not share the prevalent murderous attitude toward crabgrass, in which other more sought-after grasses have been burned to a light brown or gray, and patches of crabgrass stand out because they are the only areas of luxuriant light green.

But the murderous attitude persists, even increases. Scott, advertising a crabgrass-killing chemical called Halts, turns the situation just described on its head: "By late summer you'll have regular mats of the stuff choking your good grass." The gratuitously invidious word *choking* is used casually and without explanation (all plants try to "choke" their neighbors), just as invidious words expressing patriotism are used in wartime propaganda; and doubtless Scott's use of it evokes as little public criticism as such propaganda customarily does. (The ad goes on to mention another product, Turf Builder Plus 2, that is designed to kill dandelions and chickweed, which have attractive flowers and, incidentally, are edible.)

Let us speculate about the causes of the vindictive and apparently irrational American hostility to crabgrass. First, the hostility has at least one rational element: crabgrass is an annual plant that dies during the winter, and places where it has established itself to the exclusion of other grasses are left bare during the latter months of winter. Again, it may not be too fanciful to suggest that part of crabgrass's problem is a national subliminal memory of its origins in this country; that is, it may be thought of, in the national unconscious, as too hardy and resourceful to qualify for elegance. But the main reason, it appears, is that crabgrass, precisely through its dauntless hardihood, provides an easily visible measure of how much or how little effort and expense a homeowner has lavished on conventional efforts to improve his lawn. The verifiable presence of this plucky, lovable plant is the signature of a relaxed gardener, and therefore a mark of defeat in the neighborhood status struggle. Crabgrass's greenness when other grasses are brown has both nothing and everything to do with the matter.

Digitaria sanguinalis! Fecund, indomitable plant, asking so little and giving so much! Forgive us our trespasses.

Competitive lawn display and emulation remain a clear example in American life of Veblenism in its original, unaltered state. What, then, would parody lawn display consist of? It would be mischievous to suggest that the perfect parody would be a small suburban front-yard lawn contentedly tended by Veblen's cow. More probably, it would consist of a green space left totally to its own devices — its grasses waist-high or higher, its flowering plants coming to flower and going to seed as they will. Culturally, this would be the horticultural equivalent of Woody Hayes punching the armored linebacker who had intercepted a pass.

This does not often happen — and, of course, for reasons not wholly irrational. A short-grassed green is useful, even necessary, for children's games like hide-and-seek, and adult games like croquet and badminton; for adult sports like baseball, football, golf, and lawn tennis (which in recent years has virtually disappeared in the United States as a result of the skyrocketing cost of maintaining an appropriate lawn); for outdoor parties; and simply for sitting or lying outdoors in sun or shade, like Mrs. Trollope. But usefulness is by no means the whole story. Like Jay Gatsby, almost all of us want to feel that we have come a long way to our "blue lawn." In most American places, an untended lawn is still thought of as being to a family residence what an untended three-day stubble of beard is to a man. Lawns are too sacred for parody; we mow, weed, fertilize, and water defensively, to escape bumhood.

7

Getting Drunk

Early in his famous chapter on "Conspicuous Consumption" in *The Theory of the Leisure Class,* Veblen included a discussion of alcoholic beverages and narcotic drugs. He saw the pattern of their use in the United States as a manifestation of class distinctions — indeed, as the very best available example of "the ceremonial differentiation of the dietary." According to his understanding of the custom of his time, the working class by common consent was assigned to eat and drink only what was necessary for survival; luxuries were reserved for the superior, leisure class. Obviously, alcohol and narcotic drugs fell in the latter category. Along with the working class, the women of the leisure class were (Veblen averred) ceremonially excluded from more than token tippling or sniffing. Woman, being a chattel, should, like her cook and gardener, "consume only what is necessary to her sustenance." Her function was to "prepare and administer" her man's intoxicating luxuries. As for leisure-class men, for them drinking, up to and including enough to cause drunkenness, was accepted as a form of exploit, "a mark . . . of the superior status of those who are able to afford the indulgence." "It has even happened," Veblen went on, "that the name for certain diseased conditions of the body arising from [overindulgence] has passed into everyday speech as a synonym for 'noble' or 'gentle.' " Certainly Veblen did not mean "cirrhosis of the liver" or even "delirium tremens"; it must have been "hangover," "vomiting," or perhaps "gout," that he was specifying as the American equivalent of the Heidelberg dueling scar as a certificate of leisure-class standing.

All rather bizarre, and, incidentally, eminently subject to parody. But almost anyone who attended an American university in the first half of this century must recognize the extraordinary force of the idea of drinking as male exploit (and that idea, after losing ground in the nineteen-sixties, has been making a strong comeback in recent years, as certified in the movie *Animal House*). Undergraduate drinking patterns varied widely from region to region and institution to institution; in general, it is safe to say that the greater the status of the institution, the greater the ritual emphasis placed on "drinking like a gentleman." To "drink like a gentleman" meant to consume the maximum amount (usually in form of beer; hard liquor, being more expensive and more intoxicating than beer, was reserved except on special occasions for the few richest and most devil-may-care students) while showing the minimum effect. However, overt drunkenness was not only permitted on occasion, but was accepted as exploit, provided only that the drunk should react with comic antics and relatively harmless violence (breaking furniture, insulting strange women) rather than surliness or hostility (punching peers in the nose, insulting known, leisure-class women, such as a peer's female

friend or sister). In many instances, a successful undergraduate drinker was thereby accorded status comparable to that of a successful athlete; and, of course, the
highest status of all was reserved for the master of both
skills, the drunken athlete.

The drinking songs and games favored by undergraduates forcefully emphasize the point. One of the most
popular of the songs suggested that nondrinkers and light
drinkers live miserable lives and go to miserable, early
graves. Status and happiness are proposed in an ascend-
ing scale in direct proportion to alcohol consumption.
The man who drinks only water and goes to bed sober
"falls as the leaves do fall / so early in October." Next in
the scale up,

*The man who drinks his whiskey clear, and goes to bed
right mellow
Lives as he ought to live, and dies a jolly good fellow.*

Finally, at the Dionysian peak,

*The man who drinks just what he likes, and getteth half-
seas over
Lives till he dies perhaps, and then lies down in clover.*

A game called "Chugalug" consisted of the player
who was "it" balancing a full glass or mug of beer on his
head (a test of ability to "hold his liquor"), while the others in the group sang the following forthright ditty:

*Here's to _____, he's true blue,
He's a drunkard through and through.
He's a drunkard, so they say,*

Tried to go to heaven, but he went the other way.
So drink, chugalug!

The balancer was then required to take the beer from his head and drink it at a draft, without lowering the container from his lips. The player who could successfully complete this routine the most times was the winner, and acquired from his exploit the highest status.

Contrary to Veblen, the expense of the intoxicant played little or no part in these rituals. The cost was low — expensive imported beers were not used — and was ritually shared evenly among the participants. The only element of wealth or breeding involved was the fact that those from more affluent, and therefore generally more sophisticated, backgrounds had the advantage of having been introduced to intoxicants earlier in their lives and consequently of being better able to handle the effects. The chief Veblenian element was that of invidious competitive exploit involving risk. All exploit must involve risk, and those who habitually engaged in games like "Chugalug" realized, however dimly, that they were assuming a short-term risk of inducing conduct that would result in suspension or lesser disciplinary action, and long-term risk of impaired health. (In fact, such games created or encouraged many later cases of alcoholism, as anyone knows who played them and subsequently kept in touch with his former playmates.) Just as the primitive hunter-warrior, or even the Heidelberg duelist, knew that he was incurring risk of permanent harm to himself in his quest for status, so did the American undergraduate drinker. To show a degree of recklessness was part of the cost of being generally admired. Moreover, in line with Veblen's suggestion about the names attached to diseases of overindulgence, the practical consequence of undergraduate drunkenness had a certain honor attached to it. The news that a fellow student had been suspended or otherwise punished for drunken behavior following a drinking exploit was greeted by his fellows who had narrowly escaped the same fate with feelings of sympathy and increased respect — as if the punished one were a military colleague whose daring had led to his being shot down in combat.

The social role of drinking in American life has changed greatly over the centuries, but it has always been large. The social historian J. C. Furnas wrote of the American colonies in the seventeenth century, "A typical man of the time started the day with a pre-breakfast dram of straight rum, whiskey, or peach brandy, depending on his colony." Mencken called the years between the Revolution and the Civil War "the Gothic age of American drinking," and it was during that period that Americans coined most of the commonly used modern drinking terms — among them *barroom* (1807), *jigger* (1836), and even *cocktail* (1806).

Mrs. Trollope noted in her scolding way that "whiskey . . . flows everywhere at the . . . fatally cheap rate of twenty cents a gallon, and its hideous effects are visible on the countenance of every man you meet." It was also during that period that a great counterforce, the temperance movement, arose and gained many supporters — the State of Maine first passed its prohibition law in 1841 and reenacted it in 1858 — and the still-continuing American division and conflict between drinkers and nondrinkers became established as part of the national social fabric. As for the situation now, we have only to note the recent finding of the lexicographers of American slang Harold Wentworth and Stuart Berg Flexner that there are more American slang synonyms for "drunk" than for the sexual act itself, to realize the honor and importance that we still attach to that condition.

Moreover, the roots of the status-enhancing quality of drinking, which Veblen observed and which was later preserved in undergraduate custom, went back well before Veblen's time. A document from the Gothic age that this writer has happened upon* takes up the American custom of "treating" — the giving of liquor at any time of the day by a tradesman in appreciation of trade or in payment for physical work, or a politician to gain votes. (Veblen refers in passing to the custom of "treating," and although the word now sounds quaint, it is still used in the original meaning by some working-class Americans of rural origin.) My pre–Civil War document gives a vivid picture of the prevalence of treating, and of its status-enhancing effect. The writer says, "At our stores, in the country, in villages, in towns, where there is a brisk retail business, or where barter and exchange are carried on, we daily take notice that after a bargain is struck, or a purchase made, the parties *step into the back-shop*. In this privacy, or in the corner where a row of hogsheads and casks is standing, the cask is turned, and a small glass of liquor is given to the customer. . . . There is generally attached to every establishment where the practice is in vogue a small corps of supernumeraries, who are always dodging within call, as they have no other employment, and are known to prefer a treat to anything else. . . . Boys as well as men have their treat. . . . No harm is suspected when the lad is asked to 'drink a little.'

*See Appendix C, page 288.

It is manly, and when it flies into his head he feels doubly like a man." As a drinker for the purpose of gaining status, the pre–Civil War apprentice or handy boy is a precursor of the undergraduate of more recent times. In both cases, the drink may not really be wanted, but when it "flies into the head," it gives him an instant illusion of higher status; and, status in America being by nature subjective and ephemeral, the illusion comes close to creating the reality.

It was in the post–Civil War era, Veblen's era, that drinking as invidious exploit was taken over by the leisure class. (We have already noted how sports were similarly taken over at about the same time.) As a result, if we are to believe Veblen, leisure-class women took to serving their men plentiful and ceremonial libations, while abstaining themselves; and the lower orders began getting their treats seldom if at all. Since then, in line with the recent tendency of American display to metamorphose into parody, attitudes and practices regarding intoxicants have changed drastically.

Certainly Veblen's ideas about women and drinking, if they ever applied, do not apply now. (Mencken in his famous attack on Veblen made particular sport of those ideas. He agreed with Veblen that men do not want their women to drink heavily, but argued that the real reason is that women physiologically cannot handle liquor; therefore a man "is eager to safeguard his wife's self-respect and his own dignity." It was not one of Mencken's more engaging performances.) For one thing, women now do not customarily "prepare and administer" drinks to their husbands or lovers; the reverse is more apt to be the case. For another, although currently some four

out of five American alcoholics are men, among social
drinkers women often match men drink for drink, and
usually show little or no additional effect. Both Veblen
and Mencken to the contrary, sex does not have much to
do with the matter. But status, as ever, does.

Middle-class blacks in recent years have come to be
known as heavy users of very expensive brands of Scotch
whisky, presumably by way of classic conspicuous display and waste. But beginning in the nineteen-sixties,
many middle-class whites began cutting down on their
drinking. First the rebellious youth, and then those of
their elders who were willing to follow the lead of a
younger generation, took in significant numbers to drinking only wine or nothing alcoholic at all. (The three-mar-
tini lunch, prevalent in the nineteen-fifties, had in fact
all but disappeared long before it reached a peak in political rhetoric; similarly, the gray flannel suit disappeared almost at the very moment it was canonized in
social rhetoric. It is illuminating to note that the whole
martini phenomenon simply passed some classes of
drinkers by. Order one today in a lowdown bar, and you
will be served a villainous concoction bearing hardly any
resemblance to the real thing. It is difficult to say whether
this is a function of ignorance or an expression of parody.)
In the nineteen-seventies, it became the height of bever-
age-consumption fashion to go into an expensive restaurant and order Perrier water with a twist of lemon for four
or five dollars a glass. The new form of drinking display,
then, was nondrinking.

The substitute intoxicant was drugs. Drug use for
pleasure was, of course, far from a novelty in American
life. In the nineteenth century, the habit of smoking opium was supposedly introduced by Chinese immigrants

who were employed in the building of the transcontinental railroad. Meanwhile, use of narcotics for medical purposes was widespread and uncontrolled. Opium —grown freely and legally in the United States in those days — and its derivatives were available in both doctors' prescriptions and in over-the-counter patent medicines, and many users became addicted without realizing it. Morphine was often prescribed as a treatment for alcoholism, thus substituting one disastrous addiction for another. There was even cocaine in Coca-Cola. Gradually, as the perils became ever more evident, antinarcotic laws were introduced: the Pure Food and Drug Act of 1906, which required accurate labeling; the Harrison Narcotic Act of 1914, which outlawed nonprescription sale of narcotics; and the later total ban on heroin. As a result, the drug trade went underground and drug use assumed an entirely different character. The relatively mild hallucinogen marijuana had been a major crop in colonial America, more or less exclusively as a source of fiber for rope. Marijuana as an intoxicant is thought to have been introduced into the country early in this century by Mexican laborers and Latin American seamen. It became particularly popular among jazz musicians, including those with celebrity status.

Thus the way was cleared for the perception of some forms of drug use as risky, status-enhancing exploit, rather than as the desperate recourse of proletarians. In the nineteen-sixties — for the first time in American history, with the minor exception of earlier leisure-class cocaine snorting — drug use for intoxication became a form of conspicuous display. This was in part a response to the iron law of fashion, noted by Quentin Bell and others in connection with dress, that at a certain point whatever had been fashionable must be violently rejected and replaced with something very different if not in fact opposite. Beginning with the rebellious or self-indulgent young, and extending in ever-widening circles to the more fashion-conscious among their elders, the use of marijuana and certain more dangerous drugs such as amphetamines, LSD, morphine, and cocaine — but never extending to heroin, the use of which continued to be considered a field mark of low-status losers — came to be the answer to alcohol. The latter was now discredited on grounds of its long association with everything bourgeois, traditional, and square; marijuana was in favor because of its new connotations of the avant-garde, further enhanced by the fact that it was still illegal in the eyes of the despised state and federal governments. (Alcohol had similarly gained status during Prohibition.) By rough analogy, in the nineteen-sixties marijuana smoking in colleges and universities became what beer drinking had been earlier, and the use of more dangerous drugs what hard-liquor drinking had been. Drug use, that is, became a parody of the old form of display.

In the past few years a reaction, or cycling out, has been observable. Parody display in the matter of drug use has tended to break down into direct, classic display. (We will presently see a comparable disintegration in the field of dress fashion.) Middle-class drug use from the beginning had an element of pecuniary display, because drugs, being illegal, cost much more than alcohol for a comparable amount of intoxicant. However, in the sixties that element was subsidiary to others, particularly the implications of authority-defying and risk-taking. (That is to say, "Chugalug" all over again.) Now those implications have faded in their turn. Possession of small amounts of marijuana in many states has come to be regarded by the law as a peccadillo, of the general magnitude of a traffic violation. The constituted authorities now set a dubious example; in 1978, just after resigning as a result of having been caught writing a blind drug prescription for a colleague, the White House adviser on health affairs said that there was a "high incidence" of marijuana use among members of his own staff, and "occasional" use of cocaine. Who would keep the keepers themselves?

Even Letitia Baldridge, the Establishment arbiter of etiquette, in 1978 pronounced use of marijuana and hashish to be "marginally socially acceptable." Meanwhile, the street cost of all illegal drugs went sky-high. Cocaine in particular became so expensive as to be available almost exclusively to the affluent, and thus became an ideal vehicle for pure Veblenian display. The seal was placed on this role early in 1979, when a number of members of the Chicago Board Options Exchange were accused of conducting floor trades in cocaine along with options on the stock of IBM, General Motors, and Exxon. The next parody, presumably, would be a parody of drug use.

8

Eating and Starving

The elaborate banquet menus of the robber-baron era, some of them several pages long, and almost all of them written in French or what passed for French, were one of the classic Veblenian vulgarities of the time. Heavy eating was in favor, and not simply as a display of wealth per se. Concomitantly, approval was conventionally accorded to a marked amount of fat on the human frame. The ideal of feminine beauty was a rather narrow waist set off by a huge, voluptuous bust, similarly appointed buttocks, round, ample arms, and ample, although invisible, legs. (Earlier in the nineteenth century, the crinoline skirt had given the wearer the appearance of having a large rump, whether or not she actually had one underneath.) Veblen, not surprisingly, had his own way of putting the matter. In the course of economic development, he said, the ideal of feminine beauty among Western peoples had earlier shifted from the woman of "physical presence" — robust, large-limbed, and obviously capable of rendering the most back-breaking service to her man — to the chivalric ideal, the delicate, slender, infirm, "translucent" object to be cherished and protected; while in Veblen's own time, he believed, the ideal was beginning to shift back to the stately "woman of presence." All this was "in obedience to the changing conditions of pecuniary emulation." That is to say, in Veblen's time it was less important for a man to prove that his wife was so delicate as to be incapable of vulgar work — he had other ways of proving that — than it was for him to prove that she was so fat as to have plainly been fed to the brim.

The prevailing fashion as to male physique was different only in degree. J. Pierpont Morgan, the reigning banker of the age, perhaps just because of his own tendency to overweight made an ideal of the tall, thin, silver-haired, aristocratic-looking man, and with few exceptions chose as his partners men who met those specifications. (Incidentally, Morgan thereby established a style that still persists in the American banking business. It is entertaining to note that the tradition of hostility to fat is still honored in the House of Morgan, or is said to be, through a house rule against investing in the securities of companies headed by fat men.) But at the same time, overweight men of power like Mark Hanna and Grover Cleveland were considered not ridiculous, but rather more redolent of power, for their excess poundage; and the cartoon cliché, the invariably portly wax-mustached plutocrat with the dollar sign on his hat, was not far wide of the mark. To judge from their oil and photographic portraits, most of the leading industrialists of the time were grossly overweight by the standards of today.

It is surprising now to recall until how recently the old standards persisted. The association of thinness with health and beauty, and fatness with unattractiveness and early death, is quite new. In my own childhood and youth in the Northeast in the nineteen-twenties and -thirties, thinness was considered both laughable and medically dangerous. Between children, epithets like *skinny* were intended to hurt, and they did. Health-building ads in popular magazines presented the success story of the "ninety-seven-pound weakling," contemptuously rejected by pretty, well-fleshed women on the beach, who could with the help of the both hypermuscular and amply fleshed Charles Atlas become more or less like him, "the world's most perfectly developed man." Even among nonweaklings, to gain a few pounds was considered a sign of health and well-being; quantities of butter were used in cooking; cream as thick as treacle was poured over fruit and breakfast food; milk delivered daily by a vanishing species, the milkman, was dutifully consumed within the day, because more milk would be delivered early tomorrow; and a prime objective of treatment after an illness was to fatten up the convalescent. (It is now recognized that convalescence is a time of particular danger of excessive weight gain for those with a tendency to overweight.) True enough, fat young women dieted to lose weight in order to improve their sexual competitiveness; but they wanted to lose only enough fat to make themselves comparable to, say, the pneumatic heroines of Petty's cartoons in *Esquire*.

All this may be partly explainable in terms of the state of the medical art. Up until the Second World War the disease most feared by Americans, at least as regards children and young adults, was tuberculosis, a classic symptom of which is progressive emaciation. Conversely, an emaciated condition was believed to predispose to the disease. Youth understandably didn't want to — in the tubercular John Keats's words — "grow pale, and spectre-thin, and die." Being portly or buxom provided reassuring evidence that nothing of the sort was happening. Then in the early postwar period, medical advances at last effectively contained tuberculosis; it had been third among causes of death nationally in the nineteen-twenties and fourth as late as 1945, while today it is right off the list of leading killers. (Motor vehicle accidents passed it for the first time in 1950.)

But tuberculosis alone cannot explain the extraordinary national reversal of attitudes toward fatness and thinness. Veblenian social and economic factors were at work, too. It is interesting to note that the rise of American dieting and an American cult of thinness in the postwar years coincided precisely with a great rise in national affluence. The general availability of plenty of food and drink to make almost anyone fat deprived the state of fatness (or so Veblen would surely argue) of its role as a bodily certificate of overall superiority. Virginia Slims cigarettes in their advertising announced what the new certificate would be, at least for women: "A Woman Should Be Both Thin and Rich." A female celebrity emphasized the point by advising the world that "you can't be too rich or too thin."

Styles of American eating have also been shaped by technological developments outside the field of medicine. For example, it has been said that the modern American diet began with the invention of the can opener in 1858, which made possible the mass-produced food can; and roadside fast food began in the nineteen-thirties, spawned by an explosion of automobiles. At any rate, in the current age of thinness the problem of the unfashionably obese minority seems to stem from causes more complicated than unnatural and uncontrollable appetite. The psychiatrist Hilde Bruch reported in 1961 that her obese patients actually did not know when they were psychologically hungry; apparently during their childhoods they had never learned to discriminate between hunger and such feelings as fear, anger, and anxiety. More recently, the Columbia University psychologist Stanley Schachter and his colleagues have demonstrated that the obese do not outeat normal people at all, except when the food offered is something that they particularly relish. (Almost everyone has seen a person with a tendency to fat, who is attempting to lose fat by dieting, turn away all but a small quantity of the main course of a meal, apparently heroically — only then to engorge offhandedly, say, ten or fifteen cookies with dessert.) Schachter concluded that fat people's eating habits are largely determined by what he called "external cues" — the sight, smell, and taste of food, the knowledge that it is mealtime — rather than by hunger. Others have noted that when fat people do manage to lose a lot of flesh, they often become anxious and depressed, feeling that they have been diminished figuratively as well as literally. Whichever is cause and which effect, then, obesity is now thought to be associated with the curse of psychological disorder rather than with the benefice of having plenty of food on the table.

Nevertheless, eating — along with dressing, the most public and visible of the various repetitive activities of everyday life — continues, naturally enough, to have a large component of competitive display. As with most modern competitive display, the thing being displayed is primarily not wealth but taste and knowledge. For example, one way to gain status is by eating foreign foods in public, and in particular, by ordering and eating them with a knowledgeability that, although it may in fact reflect only careful research, appears to reflect easy first-hand knowledge of the food's country of origin. The robber barons' French (or ostensibly French) meals were only a hesitant beginning. The ordinary citizen in those days did not know a soufflé from a cakewalk, or a pâté from a bald head. First mass immigration, and later the large-scale entry of the United States into foreign commerce, introduced the public to the delights, mysteries, problems, and status-getting possibilities of eating foreign food in public.

A few holdouts among the famous, such as the late Henry R. Luce, continued stubbornly to regard food as mere fuel, and to be vocally scornful of all fastidiousness and pretension in the matter of nourishment. (After the Guadeloupe summit meeting of January, 1979, Pierre Coffe, the French chef who had presided, complained that President Carter had wounded his professional pride. "You don't ask a two-cap chef for hamburgers," Coffe said, in what may have been one of the last salvos in the traditional form of transatlantic war over culinary taste.) Meanwhile, however, the average person — or at least the average financially and socially ambitious person — now aspires vigorously to be something of a gourmet. In particular, because of Japan's new status as a world economic power and the extreme exoticism of its cuisine and table manners, Japanese food caters to this aspiration. Benihana, one of a chain of moderately priced Japanese restaurants in the United States, has one on West Forty-fourth Street in New York City that is patronized by young executives of both sexes who are energetically making their way up the business ladder. They sit around large tables, elbow to elbow with both friends and strangers, while a Japanese chef cooks on the table in front of them, with many rhythmic and flamboyant Oriental movements and gestures. (Obviously, both the style of the chef and the commonality of the table have overtones of conspicuous display.) For the American customers, once the hurdle of ordering with aplomb has been passed, the big question is whether to eat with chopsticks — a skill relatively easy to acquire — or with Western tableware. The latter usually gets the majority vote. "No thanks, honey, I'm roughing it," a brisk young executive will say to the Japanese hostess who with demure charm presses on him a set of chopsticks. In coming to Benihana in the first place, and then opting for knife and fork, the young man adopts the characteristic current American style of simultaneously embracing an alien culture and denigrating it. He can boast of the fact that he has had lunch at Benihana, and also of the fact that a full-blooded American like him is not subservient to alien custom. A twist to the Benihana phenomenon is provided by another finding of Schachter. Along with two associates, Schachter went to a large number of Oriental restaurants in New York City, and counted how many people of what physical shape used knives and forks, and how many used chopsticks. Almost a quarter of thin or normal-weight people took a fling with chopsticks, while fewer than one in twenty among fat people did. Apparently, those who are fat know that they are beaten in the status race anyhow; that being so, they are more apt to figure that they might as well pack in the calories with Western efficiency.

However, the hard core of contemporary American display in eating does not consist of toying with foreign food. It consists, more simply, of eating very little food of any kind. In the most sophisticated of American cities, it is the most sophisticated — and expensive — of restaurants that, unless the waiter is categorically instructed otherwise, serve the smallest portions. Luncheon at La Grenouille or "21," or dinner at Le Plaisir, in New York is a case in point. Part of the premium price charged at such places evidently goes for the privilege of not having to face a full plate. Absent evidence to the contrary, the patron is assumed to be tuberculosis-free, and on a diet. Similarly, some of the most dedicated and stylish hostesses, giving a little dinner party at home, make a great show of the work of preparation, inviting the guests into the kitchen to watch the seemingly endless process, all the while regaling them with the names of rare herbs and condiments — and then setting on the table a feast quantitatively fit for a bird. The result of this fashion in eating, or not eating, reached the stage of parody with the rise to world fame in the nineteen-sixties of the British model Twiggy, perhaps the first stick-shaped woman ever to become an international sex symbol.

Surely the ultimate manifestation of display by starvation is the sudden prevalence in recent years of the disease called anorexia nervosa. Anorexia is not exclusively a modern disease (something resembling it was described in the seventeenth century), nor an American disease (one case per two hundred adolescent girls was recently found in a middle-class English environment), nor a disease of adolescent girls (boys occasionally suffer from it). The fact remains that it occurs more commonly now than at any previous time in recorded medical history; that it is particularly common among adolescent girls of affluent families in the United States; and that it is a grave, frequently fatal, affliction.

The principal symptom of anorexia is intractable refusal to eat, either entirely or except in periodic binges that are nutritionally useless because predictably followed by vomiting. The typical victim, as described in the medical and lay literature on the subject, is (as Rosemary Dinnage puts it) "the odd one out in an averagely unhappy family." She is shy and lonely, hating the crudity of her adolescent growth, particularly in its sexual aspects; secretly, under her extreme lack of self-confidence, she is an ambitious perfectionist. It is crucial that, having come down with the disease, she does not refuse food out of conscious defiance of authority, as an angry baby does. On the contrary, consciously she is anxious to eat normally, both to please and reassure her parents and for the sake of her own welfare. But she is unable to do so. Nor does the disease result in a langorous fading away, as with the tubercular heroines of romantic nineteenth-century literature; rather, the typical anorexic girl is hyperactive, full of energy and hope, and as insistent as an alcoholic in denying the fact of her illness. Recovered former victims have described feeling a kind of "high," as if from drugs: "You feel outside your body. You are truly beside yourself — and then you are in a different state of consciousness and you can undergo pain without reacting. That's what I did with hunger."

It is as if, then, this terrible disease about which little is definitively known is, like drug-taking, a perverse effort to experience oneself more fully in an alienating environment. It seems safe to believe the hunch of some clinicians that the current prevalence of anorexia is directly connected with the current obsession about slimness, which serves as fertile cultural soil to nurture it. Some anorexics secretly give themselves new names; as Dinnage says, "the thin girl is going to be a new, realler self" — the shy, lonely, left-out plump girl replaced by another, triumphant and admired because so self-denying and so thin, so free of crude evidences of blatant sexuality, her name figuratively up in lights like Twiggy's.

One of the things nobody really knows is why the vast majority of anorexics are women. Perhaps it is a consequence of the tendency Veblen noted for society to use women as primary objects of display. One might speculate that the woman, who in Veblen's scheme was the evidence of family affluence with her rolls of flesh and her expensive furbelows of clothing, has in the modern anorexic's case become the victim of an opposite cultural aspiration. Conspicuous consumption has been carried to the ultimate, self-destructive extreme of consuming the consumer's own body, the very self.

Here are manners as matters of life and death. Anorexia may be looked upon as parody display carried to the point of madness.

9

Telephoning

The telephone is the most important single artifact of modern social relations. Vast and vital industries, such as the securities business and international money trading, are conducted almost exclusively over it, and so are some private lives. Not surprising, then, that it is both taken for granted and seldom out of our thoughts.

This was all true to a lesser extent at the turn of the century when Veblen wrote. The telephone was a quarter of a century old then, and several million instruments were already in use in the United States. Its effect on manners had been noted by Mark Twain as early as 1879, the third year after its invention. Nevertheless, it remained both technologically and socially in an underdeveloped state. For example, coast-to-coast and overseas service did not yet exist. The industry itself was in a state of turmoil. The original Bell patents had recently expired, freeing anyone to set up a separate system, in competition with the Bell System; as a result, many towns and cities had two or more unconnected systems, resulting in communication chaos and — not incidentally — invidious social distinctions between subscribers to the various systems in a given place. In many rural areas where Bell had not yet deigned to provide service, farmers had strung wires over trees and fenceposts and hired a farm girl to serve as central operator, thus creating their own do-it-yourself cooperative systems. These systems provided surcease from loneliness and a degree of protection from physical danger among the isolated people of an underpopulated continent. "Central" was a message center and fountain of gossip. Such functions had from the point of view of social relations a character nothing like that of the telephone today. Nevertheless, the modern characteristics of the telephone were beginning to manifest themselves. Veblen did not mention them, or it, in *The Theory of the Leisure Class* (although he later went on record as believing that the telephone's "ubiquitous presence conduces to an unrelenting nervous tension and unrest"). A pity, because of all the mechanical devices of modern life, the telephone is the one most exquisitely adapted to predatory invidiousness.

Having a telephone means both vulnerability and power — vulnerability because it lays one open to anyone, friend, foe, or stranger; power because it gives access to the vulnerability of others. Because of this characteristic, the telephone seems to create at least one problem for every one that it solves. Commercial solicitation by telephone — oral junk mail — is for many a particularly infuriating form of gratuitous assault on privacy, and one that some have for many years campaigned to have outlawed, so far without success. The insolence of telephoners who, on getting a wrong number and thereby disturbing an innocent party, then brusquely hang up rather than apologizing, causes some victims of this double indignity to seethe and fume. At a greater extreme, obscene calls, which are illegal, and eavesdropping by wiretap, which may be either legal or illegal according to circumstances, are forms of assault by telephone that point up the telephone owner's vulnerability.

The available nontechnological defenses are relatively frail and self-defeating. The principal one consists of avoiding incoming calls by leaving the instrument off the hook, switching off the bell if such a switch is available, putting chewing gum on the bell to silence it, or simply letting the telephone ring in a closed bureau drawer or under a pillow. That is to say, it consists of creating temporarily the condition of not having a telephone.

In a society of invidious predators, a telephone user is all but forced to become an invidious predator himself as a measure of survival.

This attack-and-defense aspect of the telephone, what may possibly be called its sadomasochistic quality, is sharply emphasized by the basic purpose of practically all of the technical innovations in "terminal" telephone equipment — the equipment used in home or office — that have been introduced and have become popular over the years. Ostensibly, each such innovation was intended to increase convenience. On analysis, however, the real purpose invariably turns out to be to minimize vulnerability and increase power. Michael Korda, an authority on office invidiousness, points out that "power . . . in telephoning is to have the maximum ability to place telephone calls together with the minimum possibility of receiving them." That is the basic function of practically all terminal-equipment innovations.

The first and simplest of these was the extension telephone. The industrialist E. H. Harriman early in this century seems to have been the pioneer user of multiple extensions. At one time he had one hundred of them in his country mansion, Arden House; among the rooms thus supplied was his bathroom. The multiple-extension user obviously gains the advantage of being able to place calls at any time from wherever he happens to be, and thus not only to place calls more conveniently but also to place more of them. Meanwhile, he is protected from receiving unwanted calls by a necessary component of such a system, one or more servants who screen incoming calls and pass on to the user only the calls that are appropriate and acceptable. Indeed, very early in commercial telephony the symbol of telephone authority came to be to have such a screener, so that a caller could not reach the authoritative one without first satisfying an intermediary — a clear instance, of course, of classic Veblenian invidiousness. Again very early in the game, not only businessmen but also others likely to get many unwanted calls, such as rich, attractive, and therefore highly desirable young women, took to having their calls screened for them.

Next came the unlisted number, a grosser form of roadblock against callers because it entirely screens out all who do not know the number. An additional and incidental measure of invidiousness is achieved by an unlisted number's clear implication that its possessor is in constant demand for one reason or another, and is obliged to keep away hoi polloi or go mad. Many who are not in any special demand have adopted unlisted numbers solely to make this implication. The disadvantage of the unlisted number is that, since it is impossible to keep all eligible callers properly informed of the number (some of them may have the number but lose it), many wanted calls are missed — that is, for most people it is *too* gross a screening device. (Not too gross, however, for a restaurant in Los Angeles called Ma Maison, which maintains an unlisted number. Just to call it up and beg for a chance to partake of its delights and pay its prices, one must be among the few in the know.)

The answering service — a post–Second World War development that had to wait as long as it did because it requires the technical capability of switching calls from the called number to the service — made the screening of calls available for the first time to those who could not afford a full-time hired personal screener. Another postwar development, the speaker phone, gives an additional form of power edge. It enables the user to allow a whole roomful of his associates to listen to everything the party at the other end of the line says — a fact not necessarily known to the distant party. Korda says that in the nineteen-seventies speaker phones for business use suddenly became "very status-y." To dramatize the puissant, perhaps dangerously so, advantage that a speaker phone can confer, imagine an apartment-full of delectable young women living in a big city who have installed one. Calls from foolish and ardent suitors would be broadcast to everyone present in the apartment, for their information and amusement — an elaboration of the old habit of sought-after college girls, in the all-women institutions of the past, of conspicuously displaying their desirability and insouciance by passing around the more unsolicited of their love letters.

The introduction of what is called "key equipment" — a panel of buttons available to the telephone user, the most crucial of which is the "Hold" button, enabling a called party (or for that matter, a calling party) to cut off the interlocutor, leaving him dangling in limbo, still connected but incommunicado, for as long as the button-pusher wishes — represents an important advance in telephone invidiousness. Functionally, the Hold button provides a mechanical way of achieving the same result formerly achieved by the winner of the old game between secretaries of contriving to get the other secretary's boss on the line before one's own boss comes on. The loser waits. (Lillian Hellman in *Pentimento* describes a fine exploit in the secretary game, of which she was the victim. One summer when she was in Martha's Vineyard, her telephone rang and it was Samuel Goldwyn's secretary. After Miss Hellman and the secretary had had a pleasant chat, the secretary said that Mr. Goldwyn had been trying to reach her for two days to ask if she wanted to write the script for the movie of *Porgy and Bess*. Whereupon, after a long wait, Goldwyn came on and said, "Hello, Lillian, hello. Nice of you to call me after all these years. How can I help you?")

In the simplest terms, the Hold button saves the button-pusher's time and wastes that of the person put on Hold. (If he has called from a pay booth, it also wastes his money.) It is as nakedly invidious as possible, a fact emphasized by the manufacturer's name for a forty-eight-button office panel currently on the market, which is coolly called "Patrician." Strategically, the only answer to being put on Hold is to hang up — a solution as self-defeating as that of the home user who puts the telephone in a closed drawer. No wonder Korda advises, in bloodthirsty italics, "There is no doubt that *the more people you yourself can put and keep on Hold, the more successful you will seem."*

Another fairly recent innovation is the wireless remote phone, connected to the telephone network by radio, which enables the user to make or receive calls while in an aircraft, yacht, moving automobile, or the like. It is, of course, a further refinement of the principle of multiple extensions. A refinement of *it* is the beeper, which, while up to now it falls short of allowing the user to talk or listen from wherever he happens to be, is capable of summoning him at any time to the nearest telephone to receive a call. The beeper appears to violate the law that telephone innovations, to be successful, must increase the ability to make calls and decrease the ability to receive them. However, the beeper, so long as it remained a novelty and did not become a vulgar nuisance, had a unique ability to enhance the user's esteem, at least in the eyes of some, by beeping during social occasions such as dinner parties, thus calling attention in the most conspicuous possible way to the user's importance. In recent years, though, the beeper has fallen from grace. It is now commonly in the hands of low-status persons such as messengers and couriers, and thus has lost its status-enhancing power through democratization. Thus the iron law of telephone invidiousness has reasserted itself: to be effectively predatory, a telephone appliance must make the user harder to reach, not easier.

A device designed to detect lies over the telephone, by analyzing the speaker's voice, was demonstrated at a small-business exposition in New York City in 1979, but is still in the experimental stage as this is written, and for practical purposes belongs to the future. Its possibilities for enhancing telephone invidiousness are obvious. One imagines the user, whether in business or personal dealings, saying, "Be careful how you answer. I have the voice analyzer switched on." Or, perhaps more invidiously, not saying it.

A particularly versatile and mettlesome innovation of fairly recent vintage is the home telephone answering machine. It provides opportunities considerably greater than those afforded by the answering service, chiefly because the user, the receiving party, can deal with the caller as he chooses, and immediately rather than later. To begin with, the answering machine relies on an initial tape-recorded "announcement" by the machine user, which is automatically broadcast to any caller as soon as he reaches the number. Instead of the usual "hello" of a human answerer, the caller gets some such formula as, "This is Nancy Harman. We are not available at the moment. If you wish to leave a message, you may do so after you hear the signal, and we will call back." Since the announcement can be erased and rerecorded by the machine owner at will, it gives latitude for wide variation; on different days, the tone can be forbidding, sepulchral, jocular, aggressive, humble, according to whim. It is a private closed-circuit broadcasting device, perfectly adapted to either classic or parody display.

If the machine user is actually away when the machine is operating — as he says in his announcement that he is — he simply plays back any messages on his return. The machine functions exactly like an answering service, except that many people who will give messages to services refuse to give them to machines. It is when the user is secretly at home, and the machine turned on as a measure of deception, that its versatility comes into play.

By activating the machine, turning its monitor up so that messages may be heard, by speaker, and remaining within earshot, the user may hear the caller's return message as it is being delivered, secure in the knowledge that the caller believes him to be out. However, if the user wishes he may pick up the phone, switch off the machine, and talk directly to the caller. The machine thus affords the user, without the intervention of any third party, the basic power-gaining ability to answer only the calls he wants to answer. There are, of course, difficulties. The caller who, giving a message to the machine, is interrupted by the voice of the machine owner in real life, realizes that the device is being used for call-screening and is momentarily flattered at being among the elect to whom the machine owner is willing to talk. On reflection, though, the caller may remember previous occasions when his message on the machine has *not* been interrupted, and conclude that on those occasions, too, the machine user was really at home, in which case the caller was *not* elected, but instead was blackballed. That is, a current of invidiousness as strong as that made possible by the machine superimposed on the telephone itself is subject to a certain amount of feedback.

The commercial fate of the Picturephone, surely the most spectacular of recent telephone terminal equipment innovations, illustrates vividly the rule that such innovations must increase the user's power in order to be successful. After years of research and development, the Bell System introduced the Picturephone commercially in 1970. Basically, it applies the principle of closed-circuit television to the telephone. The user has at hand not only a telephone receiver and transmitter but also a television receiver and transmitter. To make a picture call, one dials in the normal way the number of another Picturephone subscriber. After being connected, one adjusts knobs for picture clarity on one's screen, as does the recipient of the call; whereupon the two are not only in voice contact but also eyeball to eyeball. The year of the Picturephone's introduction, a popular book on business etiquette forehandedly included an earnest section on Picturephone manners — wear a colored shirt, avoid a "snarling countenance," don't worry about jewelry blinding out the lens, and so on — and the Bell System ventured to predict that one million Picturephone sets would be in service by 1980.

The fact that in 1980 the Picturephone still has to be described drives home the point that this has not happened. The Picturephone is a flop, and was recognized as such by the Bell System as early as 1975. The few set owners who acquired them at the outset, in expectation of riding the crest of a new fashion, now find them almost useless, because there is hardly anyone else with a Picturephone set to call — or perhaps one should say conjure — up.

Various reasons have been adduced for the Picturephone's failure to catch on for either business or private use. The original one, much raised when the device was in the development stage, was that it was a "mere toy," of little or no substantive value; the Bell men replied at the time that precisely the same criticism, expressed in the same words, had been directed at the telephone itself in the first years after its invention. Another theory holds that the Picturephone does have some substantive value — the capacity to convey nuances of meaning and feeling through gesture and facial expression, the capacity to display pictures and documents — but not enough to justify its considerable extra expense. But as we well know, neither uselessness nor excessive expense necessarily militates against an object's popularity in our society; rather, in the classic Veblenian canon they categorically work in its favor. Probably the real cause of the Picturephone's failure is neither of these. Probably it is closely related to the telephone's traditional and natural use as an instrument of predatory invidiousness.

First, unlike the other technical innovations that have achieved popularity the Picturephone cannot give its user an edge, because it is necessarily bilateral. The person victimized by a Hold button or a home answering machine may not have those amenities attached to his own telephone, but the party called by Picturephone must have a Picturephone, too. The power gained by seeing the interlocutor is balanced by the vulnerability incurred through being seen. (A Picturephone user can turn off his picture transmitter, but the other party will then certainly retaliate in kind.) Beyond that, is it not possible that most people simply do not want to see or be seen on the telephone — that the secrecy, and resultant feeling of power, inherent in voice contact without visual contact is a principal reason people like to use the telephone in the first place? If not, why do people so often prefer to communicate, especially if the subject is painful or delicate, by telephone rather than face-to-face? The Picturephone, out of its nature, is open and aboveboard, equitable and noninvidious — fatal qualities, it appears, in a telephone innovation.

As a natural weapon of social war, the telephone goes too far. Like sport conducted without sportsmanship, it tends to tip the balance between predatory invidiousness and peaceable savagery too far toward the former. Consequently, an unwritten telephone code, a kind of telephone sportsmanship, has arisen to redress the balance. Letitia Baldridge sets forth the basics of the code in the tone of piety once used for exhortations to sportsmanship: adopt "a voice containing a smile"; pronounce words clearly and carefully; avoid technical jargon and overfamiliarity; don't try to get the upper hand by "failing to react in any way to the person to whom you are speaking"; scrupulously apologize upon reaching a wrong number, and so on. Even Korda, the apostle and teacher of invidiousness, mentions that people don't like to be put and kept on Hold. He explains that some people must never be put on Hold — your mother, your boss, your wife, your bookie, the Number One best-seller — while many others can.

This, of course, is the opposite of traditional sportsmanship, a benefice conferred evenhandedly by the sportsman on all comers and never a means of winnowing the important from the unimportant. Korda's system of applying or not applying the Hold button isn't sportsmanship; it is bullying and toadying. Still, there are signs of an emerging code in the use of power-increasing telephone devices. Some celebrities who have ample reason to maintain unlisted phones instead maintain ordinary listed ones, presumably as proof of their peaceable savagery (in this case, with overtones of democratic declassing). An increasing number of leading corporate executives answer their own phones whenever possible. Some who have speaker phones carefully inform the person on the other end that his voice is being amplified; conversely, and equally blamelessly, people calling from yachts or private jets make a point of *not* boasting about their whereabouts; and a distinct taboo against using Hold buttons unnecessarily has grown up to the point where many who have one, just in case, nevertheless regard its use with horror, as a low blow in the social bout. They would no sooner put someone they respect on Hold than hang up on him.

We recognize these mitigations of invidiousness, predicated on power, as the equivalent of traditional British sportsmanship of avoiding what is "not cricket"; in Theodore Rooseveltian diplomacy, as walking softly and carrying a big stick; and in poker, as the maneuver called "coffee-house." They are parody display. But meanwhile, there continue to be plenty of telephonic equivalents of the Ilie Nastases and Vince Lombardis of sport.

10

Talking

Speech is a combination of communication and display. Superficially, the manner of speech — accent, syntax, intonation — is the display component, while the matter is the communication component. But the matter may be display, too: it may be a showing off of knowledge, fashionable ideas, inside gossip, or similar material with little or no communication content other than its emulative or invidious connotation.

The nearly unique factor in manner-of-speech display is that, unlike all but a few other forms of display, it is unavoidable. We cannot open our mouths to speak without betraying a good deal — often more than we care to — about our social background, education, and situation in life. In the years before the Second World War, a speech expert used to go on radio where, after listening to strangers say a few key phrases and sentences, he would try to determine their exact place of birth or residence, and he was usually not far wide of the mark. (This was a subtle exploitation of the peculiar possibilities of radio such as we seldom encounter anymore.) Attempts to alter the impression we make with our speech are very frequent, but, as has been noted previously, seldom successful. With the coming first of national network radio and then national network television, it was widely believed that American regional speech characteristics would tend to disappear, but now, after a generation of network radio followed by one of network TV, this does not seem to have happened at all. Instead, a homogenized national accent is spoken on the media (an accent that, incidentally, is spoken practically nowhere else), while the local speech peculiarities on which the expert based his detective work forty years ago continue to flourish. Indeed, one sometimes feels that in a cultural sense TV in America has swept all before it *except* regional accents.

Veblen saved manner of speaking, as a certificate of class standing, for the last paragraphs of *The Theory of the Leisure Class*, where he used it as the coda of his book. "Elegant diction," he wrote, "is an effective means of reputability. . . . Classic speech has the honorific virtue of dignity; it commands attention and respect as being the accredited method of communication under the leisure-class scheme of life. . . . The advantage of the accredited locutions lies in their reputability; they are reputable because they are cumbrous and out of date, and therefore argue waste of time and exemption from the use and the need of direct and forcible speech." This is not very complete or very good, certainly if applied to our time. It was and is true enough that the potato-in-the-mouth manner of speech characteristic of some (though by no means all) products of the leading upper-class boarding schools is "cumbrous" sometimes to the point of incomprehensibility, suggesting that the speakers are indeed exempt from the need to speak forcibly, or even understandably. But Veblen's analysis falls down at that point. It leaves out the role such an accent, with its connotations of aristocracy, can play in leadership, as it did in the case of Franklin D. Roosevelt, who achieved the presidency in part because of his accent in a time when the nation wanted an authoritarian, aristocratic leader. (The same accent worked less well for Averell Harriman when he sought the presidency two decades later, at a time when aristocratic leadership was not wanted.) It leaves out the possibility, discussed in Chapter 5, that the accent may be to its user an unavoidable embarrassment rather than a predatory weapon. And it misses entirely the rococo charm that the accent in itself has when gracefully used. It is logical to attribute Veblen's obtuseness on the subject to the feelings of one who had, and intentionally preserved, an accent of his own that did not meet the canons of reputability of his time.

In fact, despite complications and cross-currents, manner of speech can still be used as a predatory weapon in Veblen's sense, to a surprising degree. A black may gain temporary advantage over either whites or other blacks by adopting a speech manner and locutions suggestive of outlawry and terror; but that advantage is as nothing compared to the advantage that can be gained over almost anyone through the judicious wielding of a Groton accent, provided it is authentic beyond cavil and is used with confidence rather than with apology. (Lower in the social scale, speech is used to make invidious separations between the two basic American classes, the college-educated and the not-college-educated. Two sociologists of the nineteen-seventies found that Middle Americans in Kansas City singled out speech as "the way you can tell someone's social class at first meeting.") It is interesting to note that in Britain, where class accents have varied little and have been precisely recognized for what they are by everyone for centuries, upper-class-speech has long been a favorite subject for parody by lower-class comedians, while in the United States since Roosevelt's time one has almost never heard such parodies of American aristocratic speech. Either the self-assurance necessary to parody is lacking here, or the subject is now no longer considered worthy of parody.

To find the *matter* of speech — words and their meanings, if any — used for display purposes, we need not seek far. Making lists of synonymous pairs of words, in each case one word representing the higher-class and the other the lower-class way of saying the same thing, continues to be the popular game in books and magazines that it has long been. Thus in 1958 the sociologist E. Digby Baltzell contrasted *wash* with *launder, sofa* with *davenport, long dress* with *formal gown, dinner jacket* with *tuxedo, sick* with *ill, hello* with *pleased to meet you,* and *rich* with *wealthy*. The popular writer Vance Packard dutifully repeated the list for a much wider audience. In each case, of course, the first is the higher-class locution, usually because it is more direct and less euphemistic. In 1979, twenty-one years later, *Newsweek* reprinted from a British publication a whole new list based on the same principle: *party* vs. *affair, hairdresser* vs. *beautician, guests* vs. *company, curtains* vs. *drapes, relations* vs. *folks, house* vs. *home, stockings* vs. *hose, pants* vs. *trousers*. Clearly enough, the person saying "curtains" or "drapes" is not only communicating about household appointments but also, consciously or not, announcing class status.

A second stage of using choice of words for display is the habit of covering up — and at the same time, expressing — a hypocritical attitude or discreditable motive by saying the opposite of what is meant. For example (to stray for a moment from speech to writing, in general quite a different matter), a literary critic who describes a piece of writing under review as "embarrassing" is almost always being disingenuous. His real reaction is not embarrassment, with its implication of sympathetic identification with the writer; rather, it is malicious pleasure at finding the writing bad. The sympathetic implication of "embarrassing" is pure crocodile tears. Similarly, a politician whose answer to a reporter's question in public begins with the word *frankly* — Nelson Rockefeller in his prime was a notorious example — is assuredly going to say something that is not frank. Nobody is fooled in either case; the critic's reader and the politician's listener have no trouble getting the real message. The critic and politician are communicating, all right, but they are also showing off their suave expertise at being sadistic or disingenuous in socially acceptable language.

The ultimate in display talk is what might be called pure-display talk — the use of words uncorrupted by meaning and therefore free to serve solely as expressions of pretension. There is at present a small dictionary's worth of words and phrases that make their user sound somewhat learned or at least currently informed, and that even appear at first blush to convey some shadow of a thought, but that under even cursory scrutiny prove to have hardly any meaning at all. People who issue out in solemn parade such expressions as *culturally oriented, relationship, parameters, reality,* and the like, are not trying to communicate anything. They are only showing that they are masters of the words. Uttering them is an act as simple as humming a popular tune, although less innocent because more pretentious. That is, it is pure display uncluttered by communication.

Acronyms are a wildly spreading form of verbal display. They arise, of course, out of bureaucracy; they were first popularized in the United States by the New Deal, the first American government strongly committed to central planning and therefore to a proliferation of government agencies needing brief tags. Since then, they have been adopted by organizations of every sort — political groups, trade associations, corporations, volunteer groups. Meanwhile, they have evolved away from usefulness and toward archness. The ability to think them up on demand has become more or less a prerequisite for a career in public relations. Let an association of household exterminators come to a p.r. man for a catchy title, and as night follows day he will respond with Mobilization of United Social Engineers (MOUSE). Or one of psychiatrists: Society of Research Investigators of Mental Kinetics (SRIMK, a near miss). The reason for the popularity of acronyms is not far to seek. They are a particularly effective exclusionary device. The person who does not know what an acronym stands for is out in the cold, and must remain there unless he is willing to lose face by asking. In the huge bureaucratic United States military of World War II, everyone in the Pacific knew who CINCPAC was (Commander-in-Chief, Pacific). But in London, knowing the identity of such a powerful and esoteric entity as ETOUSA (European Theatre of Operations, United States of America) would get you through quite a few otherwise closed doors. Acronym users are the name-droppers of an age of bureaucracy.

Verbal display is a leading form of air pollution in our time. It is not parody; it is classic Veblenian display, differing from the kind of speech display Veblen discussed only in that — in conformity with the cultural change since Veblen's time from money to education as the principal yardstick of status — the thing being displayed is demotic, lowest-common-denominator "education" rather than elitist training in how to speak like a snob. Nor, of course, is it new. Probably people have always talked pretentious nonsense for the purpose of showing off (although that popular modern institution the cocktail party, which all but enforces pure-display talk, must certainly have increased the amount of such talk). The courtier Osric in *Hamlet* was a paragon of pure-display talk, as Hamlet recognized in parodying him:

> Sir, his definement suffers no perdition in you; though, I know, to divide him inventorially would dizzy the arithmetic of memory, and yet but yaw neither, in respect of his quick sail. But, in the verity of extolment, I take him to be a soul of great article; and his infusion, of such dearth and rareness as to make true diction of him, his semblable is his mirror; and who else would trace him, his umbrage, nothing more.

There is one more distinction to be made: pure-display talk is not the popular solecisms skewered by Edwin Newman in *Strictly Speaking* and *A Civil Tongue,* nor the "psychobabble" hilariously paraded by Cyra McFadden's characters in *The Serial*. The former are the sour fruits of incomplete education, expressing meaning however gracelessly, while the latter is, at least, a fumbling attempt to express piety toward the established religion (psychotherapy) of a time and place (Marin County, California; the present). Pure-display speech is the blowing of verbal bubbles. Always pandemic in civilized societies, it has become epidemic in ours largely because of our unprecedented availability of what passes for education, and our Veblenian passion for using the product to gain invidious advantage.

But parody? Despite the vogue for joking commercials on TV — playful irony serving the earnest ends of commerce — disproportionately little parody is to be found in current American speech, as distinguished from actions and gestures. Since words are the original home of parody, this may appear to be an enigma. Parody in discourse, as in writing, remains largely an elitist form, while in action and gesture it has become a democratic form. Perhaps parody in its original state is disqualified for democratic adoption by its connotations of intellectuality. To create parody, one must think; to utter buzz-words, only open the mouth and blow.

Praying

Veblen had great sport with what he called "devout observances," by which he meant the formal meetings and rituals of the several Protestant sects that dominated American religion at the turn of the century and for some time thereafter. And indeed, those observances presented a broad and juicy target for satire — almost as broad and juicy as the habitations and social rites of the industrial rich. What an iconoclast needs, after all, is an icon. American "devout observances" filled the bill admirably by commanding the requisite degree of reverence from all right-thinking citizens, and by seeming to incorporate the requisite amount of pretension and hypocrisy. In any case, Veblen rose to the occasion, coming through with some of his most outré and provocative ideas.

His basic notion was that the practice of organized religion is nothing more nor less than a key expression of the predatory-barbarian temperament, setting forth the attitudes and motives of that temperament just as clearly and directly as a good, murderous football game or a party at the Bradley Martins'. (In an elaborate disclaimer that one suspects of having a hypocrisy of its own, Veblen distinguished between devout observances and actual religious faith: "Of course no question is here entertained as to the truth or beauty of the creeds. . . . The subject is too recondite and of too grave an import to find a place in so slight a sketch.") Thus "devout consumption" — sacred edifices, priestly vestments, and, as Veblen blandly put it, "other goods of the same class" — must be as conspicuous and wasteful as possible, that is to say, "pecuniarily above reproach." The external architecture of the church, for example, must be more ornate and conspicuously wasteful than that of the surrounding residences. The priest's vestments, exactly like the clothes of women of fashion — Mrs. Trollope noted that women wore their best bonnets only to church — must be expensive and so inconvenient as to certify that he never does any useful work. As to his demeanor, the priest is expected to present "an impassively disconsolate countenance, very much after the manner of a well-trained domestic servant." On the other hand, in his off-duty hours the priest is expected to "consume" almost as conspicuously, wastefully, and voraciously as any other leisure-class predatory barbarian, kicking up his heels with affluent members of his congregation at, say, sports events, the difference between him and them being that his consumption is to the greater glory of God and that they are paying his bill. Women fit neatly into the scheme. The widely observed fact that they tend to be more pious than men is "an expression of the conservatism" that comes out of women's economic position as an object for men's display. Finally, even the perception of the Divinity Himself is shaped by the needs of the leisure class. The Divinity "must be of a peculiarly serene and leisurely habit of life," just like the head of the sugar trust; and His throne, like the sugar man's mansion, must be imagined as having "a profusion of the insignia of opulence and power."

There is a perverse elegance in the way Veblen adapts "devout observances" to the dimensions of his scheme. This elegance is particularly marked in the way he deals with certain obvious problems. It happens that a leading characteristic of most American Protestant worship around 1900 was Puritan austerity — on its face, just the opposite of wasteful luxury and display. For example, the benches in church pews were inclined to be unpadded, and the hardwood backs set uncompromisingly at right angles to the seats, an arrangement calculated to mortify the worshippers' lumbar and scapular areas to the maximum possible extent short of an actual bed of nails; while the facilities for kneeling in prayer usually consisted of a ratty hassock apparently filled with hard-dried beans.* Sermons were expected to be endless and excruciatingly boring. All in all, devout observances often seemed to be fiendishly designed to inflict punishment on the "consumers," as Veblen insisted on calling them. But did Veblen admit the apparently obvious point that these austerities flew in the face of his theory of devout observances as conspicuous consumption — that, to the precise contrary, they seemed to represent some-

---

*This proved to be an exceptionally persistent form of austerity that long survived relaxations in other aspects of churchly manners and customs. As recently as March, 1980, *The Wall Street Journal* noted in a page one feature that "the padded pew has arrived. . . . Seats are cushioned with springs and inches of foam, and backs are contoured." The *Journal* quoted Ross Sams, Jr., a third-generation pew maker, as saying, "Comfort in pews is in today."

thing more like conspicuous masochism? Not for a minute. Rather, he characterized the "fittings" of the place of worship as calculated to express "austerely wasteful discomfort." Wasteful of what, Veblen didn't specify — the spines and knees of the worshippers, perhaps? — but never mind. The point is that for him, the austerely wasteful discomfort was simply the other side of the coin of the sybaritically wasteful comfort of a leisure-class residence on upper Fifth Avenue.

A point Veblen emphasized, and one already touched on in another chapter, was a close association between organized religion and sports. This association was notably to be observed in undergraduate life, where star athletes (or so Veblen insisted) were not only strongly inclined to be pious but were often vociferous propagandists for piety. And how was this to be explained? According to Veblen, an "animistic propensity" is part of the sporting and gambling temperament; and the same propensity "shades off by insensible gradations into that frame of mind which finds gratification in devout observances." Moreover, just as the sporting temperament is close to the warrior temperament, so is the devout temperament close to both of them; witness how "in characterizing the divinity and His relations with the process of human life, speakers and writers are . . . able to make effective use of similes borrowed from the vocabulary of war." (To clinch that point, the stirring but indubitably bloodthirsty language of "The Battle Hymn of the Republic" was invoked.) Perhaps a bit carried away, Veblen wound up with a series of volleys into the surely already mangled bodies of the sermon-haunted, bench-tortured devout consumers of his time: all those closely related temperaments — sporting and gambling, warlike, devout — obviously share "the predatory habit of mind"; all, particularly the devout, are characterized by "arrested spiritual development"; and finally — perhaps the unkindest volley of all — the lot of them are too close for comfort to the temperament of "the delinquent classes."

So much, then, for religious devotion as Veblen saw it in his time. How true are his strictures for today?

As noted elsewhere, Veblen undoubtedly derived his ideas about the devoutness and missionary propensity of college athletes from what he saw at Yale when he was a graduate student there. Social change since Veblen's time seems to have largely reversed the situation, tending to make athletes both in and out of colleges into nonbelievers and their coaches into encouragers of nonbelief. The process of this change may be suggested by a symbolic series of events involving not Yale but rather its fairly ancient athletic rival Princeton. In 1913, there was erected at a central place on the Princeton campus a life-size bronze statue, set on a pediment of heroic proportions, of an undergraduate of handsome and serious mien in football uniform, an academic gown slung over one shoulder and a pile of books in one arm. The work of the well-known sculptor Daniel Chester French, whose other works included the figure of Lincoln in the Lincoln Memorial at Washington, the Princeton statue had been commissioned by Cleveland H. Dodge, a graduate of Princeton with the class of 1879, and was a memorial likeness of his brother W. Earl Dodge, a member of the same class, who had died suddenly at the age of twenty-five. Earl Dodge had clearly been a paragon in his time: captain of the championship Princeton football team, an honor student ranked near the top of his class, and president of the Philadelphia Society, the student religious organization. Obviously, the statue was intended not only to memorialize him but also to set forth a model of what the perfect Princeton undergraduate should be.

Almost immediately after the statue's erection in 1913, the less than perfect Princeton undergraduates of that time gave it a name. "The Christian Student," they took to calling it, or alternatively, "The Christian Athlete." A tinge of irony, or perhaps mischief, was certainly implied in those appellations. "The Christian Athlete" perfectly exemplified Veblen's notion of an association between sports and devout observances. However, to anyone with the slightest propensity to treat devout observances as expressions of faith rather than as conspicuous display, there was an obvious symbolic problem. A Christian athlete, strictly speaking, would be one who in any form of contest or competition would be inclined to follow Jesus' admonition to turn the other cheek. This is a procedure not recommended for, say, boxers. In any event, at Princeton within a few years student irony toward the French statue broadened into frank hostility. It gradually became an object of overt and seething undergraduate hatred. It escaped actual violence until 1929, when, on the evening of their graduation day, a group of seniors on a spree succeeded in tearing it off its pedestal and dumping it ignominiously on the ground. The authorities put it back up, but hardly more than a year had passed when, in the autumn of 1930, it was again torn down in the course of a riot that grew out of a football rally. This time the authorities got the message; the Christian Student/Athlete was put into storage, and never set up on the Princeton campus again. Even though academic authority was nominally asserted by the expulsion for a year of those found chiefly responsible for the second desecration, the retirement to storage of the Princeton statue may perhaps be taken as the event that marked the end of the Veblenian marriage of official piety and American sports, and the beginning of the catapulting of devoutness in America into the stage of parody display.

In the nineteen-sixties and -seventies the Protestant Episcopal Church, finding itself losing its constituency at an alarming rate, frantically set about reversing the social aloofness and doctrinal austerity traditionally associated with it. Besides making substantive structural and doctrinal changes (allowing the ordination of women, revising the long-established sanctions against remarriage of divorced persons within the church, rewriting the traditional Prayer Book, and formally granting lesbians and male homosexuals the same rights and privileges as other communicants), its individual parishes set about radically altering the style and manner of parish activities on the periphery of worship. This was particularly true at the places where the church leadership was — in particular, the two great Episcopal cathedrals on the two shores of the nation, St. John the Divine in New York and Grace in San Francisco. The former made itself available for light shows, Shinto rites, dervish dancing, special anniversary masses in honor of the rock musical *Hair,* and plays that incorporated foul language, performed in front of the high altar. At the latter church there came to be antiwar rallies, guitar liturgies, nature festivals, pagan ceremonials, and other observances well outside the traditional Episcopal realm. All this was described, ably and with relish, by Paul Seabury, a professor of political science at the University of California at Berkeley — and a collateral descendant of the first Episcopal bishop in the United States — in an article entitled "Trendier Than Thou" that appeared in *Harpers* in 1978. Describing a nature ceremony in Grace Cathedral in 1971 in the course of which the poet Allen Ginsberg had "ordained" Senator Alan Cranston as "godfather of the Tule elk" and Senator John Tunney as "godfather of the California brown bear," Seabury wrote, "The cathedral dean was dimly seen through marijuana smoke, wrestling atop the high altar to remove a cameraman, while movie projectors simultaneously cast images of buffalo herds and other endangered species on the walls and ceilings, to the accompaniment of rock music." Shortly after the article had been published, the Canon of Grace Cathedral preached a sermon in which he protested in a hurt tone that it had been "unkind," and that the cathedral had problems from the other side, too: the broadcast of its regular Sunday services had recently been taken off the air by a San Francisco radio station as being too stuffily *conservative*. "We seem to get caught between a diaphanous nostalgia for a nonexistent past, and a hostility because we haven't made everything right with the world," the canon grumbled plaintively to his congregation. "It's hard to tell which is more demoralizing and damaging. Enough to make one's head spin." Pretty clearly, the American clergy's "impassively disconsolate countenance" now stemmed from causes far from Veblen's dream.

Part of the upheaval within the Episcopal Church — the church, it is interesting to note, that has traditionally stood for social preeminence and doctrinal austerity in the American ecclesiastical scheme, and certainly the church at which Veblen's strictures were chiefly aimed — was the sudden adoption by its leadership of a radical political posture. When Episcopal clergymen had dabbled in politics in earlier times, it had generally been pretty firmly on the side of the capitalist establishment. For example, the Reverend William Graham Sumner, Veblen's own chief mentor in social theory at Yale, was nationally famous for his skill in bridging the moral chasm between God and John D. Rockefeller; and in a somewhat later time, Dr. William T. Manning, Rector of Wall Street's own Trinity Church, was fond of reassuring his well-fixed parishioners that radicals of all stripes were anathema not just to him and them, but to the Holy Spirit. (After a bomb believed to have been planted by radicals exploded outside J. P. Morgan & Company in 1920, Dr. Manning declared roundly from his pulpit that the perpetrators ought to be severely treated, and could not resist adding, "There is another class which needs to be rightly dealt with — those who call themselves intellectuals and make themselves safe by declaring that they do not advocate force." That is, no highbrows wanted in the fold.)

Recently, things have been very different. In the nineteen-sixties, at a time when its new liberal leadership was riding high, the Episcopal Church began dispensing millions of dollars of missionary funds to radical political movements having no announced Christian, much less Episcopalian, objectives — Black Power groups, migrant farm workers, Puerto Rican nationalists, and the like. In 1969, at the annual Church-in-Convention held that year at South Bend, Indiana, Episcopal leaders voted funds for a radical Black Economic Development Council — only to be informed on the spot by Mohammed Kenyatta, a leader of the favored group, that the churchmen were not entitled to consider themselves better for having done so. Mohammed Kenyatta seems to have approached the Church-in-Convention from the perspective of one sitting in for God. Seizing the microphone from Bishop John Hines, much in the manner that Jesus may have assumed the podium preparatory to throwing the money-changers out of the temple, Kenyatta sternly told his assembled benefactors, "You have forced the issue of your racism, and you have responded. The quality of your response can be judged by the degree to which you have sought what was acceptable to us rather than what was acceptable to you and your god. . . . You chose to use us to be your middlemen. That is your choice, and it is unacceptable." (The money, however, was apparently acceptable.) Meanwhile, on the foreign-policy front, Grace Cathedral in 1969 began being used for rallies that were not only anti–Vietnam War but also pro-Hanoi, while on the East Coast in 1971 Paul Moore, Jr., the millionaire liberal Bishop Coadjutor of the Diocese of New York, allowed *his* cathedral to be used for an antiwar rally organized by a possibly rather surprised group of pro-Maoist Marxists.

Veblen, it certainly seemed, had been permanently right about one thing: devout observances in America are often about *something* other than worshipping God, and that "something" would seem to be showing off in one way or another. Just as showing off wealth and ignoring poverty had been in fashion around 1900, so incitement to revolt against society — more categorically, against oneself — was in fashion in 1970. In the years following, this masochistic form of parody display, perhaps remotely related to the doings of the American artist of the same time whose works of "conceptual art" consisted solely of bloody assaults with a knife on his own manhood, tended to gradually tail off, in devout observances as in society at large. Episcopal political display gradually simmered down principally to the matter of voting church-owned corporate stock against incumbent management if that management did things that the Episcopal leaders disapproved of, such as investing in South Africa.

And this new corporate-proxy approach to institutional devotion brought new devotional comedy. Back in the old days, we had had not just divines but also leading figures in government and politics — John Foster Dulles perhaps most memorable among them — fulminating against the evils of "atheistic Communism." Dulles was criticized at the time by a few diehard grammarians for being repetitive; after all, they asked, had anyone ever heard of *religious* Communism? Most certainly not. In 1979, though, we had Donald J. Kirchhoff — president of Castle & Cooke, Inc., a billion-dollar multinational conglomerate — complaining to the New York Financial Writers Association about a Protestant church group that held a block of Castle & Cooke stock, and whose representatives were always snooping around the company offices trying to get data about pay scales, union contract provisions, and other information that Castle & Cooke considered to be nobody's business but its own. According to President Kirchhoff, one of the institutions behind the church group "counts on extensive research support from the North American Congress on Latin America, a pro-Castro organization . . . as well as other organizations in the new-left camp." Kirchhoff summed up, "Those Marxists who frankly want to end political and economic freedom, and to impose their own values on society, are engaged in a constant search for divisive and abrasive issues that will destabilize free societies — and are today using corporate annual meetings as a primary battleground."

What, we may ask, ever happened to atheistic Communism? Gone the way of Fifth Avenue mansions, amateur sportsmanship, Christian students, right-wing bishops, and other forms of Veblenian direct display. Now, apparently, the threat to society is religious Communism, and society's doughty defender, we must presume, is atheistic capitalist corporate management.

That is to say, parody display exemplified. True enough, evangelical religion, epitomized in the Bible-thumping and power-loving Billy Graham with his surprising propensity for finding spiritual merit in Presidents of the United States, has recently been rapidly gaining members and influence in relation to the more traditional and highbrow sects; and true enough, the evangelical style of devotion is a lot closer to what Veblen described than what Bishop Moore and Mr. Kirchhoff's nemesis exemplify. But before we conclude that there is no parody in evangelism, let us attend to the Reverend Bill Sharp of Las Vegas, Nevada, as quoted by Robert G. Kaiser and Jon Lowell:

> We're planning to build a Christian nightclub [in Las Vegas] which will be a space needle. We've been approved by the Federal Aviation Administration to go two hundred and thirty feet in the air. We're going to put in a hotel. . . .
> This is the city of weddings. That's why we're building the wedding chapel at the top of the Christian nightclub. You'd be able to walk up a ramp from

the restaurant. Of course, you could have a reception there. There'll be smorgasbord in the daytime. It'll be a revolving restaurant like the space needle. It'll seat five hundred people. . . . At the top we'll have our wedding chapel. . . . This is going to be the world's most unique wedding chapel when we finish. We've going to advertise in all the national magazines. . . .

I maintain this: that if Jesus of Nazareth was in the physical form today . . . he would not, contrary to what some of my peers say, take a whip and go in and whip all of the people at the crap table. . . . Don't get me wrong. I'm not saying that if Jesus was walking around the Strip he'd be in at all the dice tables or playing baccarat. But I believe he'd be in there manifesting the spirit of love.

Giving

The person engaged professionally in giving away other people's money — the philanthropoid, Dwight Macdonald named him — is largely new in this century. Veblen would have had a heyday with him; let us see if we can.

His rise has, of course, come about along with the general institutionalization of industrial life, which has called for an institutionalization of its good works along with its not so good ones. Andrew Carnegie, who managed largely without institutions or even assistants when it came to philanthropy, still stands as the greatest of American philanthropists; but even a moderate-scale giver today would not think of trying to get along without a properly registered charitable foundation staffed with trained, well-salaried professional counterparts of what a panhandler refers to as a mark. For one thing, if he tried to go it alone as a giver, he might find himself in trouble getting tax deductions on his gifts. (The imposition of the income tax in 1913, and the subsequent piecemeal exclusion of charitable contributions, whether individual or corporate, from taxability under it, has done more than anything else to determine the character, including the moral character, of modern American philanthropy. Hardly anyone gives large sums away today without the sure knowledge that he will get part of it, sometimes almost all of it, back.) For another thing, he would lose face. A foundation to a large giver has become a required item of public attire.

A typical member of the new subclass, the executive of the foundation, has the striking characteristic, which would have been impossible before the era of parody display, that he tends to rank higher in society than his employer does. The modern philanthropist, as often as not, is a poverty-bred, obsessed achiever who has acquired a good many of what even he regards as moral debts in the course of his heedless rise to power and riches. These this rough-hewn man of goodwill now proposes to discharge through his foundation. The people he hires to handle this responsibility on his behalf are very different from himself. Generally speaking, they come from the well-bred, relatively impoverished gentry. They are better educated than their employer, and consequently speak and write the English language better; they are more at ease socially; they tend to have better manners; and they have easy access to circles where he would be received warily if at all. What they lack is his shrewdness, ruthlessness, and driving ambition. They may secretly hold him in ridicule or contempt, but they are glad to make a comfortable, high-prestige living dispensing his dollars.

Veblen noted the existence in his time of precursors of this kind of foundation executive (of course, there are other kinds) when he spoke, not in connection with philanthropy, of relatively impecunious gentlemen of leisure who tend to become "hangers-on of the patron," and therefore "vicarious consumers without qualification." However, in the society Veblen described, the "patron" by virtue of sheer wealth ranked easily above the well-bred hanger-on. He does not necessarily do so now. Veblen could not foresee the paradoxical (and parodic) reversal of social rank between employer and employee that modern institutional philanthropy has brought about.

For the executive of a large and celebrated foundation is indeed a man of mark. He commands a salary smaller than the one paid his counterpart in the for-profit sector, but it is a thumping big salary all the same, fully adequate to allow him to enjoy the perquisites of life appropriate to a man of his manifest taste and great (although vicarious) generosity. He is able to dash off frequently to international philanthropic conferences in the Rockies, or on the shores of Lake Como, or in some well-appointed French chateau, English manor house, or Tyrolean Schloss, at which — as a recent commentator, David Heaps, formerly of the Ford Foundation, has remarked — a plethora of experts abounds, especially experts with Oxford accents. Some pressing topic of world concern is discussed, with graphs and charts, for three days or so, at the end of which (according to Heaps) fine moral and legal distinctions are made between political rights and economic rights in distant countries actually deprived of both; or it is concluded on compelling evidence that the poor nations are less well off than the rich.

These conferences and other reminders of his status of professional high-mindedness give the foundation executive a distinct social edge over a profit-grubbing corporate executive with his gaze mired in the bottom line. That is to say, the noninvidiousness of his work is itself invidious. It may be to mitigate this invidiousness that the foundation executive, as we shall see, frequently expresses a kind of *nostalgie de la boue* for the profit sector.

In the old days, it was the patron who did all the patronizing. In the new ones, the patron, if he isn't careful, will find himself being patronized by the elegant and learned hirelings who dispense his patronage.

Despite all this, the pure, unsullied urge to do good works for their own sake — a classic reversion, in Veblenian terms, from predatory barbarism to peaceable savagery — lives in our time, as it did in his. (Veblen also noted how that pure urge was sullied by several factors since then mostly gone from the philanthropic scene. For one thing, most charitable organizations in those days had a more or less religious character, suggesting to Veblen that charity was after all just an extension of predatory devout observances; and the fact that most charitable work was then done by women suggested equally clearly that such work's hidden purpose was merely "vicarious consumption" — that it was merely a devious way of enhancing the social prestige of the women's husbands.) New and old rich alike often distribute their largesse out of higher impulses than to make them eligible for a tax deduction. Indeed, saving money otherwise due to the government by giving it to charity is occasionally specifically rejected on moral grounds. When the Texas magnate H. Ross Perot had first made many millions, indeed momentarily a billion or two, out of installing and programming computer systems for state welfare programs, he announced that he would take no deductions on his numerous charitable contributions because he did not want to take tax revenue away from a government that was ineffably dear to him. Other philanthropists, while protesting *their* affection for their government, nevertheless concluded that Perot was mad. And it does appear that he soon changed his mind and began taking deductions, along with the other angels. It took this relatively naive East Texan to recognize formally the moral fudge inherent in tax-deductible philanthropy, and, if briefly, to act on his recognition. The act showed clearly that the original peaceable-savage motive for sharing what one had acquired has not been entirely eroded by the onward march of industrial specialization.

What has been most seriously eroded, it appears, is the ability of the giver to feel, deep down, that he is or should be really acting charitably at all. This is most conspicuous in corporate philanthropy — giving for the general good not by individuals or philanthropic foundations but by corporations nominally devoted only to accumulating money. Small groups of churlish stockholders resent this imperious distribution to community projects, cultural TV programs, and the like of money that they consider to be properly theirs. The corporations, living as they do in a legalistic atmosphere, have to defend themselves on practical rather than on moral grounds. They argue that their philanthropy is necessary for the promotion of good public, community, and government relations. If, say, an oil company did not sponsor exhibitions of avant-garde art, the public might come to loathe it so much that the government would be forced to crack down on its pollution or its profits. (But does the public really love avant-garde art that much? No evidence exists that it does. There sometimes seems to be a lack of communication between corporate philanthropists and their constituency.) The corporate giving department becomes, often literally, part of the public-relations department. Charity is at last reduced the ultimate step, to the status of a form of institutional advertising.

Nevertheless, the corporate philanthropoid is very much the same breed of animal as his counterpart the foundation executive. He, too, revels in talky meetings; he, too, may get to go and ruminate and rusticate at Aspen, Bellagio, Arden House, and Royaumont. The difference is that the corporate man is part of an organization where his form of activity — giving rather than getting — is a sideshow rather than the main tent.

This situation leads him to a curious perspective. The corporate philanthropist often has past experience as a worker in the main tent; that is, he may have been promoted (or sidetracked, depending on the values of all concerned) from a position in the for-profit part of the company. The early days of his career as a corporate philanthropist turn out to be a honeymoon. No more sales quotas to meet! He revels in his new role as a peaceable savage living in the heart of the Barbary Coast. He may even develop a tendency to trade on that role, treating in a faintly condescending way the old colleagues whom he has left behind in the grubby world of getting and spending. After all, he is doing good and they aren't, although his salary and fringe benefits are more or less on a par with theirs. But gradually a startling insight overtakes him. The corporate giving department, it turns out, has problems that are more than vaguely familiar to him. The people in the department, although now certified practitioners of the Golden Rule, are human. Managers drink too much, or stay at lunch too long; secretaries come to work late or not at all; petty cash disappears. Analyses by management consultants reveal that the corporate giving department is operating inefficiently, and ought to be reorganized in order to increase its output-to-cost ratio.

Meanwhile, something not unrelated is happening to the corporate philanthropist himself. Partly out of old habit, partly out of emulation of his new peers, he finds himself acting in certain ways less like the Platonic idea of a philanthropist than like a commonplace man of affairs. Simply approving a grant request and sending a check to the applicant is not, he learns, the way things are done in his office. Such conduct is apparently too far out of the American corporate mainstream. There has to be a dicker, a tradeoff of one sort or another. When a promising application is received, there is a conference of the department, or a series of conferences, at which the application is discussed and ways proposed by which it can be remolded to serve better the goals of society as perceived by the pooled brains of the corporate giving department. The applicant is summoned, and asked to resubmit the proposal with changes to conform to the various whims and notions of the corporate givers. (Or, perhaps, the "vicarious consumers without qualification.") The applicant, idealistic or foolishly stubborn, may balk. Now the corporate philanthropist must go carefully, because the applicant has great public prestige and is so successful that he does not really need the grant. Not really needing a grant is, of course, a prime qualification for getting one; such a position gives an applicant status as a highly desirable grantee whose association with the department would be a feather in its cap. On that account, the applicant under discussion must not be allowed to slip away as a consequence of too hard bargaining on the exact nature of the project.

In the bargaining, the philanthropist discovers that he is enjoying himself. It is like old times. A certain crafty look comes into his eye as he attempts to charm, threaten, or cajole the applicant into moving another inch his way. When the bargain is finally struck and the petitioner leaves with his largesse, or at least with a signed agreement, the members of the department go out to celebrate with the sense that they have brought to the corporation a nice piece of business.

American philanthropists both corporate and independent are fond of saying that, sum for sum, giving away money is fully as hard as earning it. Beyond that, giving away money, American-style, has become very much *like* earning it. The same problems are encountered, and the same methods used. Charity, in its institutional form, tends to take the shape of a parody of commerce.

13

Vending Wisdom

*T*elling *other people* their business has always been great sport. In recent years, it has become big and lucrative business. There is some logic to this development; as professional and commercial life has become more and more fragmented and complex, and as the total sum of information bouncing around at large has grown even faster than the money supply, people and organizations have increasingly been forced to turn to experts for advice in particular areas. But other, less rational, causes are also at work in the growth of consulting. As affluence has become so widely distributed that money has lost much of its value as currency for competitive display, the display of expertise has moved in to fill the gap. Expertise, that is, or what will pass for it. In the old days of pecuniary display, those who didn't have much money sometimes managed respectable displays anyhow; witness those pretentious fake fronts on turn-of-the-century houses. We should not be surprised to find that in the new days, some ostensible experts are driven to display what they haven't got. Expertise is much easier to fake than money.

Since most forms of consultancy require no official licensing of any sort, the field provides rich opportunities to mountebanks. Some psychological consultants, or counselors, have degrees of one sort or another to back them up, but many have not. In these and other areas of consulting, the sole prerequisite to becoming a consultant is, literally or figuratively, to hang up a sign. The sole certification of success is satisfied clients, who are counted on to spread the word. The extreme ease of entry into consulting makes it a convenient basket to catch people temporarily or permanently in need of a calling with a name, for display purposes. That is to say, it attracts people who have lost their jobs because of incompetence. An insurance man who spreads the word that he has left his job and set up shop as an "insurance consultant" may fairly confidently be read to mean that he has been fired and is looking around. Astonishingly enough — since the current demand for consultants with or without credentials is almost as great as the supply — many such consultants-of-convenience actually have clients who pay them real fees.

Consultants themselves often hire consultants; indeed, for-profit corporations often pay people to do little else. Just *finding* a consultant, a task apparently as onerous as finding blueberries in a blueberry thicket, is good for a fee or salary. A few years ago, when the investing of corporate pension funds was first becoming big business, there grew up a satellite business of pension consulting. Pension consultants earn their keep by finding somebody to manage the investments of corporate or other pension funds. Since investment management is a richly rewarding field of endeavor, there were fully as many investment managers waiting to be picked as blueberries in a blueberry thicket. One would have thought that the corporate treasurer, after interviewing a few of them, could have picked one all by himself. Not at all. Instead, he would pick a pension consultant to do the picking, and go out for coffee. As often as not, the chosen consultant had an umbilical-financial connection with a stock brokerage firm. Being a resourceful fellow, the consultant might manage to pick for his client, the corporation with the pension fund, an investment manager who would privately agree to make most or all of the pension fund's investment transactions through the brokerage firm with which the pension consultant was affiliated. The outcome of this arrangement might or might not turn out to be to the benefit of the pension fund's beneficiaries; what is certain is that it would be twice to the benefit of the consultant — once through his consultant's fee for selecting the investment manager, and once through his share of the brokerage commissions steered to his brokerage house by the chosen manager.

Such a consultant had better not get caught doing that, since it constitutes fraud. Still, it has been known to happen, and to go unpunished. To the extent that being a consultant is showing off, it is showing off in an impure form; unlike the pure competitive displayer, who presents his show free, the consultant charges admission for his.

The wonder is that there are so many takers. The appetite of consulters for consultants is apparently voracious to the point of insatiability. Let the slightest thing seem to be amiss in a corporation, foundation, cultural institution, bureau of government, or personal life, and the all but reflexive response, in many cases, is to call in a consultant.

The outcome of this response has been to call into being a huge industry — one with an emergent literature of its own, designed to provide expertise on the expertise business. Bermont Books, Inc., of Washington, D.C., recently published a catalogue offering a collection of books called The Consultant's Library. The lead item — written by Hubert Bermont, president of Bermont Books and founder of The Consultant's Library — is entitled *How to Become a Successful Consultant in Your Own Field*. It suggests that people who are working for corporations, and for one reason or another find themselves misfits there, get out and become consultants. The catalogue copy for *How to Become a Successful Consultant,* also written by Mr. Bermont, lays the matter on the line, as follows: "Many people are amazed when they discover the tremendous amount of professional experience and specialized knowledge they've accumulated — experience and knowledge that others will gladly pay for." Especially, Mr. Bermont goes on, middle-aged corporate executives who feel that they have come to dead ends in their jobs: "There are other books which deal with 'the executive dropout,' with 'alternative life styles,' etc. This is not one of them. I address myself to the individual who has gained a goodly amount of expertise and experience in a given field, who has been aware for some time of being trapped in an uncomfortable working situation, who realizes that changing employers will only be more of the same because house rules are stacked against him by the very nature of the system, and who has at least once thought, 'Maybe I ought to try consulting.' "

If the individual Mr. Bermont addresses himself to were to take his advice and become a consultant, what advice might the newborn consultant then be expected to give to his corporate clients? Why, that they recognize that "house rules are stacked against them by the very nature of the system," and get out of the corporation. To do what? Why, to become consultants. (Similarly, many psychotherapists directly or by implication encourage their patients to become psychotherapists, and many do.) The secret, parodic goal of consultancy thus appears to be not to impart expertise but to create a world of wall-to-wall consultants.

14

Male Bonding

The elective, or "exclusive," club is repeatedly pronounced obsolescent or moribund as the nation theoretically becomes more democratic, but in fact it survives as one of our characteristic institutions. It flourishes most vigorously in the form of the country club; but that kind of club is so close to being an extension of suburban family life that it ought to be treated under that heading, and will be ignored in this discussion. Our focus is on the club in its older and purer form, the one-sex urban social club.

The membership of the strongest of such clubs is male. There are women's urban clubs, including a few that are much sought after, but in general they are less successful and command less devotion from their members — possibly because, as Lionel Tiger insists in his book *Men in Groups*, men naturally "bond" with each other in nonsexual social relationships better than women do. It is interesting that the recent women's movement, with its emphasis on "sisterhood," seems to have had little effect on the popularity of women's clubs, unless we

are to include transient, ad hoc groups such as those devoted to "consciousness raising." It has, on the other
hand, had a noticeable effect on women's desire to become members of what have heretofore been exclusively
men's clubs. Of that more anon.

Clubs are by their nature invidious in the classic
Veblenian sense. (Perception of them is largely, and logically, defined by the perceiver's own condition: clubmen
are in favor, nonclubmen indifferent or against.) The act
of excluding someone who may wish to join — which is
the essence of the club — is of course invidious. An ad-
missions committee, each time it decides on such an exclusion, has (privately, to be sure) declared its members
to be better, at least by the standards of the club, than the
candidate. (Not "applicant"; it is characteristic of the
best clubs that anyone who would "apply" is by that token
unacceptable.) The blackball is the very quintessence of
barbarian invidiousness. It may therefore be regarded as
curious that Veblen never wrote about men's urban clubs,
which flourished mightily — indeed, probably reached
their apogee as a part of life among Americans of
means — in his time. Probably the explanation is that he
knew little or nothing about them except in a special and
uncharacteristic manifestation, the university faculty
club, which usually makes membership decisions entirely on the basis of professional status.

The paradox of the club is that, within the context of
its innate invidiousness, it makes an ideal of noninvidious conviviality, which was precisely Veblen's ideal of
human conduct under the name of "peaceable savagery."
In its highest manifestation, the club by written or unwritten rule forbids or discourages any discussion of
business affairs, and in particular of money-making,

anywhere on its premises except in private rooms behind closed doors, where such discussion will not contaminate the noninvidious conversation of other members. It forbids, often categorically, the taking out of business papers in public rooms (although an exception may be made in the case of papers concerning the business of acceptably peaceable forms of activity, such as philanthropy or the arts.) It maintains no athletic facilities, which might attract predatory-minded members or encourage the suppressed predatory impulses of members who are otherwise acceptable. It eschews such useful but mundane accouterments as an in-house barber shop, to avoid the implication that it is a useful facility rather than a secular temple. It forbids members to take any action that might involve the club in publicity, good or bad, and in particular, forbids them to invite people of the press to it for the purpose of conducting interviews with newsworthy members; the purpose of these injunctions is to keep at arm's length, or at least outside the door, the invidious business of achieving and maintaining fame and reputation. Without a written rule (which might itself be considered invidious or even ridiculous), it tacitly discourages conversation among members about women, with the exception of public figures (writers, artists, actresses, political figures) or members' wives of long and stable standing; the reason for this seems to be that mention of women not in those categories might introduce a note of sexual competition, which is always invidious. Finally, it discourages members from so much as speaking their club's name outside it in the presence of nonmembers, an act that is construed as using the club's good name, and its exclusiveness, to gain social or commercial advantage. All in all, the house rules of the highest form of

urban club, along with their unwritten adjuncts, constitute the strictest and most categorical code of noninvidious behavior that we have in our society. (The code
has its counterparts, entirely unwritten but not necessarily less stringent, in other more generally accessible predominantly male groupings: for example, in barrooms
regularly frequented by a certain clublike clientele,
where discussion of, say, marital difficulties may be tacitly forbidden, on pain of ostracism. I recall some years
ago hearing one member of one such circle say of another — with the very air of defending the ramparts of
civilization that a club member uses in censuring a vio-
lator of the house rules — "One does not knock down
one's wife in Bleeck's.") The club is a hot dog of peaceable
ble savagery wrapped in a bun of predatory invidiousness.

Of course, not all urban clubs are like the one just
described. Some comport themselves in an almost dia-
metrically opposite way. They may feature competitive
games — the one most compatible with an urban environment is squash — as their very raison d'être. They
may provide useful facilities like barber shops. They may
more or less unashamedly encourage business discussion, and have business status rather than capacity for
interesting general conversation as their chief criterion of
admission; thus their social function comes to be to provide a comfortable (and tax-deductible) ambiance for
business meetings, and a visible rung for members on the
ladder of business success. However, it is interesting to
note that in recent years, the popularity of such clubs has
declined more noticeably, and their resulting financial
problems have often been greater, than has been the case
with the few "purer" clubs that look askance on business,

sports, and barber shops. That is, the overtly status-shunning clubs have tended to become the prime status symbols.

This situation suggests, correctly, that there is a worm in the apple of Eden. Within the "pure" clubs' paradise of peaceable savagery, subtle intimations of predatory attitudes intrude. Among those engaged in blamelessly nonpredatory work, predatory characteristics make their appearance. Executives of philanthropic institutions may act smug about pulling off a philanthropic coup bigger than the competition can engineer, or an arts administrator who has received a particularly "important" grant may lord it over others in his profession who have lost out. The head of a large philanthropic foundation has more direct, naked power over people he deals with than the head of a large corporation has: the latter can hand out or withhold on whim jobs or contracts, but the former can hand out or withhold actual money. It is approximately the difference between giving a panhandler a slip of paper containing a job recommendation, and giving him a dollar bill. Most panhandlers, given the choice, prefer the latter. Yet the foundation executive is ex officio acceptable to the most noninvidious club, while the corporation head, unless he can display special non-business qualifications, is not. Thus the coarse warp of competitive society finds its way into the most carefully woven and preserved fabric of the superior club. Strains of predatory activity intrude unasked into the sanctuary.

It is further interesting to note a tendency of the more cosmopolitan members of the superior clubs — those who out of predilection or professional necessity want to present themselves in a favorable light to a wide public — to apologize for or even deprecate them (not by name, of course, but generically) in public. Such members may hold their clubs very dear, but they would like to appear not to. A leading politician who belongs to a club that excludes women has, as of recently, got a problem. He may have to resign; it is a matter of priorities to him. Others with a not wholly dissimilar problem may not need to take such drastic action. The newspaper columnist noted for his wit who drops hints in print about the boredom, stuffiness, and snobbery of club life may well belong to, and cherish, a very good club. His public lines deprecating clubs in general are a measure of compromise with his readers; they may also be written in part to his fellow members of the club, to assure them that he has a wider perspective on the matter than they.

The past decade has seen a rising tide of agitation, both among the members of male clubs formally pledged to noninvidious behavior and among the women of their milieu, to admit women as members. (The exclusion of otherwise qualified candidates or potential candidates from the best clubs on grounds of race, religion, or ethnic background has largely ended since Veblen's time, when it was the general rule. Today, any club that can be plausibly convicted of such exclusion is automatically eliminated from the top category. "Tokenism," however, in many cases survives.) Minority groups of male members of such clubs have upon occasion petitioned their governing bodies to change the rules and admit women. Local governments, such as New York City's, have proposed laws designed to discourage all-male clubs. The argument in favor of such a change is that many women in the present state of society (or, many women would say, in any other state) are just as well qualified as men to engage in peaceable, learned schmoozing. The arguments on the other side tend to be irrational, invidious, or simply re-actionary. Male club members are on particularly shaky ground when they draw attention to women they know who hold that women should not be allowed to join; this argument suggests a slaveowner defending the institution of slavery by pointing to Uncle Tom.

The weakest aspect of women's case for being let into the male preserve is the ground on which it is com-monly based. Women in the acceptable professions, like law, publishing, writing, or the fine arts, sometimes take the stand that their exclusion puts them at a competitive disadvantage in their profession. "You can take clients to lunch there, and I can't. It's unfair," they argue. This argument answers itself. Members of whatever sex aren't *supposed* to take clients to lunch there. The members the aspiring women would emulate are miscreants who are violating the letter and the spirit of the rules. True, such violations take place, and quite frequently. But such women, the most misogynist members in their safe citadel can argue, miss the whole point. On the basis of their stated reason for wanting to join — the nakedly preda-tory one of hoping to improve their professional stand-ing — the acceptance of women as members would be certification that the club's nature, underneath its peace-able facade, is predatory. What had been the club's most precious feature would thus be lost.

It stands to reason that something like this will hap-pen — that the near-term future of the supposedly peaceable-savage male club lies in mixed-sex member-ship, and in filling an unabashedly predatory social role. But as Tiger has explained and documented, male bond-ing is as old as the human species; it will not be brushed

aside permanently by social reforms undertaken in reaction to a passing fashion. All-male associations of one
sort or another will arise out of the ashes. That is, the
peaceable-savage male club will survive.

15

Counter-Manners

"*I*'m an Anglophile," the black jazz trumpeter Lawrence (Bud) Freeman told the writer John Bainbridge in 1979. "In fact, some people call me an Anglomaniac. . . . When I was growing up [near Chicago], my brother, my sister and I all had one idol: the Prince of Wales, later Edward VIII. We were knocked out by the way he dressed. The Windsor knot. The peg-top trousers. The whole thing. So we started dressing that way. We copied his walk, his mannerisms, his accent. To help cultivate our English accent, we went to see 'Journey's End,' the British play about the First World War. There's one line in that play that absolutely killed us. In the dugout, the officers' cook serves a cup of tea to the young captain, who's a heavy drinker and very distraught, and asks. . . . 'Would you like a nice plate of sardines, sir?' The captain replies, very slowly, 'I should *loathe* it.' That became our favorite expression for anything we didn't like."

Probably members of minority groups have always tended to parody the manners of the majority group surrounding and perhaps oppressing them. Certainly American blacks have long tended to parody those of American whites. Even in slavery, where a tiny technical mistake of a literary nature — accidentally letting the parody come out too biting or insufficiently respectful — might subject the parodist to a whipping or worse, put-ons of the master, his family, and his friends were freely practiced. Particularly for the oppressed, social parody is an art with such great psychic rewards that it is worth great physical risks.

The subtle point about the art in this form is that to the parodied it must not appear to be parody. Rather, it should appear to them to be inept but slavishly admiring imitation. Malice and ridicule are artfully disguised as ineptitude. Mr. Freeman describes himself as a child (since then, of course, he has become a rich and famous man) as "an Anglophile . . . some people call me an Anglomaniac." "Anglophile" implies slavish imitation, but "Anglomaniac" gives the game away: it implies parody. Grown-up Freeman talks to Bainbridge in terms of imitation, but it is fairly safe to assume that young Freeman and his brother and sister, in copying the Prince's mannerisms and cultivating his accent, were more or less consciously applying a cultural twist of their own —adding to their worshipful mimicry that touch of zestful exaggeration that pushes imitation over the delicate line to parody. The irony that the subject thinks he is being subtly imitated, while the artist knows that he is being devastatingly parodied, gives the situation the tension that makes it so delicious.

Modern American blacks and Hispanics are expressive people, very much concerned with styles of expression, otherwise called manners. White Americans, particularly those of the upper social and economic strata, often allow themselves the provincialism of believing that most blacks and Hispanics have bad manners, or lack manners entirely. On the other hand, blacks and Hispanics make it clear by certain of their styles that they believe upper-stratum whites have bad manners. Both sides are wrong. There are no absolute values in manners; they are ethically relative. (Some blacks and Hispanics illuminate the point by using the word *bad* to mean "good" when referring to matters of style.) To be sure, most people would agree that a street mugging is bad form; to be fair, the same people would have to agree that it is equally bad form (as well as bad sociology) to assume that all muggers are black. But peaceable, noncriminal manners are neither good nor bad but thinking makes it so. Either way, they are still manners, expressing, perhaps more eloquently and certainly more subtly than headline events, the temper of people in their time and place.

(Mrs. Trollope wrote in 1832, "The total and universal want of manners, both in males and females, is so remarkable that I was constantly endeavoring to account for it." What the English lady meant was the want of *good* manners as she understood them. America in 1832 had plenty of manners, and they were, of course, the subject of her book.)

Minority adaptations of establishment manners are parody, all right; but as practiced in our particular time and place, they often deviate from normal parody in two opposing directions — on the one hand toward simple imitation, on the other toward deliberate reversal or contradiction. Imitation — of an outlandish form, to be sure — is the tendency described, for example, in the sociologist Elliot Liebow's *Tally's Corner,* a study of black streetcorner men in Washington, D.C., in the nineteen-sixties. The men Liebow describes, when they work at all, work as janitors, laborers, countermen, truck drivers, parking-lot attendants, and the like; meanwhile, petty crime is a settled part of the lives of many of them. They snatch purses. They take goods from their employers — up to a point, with the employers' tacit permission. What is interesting to note is that these criminal activities are subject to a more or less strict self-imposed moral code. One of the men, for example, earns thirty-five dollars a week, and systematically steals from his employer or from others another thirty-five dollars' worth of goods — no more. By unstated mutual agreement, the employer allows that much theft, but no more. If the employee were to steal more than that, he would both subject himself to the risk of reprisals by the employer and violate the manners of his own group. However, for competitive-display purposes among his peers, his ridiculously inadequate salary rather than his total income is the controlling factor. So far as his streetcorner colleagues are concerned, he is a thirty-five-dollar-a-week man, not the seventy-dollar-a-week man that he is with the theft included — just as, in conventional executive life, a fifty-thousand-a-year man is for status purposes just that, rather than the seventy-five- or eighty-thousand-a-year man that he may be if you include his pension, profit-sharing, and expense-account padding. The last is, indeed, precisely a systematic and tacitly condoned form of theft from the employer, just like the streetcorner man's. The latter's tacitly condoned thefts are his form of fringe benefit; without meaning to he has, while apparently being engaged in a frontal attack on middle-class values, constructed a kind of skewed mirror image of them.

The men of Tally's Corner engage in predatory invidiousness quite worthy of a rising advertising executive or a socially ambitious suburban wife of the fifties. They flaunt white Cadillacs when they can. (The Cadillac, interesting to note, was at the time Liebow described largely a *former* status symbol among socially ambitious whites; it had by then been discarded in favor of more esoteric high-priced vehicles). They adopt bizarre styles of clothing and behavior to make a distinction between themselves and the rest. They depict themselves to each other as ruthless, sexual and financial exploiters of women. At the same time, as Liebow describes it, peaceable savagery flourishes on Tally's Corner as it seldom does or ever did in polite suburbia. Friendship between men — nonsexual, and free of ulterior motive — is near the top of the scale of values. Men "go for cousins" — that is, behave toward each other as if they were cousins — or, as a further step, "go for brothers." Loans of up to two or three dollars, or even more, are constantly asked for and freely given. The exploitation of women that the men constantly boast of is, Liebow says, nothing but a pretentious fraud; in fact, although most of the sexual relationships are short-lived and many end violently, in the early stages the men are solicitous of the women to the point of abjection. Thus the society of Tally's Corner, at the same time that it imitates or parodies the predatory aspects of the majority culture, manages to embody Veblen's abstract ideal of the peaceable savage to an extent that the majority culture never approached in either Veblen's time or later. Indeed, Veblen, who admitted that peaceable savagery as he conceived of it was largely a dream, might have been amazed at how nearly his dream came to realization at Tally's Corner.

In a more recent study of black street life — *A Place on the Corner*, by the black sociologist Elijah Anderson, about ghetto life in Chicago in the early nineteen-seventies — there is described a much more categorical takeoff on white manners, particularly the manners of urban clubs. The men who frequent this gathering place, a bar and liquor store called Jelly's, divide themselves by common consent into three classes, just as if they were sociologists themselves. The three classes — "regulars," "wineheads," and "hoodlums" — rank, again by common consent, in that order; conventional respectability is the universal criterion of status, accepted even by the lower-status wineheads and hoodlums. Deference is granted to those who hold steady jobs, and marriage, surely the key institution of respectable society, is honored, even though chiefly in the breach. Listen to Ollie, generally and respectfully considered to be the group intellectual, as quoted by Mr. Anderson:

> "Now, I know I'm a single person and ain't never been married, but I'm under the considered opinion that that's one of the things that hurts the society we live in — lots of people don't know, but we as black people have always suffered under this thing about the broken home. We always have. We've always suffered under this. But I say this, no civilization will ever exist for any length of time without a strong base of family life. And the family structure in America is gone to pot. In other words, like I don't mean reefers . . . ," said Ollie.
>
> "I know where you comin' from!" interrupted Herman.*

*Anyone who remembers the ill-fated Moynihan Report of 1965 — a government paper written by the white sociologist, government official, and later Senator Daniel Patrick Moynihan — will surely note that Ollie's ora-

Does not one discern in this the very tone and content (if scarcely the language) of a bore at the bar of a
white suburban country club devoted to some such notion
as that "the family that plays together stays together" —
or even of an urban club devoted to intellectual pontifi-
cation? A crucial contrast, of course, is that the house
rules at Jelly's permit discussion of specific women and
members' specific problems with them ("My wife done
told me she don't have no sexual feelings for me no
more"), whereas the better class of white Establishment
club regards discussion of this nature as just a notch or
two above infanticide. But in several other respects, the
analogies are striking. For example, Herman, an established regular, introduces the sociologist Anderson by
saying, "Hey, here come my friend Eli! He al'right. Hey,
this the stud I been tellin' you about. This cat gettin' his
doctor's degree." Here is a member's letter proposing a
friend for membership, complete with pro forma personal
endorsement and curriculum vitae to impress the admis-
sions committee. Presumably, the committee will deliberate, however informally, in due course. Again, the
wineheads ruefully accept their second-class status
based on such minor discrepancies from propriety as
their habits of begging and urinating in public, while the
hoodlums struggle against their hoodlum natures to re-

tion is a precise restatement of its thesis. The Moynihan Report was instantly
excoriated by black leaders, who pronounced it condescending and therefore
antiblack. Yet the Report itself was principally based on an earlier work by
the black sociologist Franklin Frazier. So here we have a black streetcorner
philosopher stating an idea that had first been put forward by a black scholar,
then officially promulgated by a white Establishment official, then violently
rejected by the black Establishment. The perceived truth or falsity of the
thesis seems to be a function of the skin color of the current speaker. Never
was there a clearer instance of the parody — perhaps closer to travesty —
that characterizes discourse on race in America.

form themselves sufficiently to permit them to qualify as regulars. Thus also do scapegrace members of white Establishment clubs long to stop violating the antitrust laws or cheating on their income taxes, or whatever they do wrong more or less regularly and compulsively, not so much for the moral as for the social advantage such abstinence might confer on them.

Yet again, the members of Jelly's close ranks to provide what support they can for a fellow member who is slipping into habits that may eventually damage his status and therefore theirs — for example, Herman, who is sleeping with a woman believed to be promiscuous and grasping. ("You know all she gon' do with Herman is take his money. . . . He gots to be dropping some iron [money] to spend that ho's [whore's] time." Similarly, if legend is to be credited, the Yale secret society Skull and Bones, an epitome of elegance and power within its context, used to maintain a secret camp devoted solely to the rehabilitation of members who had shown signs of losing at the game of life. A Bones man must not drop iron to spend a ho's time.

A final note on Jelly's: Anderson makes clear that there, as in the superior white urban club, a very high value is put on the peaceable-savage spirit. Casual joking, nonthreatening arguing, and good-natured grumbling make up most of the discourse; nothing is at stake in such discourse except friendship. At least among the ruling-caste "regulars," friendship is constantly and pointedly put above money; hence the customary readiness to lend small sums with no haggling.("At one point Otis said, 'How much money you got, Bill?' 'Oh, bout a couple million. What, you want some?' Bill replied. 'Yeah,' Otis said. 'Lemme hold twenty dollars.' With no further questions, Bill took out his wallet, picked out a twenty-dollar bill, and handed it over to Otis. Everyone in the room observed this transaction, but no one commented.") Wineheads do their bleary best to act like peaceable savages, though they seldom succeed very well on account of their apparently uncontrollable social misfeasances. As for hoodlums, of the categories of Jelly's members they are the most money-oriented, the most competitive, and the most prone to violence. That is, they are the most predatory-invidious — and in the elaborate and precise grading system of the club, they have the lowest rank for just that reason. The social values of Jelly's are those of Veblenian society turned on its head.

The "writing" that for more than a decade has covered the inside and outside walls of many subway cars in New York City — intricate designs, monograms, and messages in more or less art-nouveau style done with spray paint at subway barns and marshaling yards in the dead of night — is a socially complex form of minority self-expression in that it means such different things to different groups. To the Metropolitan Transit Authority and the run of subway riders, it is offensive and potentially threatening vandalism; to liberals among the riders, it is a harmless safety valve for ghetto anger; to a few radical-chic highbrow critics, it is naive art; and to the artists (or, as they prefer to be called, writers) it is competitive display, intended to impress colleagues rather than outrage clerk-typists, salve liberal consciences, or please critics. A group that signs itself, say, "Top Stars, Inc." is indulging in the only form of media hype available to it, and, incidentally, parodying the billboard ads that the writing surrounds in an abandoned embrace. (It is interesting to note that, under one of the rigid rules that subway writers impose on themselves, the ads themselves are seldom defaced or touched in any way, as if advertising were the one aspect of white society that the writers can respect.) But perhaps the paradigm of American countermanners is to be found in the Californian Mexican-American custom of "lowriding," which has been vividly described by Calvin Trillin and Edward Koren. The sine qua non of lowriding is a car — almost always a product of the most basic of suppliers for suburban America, General Motors — that has been customized in such a way that its chassis rides only a few inches above the ground. This is accomplished by cutting some of the coils of the springs, or by melting the springs with a blowtorch. A further refinement is the installation of hydraulic lifts that enable the driver at will to raise front or rear ends of the chassis, or both, from two or three inches above ground level to eight or ten inches, thereby enabling the driver, the lowrider, to go over a bump or to pass muster with a policeman. The prescribed style of lowriding is to go as slowly as possible — perhaps three or four miles per hour, or about the speed at which normal cars involuntarily proceed when caught in a highway or expressway traffic jam.

"Low and slow — clean and mean," Trillin and Koren explain that lowriders say, by way of motto. "Clean and mean" presumably refers to the special features of a lowrider's car apart from its lowness and slowness, which ideally include a multicolored lacquer paint job, tires much too narrow for the car, chrome side pipes, crushed-velvet interior lining, a small steering wheel made of welded chain, and every conceivable electronic audio and video accessory that can be operated in a car. There are lowrider clubs in various California cities, and a magazine, *Low Rider*, published in San Jose, a leading lowrider center. In spite of a vague air of outlawry — or perhaps because of it — lowrider clubs, according to Trillin and Koren, "seem intent on respectability, holding family picnics, raising money to combat muscular dystrophy," and the like.

That is to say, the primary object of the whole elaborate exercise is evidently not to outrage or threaten Anglo society. Is the object rather to comment on that society? The answer is equivocal, and pointedly so. No Californian of any race who has the slightest interest in cars can fail to notice that the style long favored by white customizers of cars in that state features an outrageously jacked-up rear end, making for high rather than low riding; outlandishly wide, rather than narrow, tires; and a souped-up motor designed to propel the car unreasonably fast, not unreasonably slowly. It takes no great leap of the imagination to conclude that the Chicano lowrider car has been contrived, with extraordinary effort and ingenuity, as the most specific possible contradiction of the Anglo custom-car style and thus by extension of the Anglo cultural style.

Contrived consciously, or not? In general, Trillin and Koren think not. They say, "It may be that Chicano car clubbers alter their cars in whichever ways would be most offensive to Anglo tastes. If so, the car clubbers don't seem to be aware of it. Asked why they favor tiny steering wheels or chrome side pipes or lacquer paint jobs, they are likely to say something like 'Oh, it has a clean look.'" On the other hand, when the interviewers asked a member of a San Jose car club why its cars are low, he replied by saying, "Whose cars are high?"

Overtly, the audience for lowrider conspicuous display — like the audience for New York subway-writing display — is the peer group, the fellow minority members, rather than the opposing majority culture. "You got pride. You got a nice ride," a lowrider told the interviewers. "You show off. They check it out. They say, 'That's the way. Look at that. That's sharp to the bone. That dude's got a bad ride.' " The parody isn't intended principally to impress the parodied; nevertheless, both subway writing and lowriding are noticeably practiced in places where the parodied have maximum opportunity to see it, in fact can't escape doing so. Countermanners in America are as elegantly worked out, and as stringently corseted by intricate rules, as those other manners codified by Letitia Baldridge.

16

Nesting

The castles and palaces of the robber barons were certainly one of Veblen's starting points, one of the phenomena of his time that originally suggested his theory. It is true that in *The Theory of the Leisure Class* he had little to say about them. While expatiating at length on public grounds and buildings, as to domestic architecture he confined himself to a passing comment that it provided an especially rich lode of "honorific waste" and "expensive discomfort." The reason for this slighting seems obvious. The evidences of competitive display in the domestic architecture of Veblen's time were so blatant, pervasive, and well publicized as to need no more than passing comment from him. In this particular matter, he held a sure-winner hand, which he was too shrewd to overplay.

Indeed, Veblenian home-flaunting at the turn of the century had given rise to pockets of counterdisplay, where some of the old-rich sought to show their disdain for the new-rich by maintaining *in*conspicuous domiciles. (Veblen took due note of this phenomenon under the rubrics "exaltation of the defective" and "veneration for the archaic," but not in connection with house styles.) Jane Davison tells how at Newport, the nation's most revered summer resort at the time, the old well-to-do families clustered in the generally unpretentious Georgian houses in the area known as "the Point," leaving Bellevue Avenue to the new-rich and their preposterous new piles. "People who lived on the Point . . . found such display both vulgar and comical," Mrs. Davison comments. "Tongues clucked along Washington Street [main drag of the Point] with each new excess reported." She goes on to remark that her grandmother "recorded one summer's joke, the news that one of the gilded matrons had decreed that the kindly Newport cow assigned to produce milk for her darling child should drink nothing but Poland water." It needs only to be added that the Bellevue Avenue people were as necessary to the invidious purposes of the people of the Point as vice versa. If the Point had not had Bellevue Avenue, it would have had to invent it.

The use of the dwelling as a weapon of social warfare has had its ups and downs over this century. The coming of the income tax and the First World War brought a temporary end to the Bellevue Avenue phenomenon of the eighteen-nineties — the boastful phantasmagorias of the new-rich coming up every spring like asparagus shoots. There was a revival of that sort of thing in the nineteen-twenties, but that era's robber barons — this crop not the homegrown yokels of the earlier time, but exotics fighting their way into the American mainstream — characteristically chose *old* mansions for their homes. (Jay Gatsby's "huge, incoherent failure of a house" is a fictional example. The financier Robert R. Young's later lust for and eventual possession of The Breakers, formerly the Vanderbilt family's Newport retreat, is a factual one.) Suburbia was rising, and with it architectural competitive display with a broader national base. Davison: "The new and enlarged class of housewives found a romanticized national past more appealing than their own individual backgrounds. Gracious living in a traditional house in Short Hills or Wellesley — a costume drama — became a typical cultural and economic goal for a young couple. . . . I would describe the nineteen-twenties as the reign of the large neo-Georgian house as an upper-class phenomenon and a middle-class ideal."

The row upon curving row of flimsy new suburban boxes that went up in the early postwar years, mostly to accommodate the young families of the middle-class parents of what would become the baby-boom generation, were almost pure function, with scarcely a hint of competitive swagger. In such a homogenized mass, display was a shy bird that showed itself naively and inexpensively — through an iron jockey on the lawn (his skin first painted black and then, after a rise in social consciousness had occurred within the house, repainted white) or the biggest Christmastime light show on the block. Gradually, though, as the young couples waxed not so young and their incomes rose rapidly along with the national income (in those blessed years of insignificant inflation), display began to reassert itself in the new, massified postwar form. By the end of the nineteen-fifties, Vance Packard saw "the home" showing signs of supplanting the automobile as the "symbol most favored by Americans for staking their status claims." Real-estate advertisements began appealing to snobbery, often with an antic simplemindedness. They made grandiose self-parodying claims: "Huge ⅓ acre Estate Sites." The living room became a "Reception Galleria," the bedroom a "Sleeping Chamber." French, the status-attesting language of the robber barons' dinner menus, was again pressed into halting, indeed almost ataxic, service: "C'est Magnifique! Une Maison Ranch très originale avec 8 rooms, 2½ baths . . . 2-Cadillac garage . . . $21,990." In earlier times the various ethnic and religious groups had sought to suppress their differentness in architectural display, but now they sought to emphasize it, adopting characteristic styles. Polish-Americans were said to go in for garish colors, and Jews to favor modern architecture over colonial and, in contrast to land-proud Anglo-Saxons, not to care about having a big backyard.

Little of this was parody. Seldom did any note of playfulness alloy the grim search for social advantage of this post-Veblenian horde — "striving, frightened people," a Chicago developer categorized them to Packard. Life was what Veblen had said it was for the "doubtful leisure class" in any barbarian culture: "an unremitting emulation and antagonism between classes and between individuals." For a few of the Levittowners of the nineteen-forties and -fifties this would change in the sixties, when they would graduate to being conglomerateurs and go-go fund managers and could indulge themselves in whimsical palaces as of old, though with a new Hollywood touch. (Eugene Klein, head of the parodically named National General Corporation, decked out his Beverly Hills mansion with a Marie Antoinette footbath and a desk set once owned by a czarina, and was scrupulous to let it be known that the former owner of his used Rolls-Royce had been Queen Elizabeth II.) But for most of the early postwar generation the old grind went on; emulate, emulate, antagonize, antagonize was still the rule of the home. ("Home" indeed. Two eminent authorities, the poet Edgar A. Guest and the courtesan Polly Adler, have both long since, in their different ways, instructed us that a house is something different from a home. The word *home,* insensitively used to mean "house," was foisted on the world by the real-estate trade, and accepted by all but a fastidious minority. And that acceptance is instructive: where we find the algae, euphemism, we will usually find the pollutant, pretension.)

Demographic and economic changes in the nineteen-seventies brought about a new situation as to real-estate and architectural display. The coming to potential house-owning age of the huge and never-fully-explained population bulge called the baby boom gave rise to a wild inflation of real-estate prices. (The problem was exacerbated by the coincident and probably related arrival of a vogue for living alone, resulting in a demand for many more housing units. In 1980 sixteen million American households consisted of a single person — one in five of all households.) The phenomenon of prices for houses doubling within a year became commonplace in such areas as New York, San Francisco, and their environs. In the climactic year of 1978, over eight hundred thousand new houses were built, almost four million existing houses were sold, and the sum spent on residential houses, one hundred and forty billion dollars, came to as much as had been spent over the whole decade of the nineteen-sixties.

The result, if not parody, was sociological tragicomedy: the nation at large had priced itself out of its housing market. In 1970, according to the Department of Housing and Urban Development, half of United States families could afford a medium-priced new house; in 1980, 13 percent could. Where was competitive house display now, when seven out of eight could not buy a house at all? Some of it, of course, was to be had through purchase of the new substitute for a house, a condominium, or "condo" — word to conjure with in the singles bars of 1978 or 1980. More of it had retreated into its old realm, that of the rich. But whether or not the rich are inherently different, as F. Scott Fitzgerald is supposed to have asserted, the rich were different now. Some were imaginary rich. Particularly in southern California, residential real estate tended to become a play-money game.*

Richard Reeves in 1979 described the Los Angeles real-estate bubble, which began in a big way in 1975 and reached its peak in 1978 and 1979. As with previous speculative madnesses in this country and others, prices entirely took leave of reality, and the sole or principal purpose of buying became not to use the thing bought but rather to resell it later — not much later — at a higher price. History has shown that such a bubble game tends to need a magic number as the counter signifying victory. In this case, the magic number came to be one million dollars for a house. By the peak, there was one Los Angeles agency that handled only million-dollar properties, like a croupier who deals only in blue chips. When Reeves visited it in 1979, it had twenty-nine listings priced from $1.1 million to $4.2 million. The same agency had over fifty sales agents who had sold more than $3 million worth of real estate each within the past year, and had thereby, according to Reeves's calculation,

*" 'The great American game,' they say, is Poker. Just why Real Estate should not come in for honorable mention in that way is not to be explained offhand." — Thorstein Veblen, *Absentee Ownership and Business Enterprise in Recent Times*, 1923.

earned commissions of ninety thousand dollars each. Among the accepted requirements for the million-dollar price, under the game's rules, were double baths and dressing rooms, although not firm walls, solid foundations, or pleasant locations. A tennis court, all agreed, added between $100,000 and $200,000 to the price, while an address technically in Beverly Hills, whether or not next door to a trash dump, automatically tacked on $100,000. Naturally, there were people standing ready to buy places without double baths, dressing rooms, and tennis courts for less than one million dollars, install those amenities, and sell for one million dollars. Such an entrepreneur told Reeves that in a few years he had run an initial stake of $7,000 to ten million.

A familiar American type of recent times, the housewife or divorcée turned real-estate agent, reached apotheosis in the southern California boom. Characteristically, such an agent was college-educated and had previously worked in a Jerry Brown campaign or taught classes for poor black or Chicano children. The latter activities had been temporarily fashionable expressions of noninvidious goodwill. Now — still fashionably, for what is fashionable as between being paid for work and not being paid for work is notoriously subject to overnight reversal — the women had opted for invidiousness, in the form of making money. And indeed, in some cases they were making it hand over fist. Reeves found one woman who had adopted the habit of treating herself to a diamond every time she pulled off a million-dollar sale. She had eight diamonds. Presumably, she also had a quarter of a million dollars in commissions, less the cost of the diamonds. One such woman agent grimly explained that the price of being a success at selling million-dollar houses was twenty-four-hour work days and, when the going got hot, "being at the door with a buyer when they put up the For Sale sign." Thus, apparently, the old work ethic operated, or at least was admired, within the iridescence of the real-estate bubble.

Who, then, was buying the houses? The agents said that nearly half the big-ticket sales were to foreigners — a code word for Arabs, the rich few among whom had selected southern California as a new secular Mecca. Housewives reported agents coming to their doors and saying, with a straight face, "Madam, inside that car is a genuine Arab who has authorized me to offer you cash for your house." But Arabs couldn't buy all the houses, and they didn't even bother with the formerly low-priced items, the Levittown-style bungalows that a few years earlier had cost $20,000 and now cost $80,000 or $100,000. As a result of the boom, Americans of modest means who wanted to own their own place now had to nail themselves to a financial crucifix to do so. Families with incomes of under $20,000 a year were buying houses costing more than five times that much. They were doing so, of course, by taking huge mortgage loans at sharply rising interest rates. The average down payment was twenty percent of the sale price, with the rest covered by an array of mortgages. Since a family earning $20,000 almost never had $20,000 in cash ready to put down, even the down payment was obviously often borrowed in whole or in part. The resulting interest payments amounted to most of the family income.

Particularly in the case of middle-range transactions — say, from $100,000 up to $1 million — sometimes the seller was willing personally to grant the buyer a purchase-money mortgage covering nearly all of the sale price. Occasionally, in a deal called in the trade's charming jargon a "wrap," the seller was willing to grant the buyer a purchase-money mortgage covering *all* of the sale price. In such a case, the buyer immediately paid no money. And, of course, the seller immediately received none. The house being "conveyed," so the bill of sale said, for $800,000 might be a nasty, leaky little box of plasterboard and asphalt tiles, standing on adobe earth subject to swelling, sinking, and, if it happened to be near the San Andreas fault, sudden engorgement by the earth. It was all very appropriate. The transaction by which this residential disaster area changed hands required no money to change hands. The structure and the conveyance were a match — both were cheerfully transparent lies. Southern California had brought the Monopoly board to real life.

Obviously, all this had overtones of parody; these were by implication noted by Senator Alan Cranston (of California) when he airily observed, "Inflation is not all bad. After all, it has allowed every American to live in a more expensive neighborhood without moving." In truth, the owner of a $20,000 house that changes on its own initiative into a $150,000 house has improved his conspicuous-display standing without his wish or act. But an event like the southern California boom is not a joke. It is a social tragedy that will end in many ruined lives. Some way back, I observed that parody can be a matter of life and death. When the subject is human shelter, the life-and-death component tends to smother the parody component. In southern California real estate, the parody display was largely in the sale price itself rather than in the thing being sold. To whatever extent a huge financial obligation is incurred as a joke, the joke is guaranteed to go sour. The southern California real-estate case is evidence that competitive display is capable of ending in social disruption and perhaps in human misery.

A subject more compatible with parody is that of "second homes," which postwar distributed affluence has made available to many more Americans than ever before. A "second home" is, of course, a nominal luxury, a discretionary rather than a necessary form of shelter. (Since, as noted, euphemism tends to live symbiotically with pretension, we may expect it to flourish here. And it does. As to "second homes," the smarmy usage "home" has won the day almost entirely. People who would not dream of calling their first house a home are reasonably happy with "second home.") In any time and setting, we will find the Veblenian fieldmarks more clearly evident in second homes than in first houses. Those turn-of-the-century mansions on Bellevue Avenue, Newport, were built as second homes. The fact that everyone knew this gave them unique leverage as items of competitive display. If a robber baron could spend so much on a *second* residence, what must be the incomparable splendor of his first? For purposes of display, a second home had the special advantage of appearing as the tip of an iceberg.

It still does, although here as in so many other areas, the number of displayers has swelled from a handful to a mass and the quality being displayed has changed to a marked extent from wealth to taste. Whole communities on Long Island consist largely of the second homes of retired New York City police, fire, and sanitation men, each with its breezeway and semiattached power boat. Higher up the economic scale, the prevalence of second homes is certified by what has become a standard national form of such certification, the existence of a magazine devoted to the subject. *Holiday Homes International* features the expressions *life style, carefree, easy living, gracious,* and *luxury,* and pictures of estates with prices in six or seven figures. Also some less familiar expressions; in 1979, for example, the magazine described "a prestigious aero community" near Chicago. What is an aero community? One in which people with their own airplanes may be sure of places to land them, take them off, and park them. Attached houses with private airplane parking were going for $155,000 and up, while private hangars started at $250,000. (Spending more on transportation than on habitation is of course nothing new. In the luxury-automobile era of the nineteen-twenties, some people had paid considerably more for their cars than for their houses.) Again, *Holiday Homes International* made much of a hideaway in La Jolla, California, with a living room bigger than the average hotel lobby, a swimming pool with a bridge over it, and a "sunken cocktail area and bar looking out on golden pool and ocean." The atmosphere was described as "friendly," a characteristic perhaps certified by the asking price, $4.5 million. One last one: a San Antonio, Texas, offering at $390,000 was promised to be a sixty percent scale model of the White House. Its owner could, if he wished, fancy himself to be sixty percent President of the United States. As Paul Goldberger pointed out in *The New York Times,* the intended audience for *Holiday Homes International* was not just potential buyers of such houses; it also included those who just like to imagine themselves as such. "Everyone fantasizes to some extent about houses," Goldberger said. The point is hard to refute; houses play a major role in almost everyone's actual dreams.

All, of course, painfully familiar instances of the impulses we have come to associate with the name of Veblen. We also tend — as Veblen categorically did not —to associate them exclusively with capitalist societies, our own in particular. But second homes flourish behind the Iron Curtain, too. Anthony Bailey has described how in Prague in 1979 there was a desperate urban housing shortage that led to an official floor-space allocation within the city of twelve square meters — a room roughly ten by twelve feet — per person. Yet many of the weekday occupants of such warrens were able to go on pleasant weekends to outside-the-city summer cottages which they capitalistically owned, just like a New York City fireman. "Just about everybody in Prague seems to have one, or the hope of having one," Bailey wrote. "In the small apartment building where one woman I know lives, and which is occupied by people in a thorough mixture of occupations, nine of fourteen households have a summer cottage. . . . It is felt that government tolerates the summer cottages because of their value as a safety valve." Government also seemed to be in the habit of taking advantage of the phenomenon to make unpleasant official announcements on weekends when everybody was away. The clear implication is that competitive display is no capitalist patent, and that it is no longer invariably looked upon by Communist ideologists as a hallmark of decadent capitalism. In the famous Marxian canon "to each according to his needs, from each according to his abilities," a summer cottage, at least in Czechoslovakia, seems to qualify under "needs."

In this country, the rise of the mass-produced second home has led to a new form of competitive display, a by-product of the escalating cold war in summer-cottage communities between the summer people and the natives. It is characteristic of the new age of display that this war is not primarily economic. Rather, the principal points of dispute in it are taste and style, and the principal weapon is coming to be political action. The summer people think of the natives as simpleminded, backward, recalcitrant peasants, although a certain civility must be shown toward them because they are needed to perform essential services. The natives, for their part, think of the summer people as affected, pretentious, and in politics dangerously radical.

Except for the last characteristic of summer people — the innovation of radical chic — this was all true in Veblen's time. The change that has taken place in the climate of the class war has its basis in economic and political changes. In Veblen's time the summer people were generally rich although few, and the natives poor although numerous. When the summer people dominated a resort town, as they often did, it was through naked economic muscle. Local political power had to be directly or indirectly bought. Now, in many resort villages the summer people may be only marginally richer than the natives, but what they have lost in economic they have gained in political leverage. Sometimes the summer-people voters in such a village are about equal in number to the native voters, and therefore are able to challenge the latter for control by traditional democratic means.

Thus the form of the battle has changed, while its cultural content has remained much the same. The two sides differ by instinct and training, without the need for recourse to logical thought, on almost every issue. The summer people favor conservation of wildlife and wetlands, while the natives favor economic exploitation. The summer people favor zoning that preserves open space; the natives want residential development of practically all available land. The summer people want highways to bypass villages, leaving them quiet and pristine; the natives want cars to be funneled down Main Street, bringing it additional business and squalor. These battles, while cultural in content, are political in form. The newly numerous summer people find themselves deep in summer-town politics, in which they are now sometimes victorious. The natives parry with such moves as scheduling the key meetings in deep winter, to screen out the summer people; the latter riposte by changing their voting residences and their residential habits, keeping their houses open in the winter so that they can attend political meetings. Meanwhile, the situation becomes nomenclaturally absurd. The summer people, although still so called by the natives — once a summer person, always a summer person is the ironclad rule — are now in fact year-round residents. Conversely, many of the natives, especially those whose livings are made in the summer from services to the summer people, have taken to going away regularly for part of the winter. They are therefore factually less native than the summer people. The sets of players are playing on each other's teams while still wearing their old uniforms.

What is observable about all this is that the form and the substance of the struggle are separate. Often the real, underlying struggle is not about conservation, development, zoning, or highways, but about the self-esteem of two groups that are culturally and temperamentally in conflict. Each group's political activities are a form of competitive display. The summer people are showing their superior sophistication, education, and, at least from their perspective, public-spiritedness. The natives are showing their practicality, "Americanism," and self-reliance. Of course, at the same time they are also showing that they have been there longer. The force of this crushing argument — which is usually accepted without a whimper by the summer people, who eagerly compete among themselves for priority in residence — is interesting to note. It takes precedence even over the traditionally sacred value of land ownership. A native of long residence need not own land, or even have had land ownership in the family, to be qualified to argue effectively on the residence priority issue. Tenancy over a sufficiently long period will do amply well. In the summer-people-vs.-native struggle, it is not even necessary to own real estate in order to use it for competitive advantage.

All booms are followed by busts, and early indications are that the character of the national real-estate market in the nineteen-eighties will tend less toward economic fantasy and more toward reality. Recession and scarce or expensive mortgage money may be expected to force competitive display in the direction of boasting about originality of style rather than about enormousness of price. We are entitled to hope that, as a by-product of this change, peaceable savagery will gain ground at the expense of predatory invidiousness, as it did earlier during the Depression of the nineteen-thirties. Meanwhile, invidiousness rules supreme.

Working

It should not surprise us that manners in business and professional offices are among our most straightforwardly and classically Veblenian. Business and professional life, after sports, is probably the area in our lives most forthrightly devoted to unremitting invidiousness accompanied by force and fraud. Indeed, the amount of lip service paid to peaceable-savage conduct is markedly less in the case of business than in that of sports. Does any Harvard Business School professor or management consultant rise to tell students and practitioners of business that what really counts in the boardroom is "how you played the game"? Indeed not. What counts is winning or losing, and no bones made. "Ethics" is encouraged by the more elevated of these arbiters of business conduct, but never generosity, unselfishness, gallantry — the qualities that make up the much-dishonored but still much-promulgated ideal of "sportsmanship." No credit accrues to one who habitually applies those qualities in business dealings; rather, he is apt to be patronized as a romantic fool, and handed a pink slip on Friday afternoon. Even a sense of "social responsibility" — the appropriateness of which in a corporate leader is the subject of sharp debate among business theorists — is usually defended not for its own value but on the pragmatic ground of its long-term service to increased profit. In sum, in the business world predatory invidiousness is universally accorded the highest value, while there is no code, not even a dishonored one, to embody the values of peaceable savagery.

Nevertheless, those values do exist in business, ever fighting a rearguard action. Practitioners of business recognize that this is necessary. Here as elsewhere, some sort of balance is needed to make the institution work. Evidence of the workings of this rearguard action is to be found in the ambiguous character of some of the many books of advice to executives that flood publishers' lists. True enough, some of the most successful among such books — *Looking Out For Number One, Winning Through Intimidation,* and so on — singlemindedly and without apology advocate unrestrained predatory office activity, at the risk of (or perhaps for the purpose of) offending delicate sensibilities and disrupting delicate balances. But another very popular strain of such writing, exemplified in the books of Michael Korda,* takes a different tack. In such books, when explaining to the reader in meticulous detail how to flummox, defeat, and crush the office opposition, the author hints that he is only kidding. This hint is an appeal or a concession to the peaceable-savage component in the character of the reader, and of the writer himself. However, whether the writer is really kidding or is only pretending to be, and whether or

---

*But not in his delightful family memoir, *Charmed Lives* (1979).

not the average reader is intended to believe he is kidding, are other matters.

In his book *Power!* for example, Korda gives the following pieces of advice.

When it is necessary to face down an office opponent, "it is possible to prevent involuntary twitching at the corners of the mouth by applying Xylocaine anesthetic ointment before an important meeting." It is important, however, not to overdo the treatment: "If too much ointment is used, the lips become numb and speech is slurred."

"Executives who sweat heavily may find it worthwhile to invest in a powerful air conditioner," since perspiration is "usually considered a sign of tension or lying." (Note that the undesirable by-product of sweat that is to be avoided is an impression of stress or prevarication — not an aggressive locker-room odor, which, we may suppose, may even be an asset.)

"An office calculator on the desk is . . . a sign of weakness and overattention to detail. . . . The only IBM product that serves as a power symbol is the IBM Selectric II typewriter."

"All the leather and chrome in the world will not replace a truly well-thought-out power scheme."

The reader so professionally secure as to feel no need for such office tactics — that is, the one able to afford the luxury of a sophisticated attitude — will take this as cynical wit. The thought of someone smearing his or her lips with a drug preparation to induce partial paralysis strikes such a reader as charmingly absurd, like the ultraelaborate technological aids to violence in James Bond movies. On the other hand, on reading Korda's passage, the dedicated office striver who needs all the help he can get and knows it will probably go out to the drug-store and ask for a jar of Xylocaine. What is parody to one reader is serious advice to another.

Moreover, the general thrust of Korda's whole book, as well as the way it was promoted, strongly suggests that at bottom the author is serious: he really does mean the reader to get Xylocaine to keep his lips from twitching, an air conditioner to forfend the appearance of lying, an IBM Selectric II as a power symbol, and strategically correct office furniture as a power scheme. The hint of parody is there to take the curse off.

What is significant to us is that the curse must be taken off, or this popular author believes that it must. His irony is a sort of apology. The question of whether or not he is kidding in prescribing Xylocaine before important meetings describes the knife-edge on which the matter rests. All-out invidiousness is encouraged in office competition, all right — but encouraged nervously. A still, small voice tells the encourager that he may be going too far. Anyone who has ever been privileged to visit Korda's own office at the publishing firm of Simon & Schuster knows that Korda himself is a master of lighthearted invidiousness, gaining an edge over the visitor by throwing out outrageous ideas with elaborate calmness, gesturing and jumping around like a comedian on a major gig, and sometimes boosting the act by wearing an in-from-the-country costume that includes riding boots, although not quite carrying a whip.

Another piece of counsel from closer to the heart of big business than Michael Korda's office may serve to clarify the matter further. Writing in the *Harvard Business Review* in 1979, Michael B. McCaskey, associate professor at the Harvard Business School, undertook to analyze "The Hidden Messages Managers Send." Mc-Caskey described a situation in which one manager feels that another has "violated his expectations or values" — perhaps by the action that is often more vulgarly described as "chewing him out" — and the second, in view of the fact that "status differences make it unwise to express disagreement or doubt verbally," reacts with "nonverbal stumbles." To wit: "There will be a burst of movement, almost as if both are losing balance. Arms and legs may be thrust out and the whole body posture changed in order to regain balance. Stumbles signal the need to regenerate what's being discussed."

They would also seem to signal that predatory office activity may sometimes have about the same physical effect as physical aggression. The victim in Professor McCaskey's vignette acted very much as he might have if he had been flicked by Muhammad Ali's left hook. McCaskey suggests that one way managers can "increase their listening skills and sharpen their appreciation of body language" is by replaying videotapes of their in-office behavior. If the manager who with a well-chosen few words had caused his colleague's arms and legs to fly around and his knees to buckle happened to have videotape of the event, by playing it he could learn that his words had had a powerful effect. But would that knowledge dismay him and consequently mitigate his invidiousness in the future? It would be naive to think so. Rather, it would more likely encourage him to try for a clean knockout next time around.

Whether or not they aim for a degree of irony as Korda's do, the many recent books on intimidation and self-preservation in office life — what might well be called books of invidiousness training — have a dominant theme in common. It is that in business competition, it's OK to be an utter heel. Such advice is, of course, part of a larger movement toward legitimizing self-serving activity in a larger context as embodied in such recent forms of psychological therapy as Primal Screaming and est. Just as the latter give sanction to invidiousness in personal behavior to a degree seldom matched before in our society, so in business life do such books as those of Robert Ringer, and, to a lesser extent, Korda.

Of course, the exact state of the tradeoff between barbarism and savagery in the office varies from industry to industry — there is probably more office subtlety in the "clean" and intellectually oriented businesses like publishing and computer programming than in steel or automobile manufacturing or meatpacking — and, even more, from one era to another. In Veblen's time, class rank in American office life was so well defined, and the likelihood of an employee transcending class lines so remote, that only a limited amount of invidiousness was necessary. (Veblen never touched on office life in *The Theory of the Leisure Class,* even though the male members of the "leisure class" as he conceived of it were men who went to offices, although not to do what he considered useful work.) Two vignettes of the office behavior of turn-of-the-century office bosses will serve to describe the tone they set. Lincoln Steffens relates in his autobiography how, as a Wall Street reporter in the eighteen-nineties, he learned about the office demeanor of J. Pierpont Morgan. Morgan, Steffens relates, sat at an open desk, unprotected by walls or doors or a guardian secretary, in plain sight of the bank's main business floor. However, his apparent accessibility was an illusion, for he had his own interior walls.

It looked as if anyone could walk in upon him and ask him any question. One heard stories of the payment of large sums for an introduction to him. I could not see why the tippers with business did not come right in off the street and talk to him. They did not. . . . His partners did not go near him unless he sent for them.

Steffens asked a Morgan partner what would happen if he were to dare to approach the great man without an introduction. "Oh," the partner replied, "then you would have seen an explosion."

Again, there is a story about John Elbridge Hudson, president of the American Bell Telephone Company (predecessor of AT&T) during the eighteen-nineties, and a ranking candidate for the title of coldest fish ever to occupy the chief executive's chair of an American corporation. A nominal classical scholar like many gentlemen of his time, Hudson enjoyed reminding himself of his status — reminding others was, of course, unnecessary — by writing memoranda to himself in Greek. Like Morgan, he was impossible to get an appointment with, but his technique in protecting his isolation was different. Unlike Morgan, he occupied an office with a closed door. Once, according to an office story of the time, a petitioner seeking his presence sat in his anteroom every day for several weeks, leaving only for lunch; during this period Hudson would periodically pass through the anteroom, neither encouraging the petitioner nor advising him to give up. The interview never took place. (Another Hudson story, not strictly relevant here but irresistible all the same, concerns the custom of American Bell at the time of giving each director a gold piece after each board meeting, in appreciation of his attendance. The directors, well heeled to a man, were in the custom of giving their gold pieces to charity, or back to the company; but after their leader's death there was found among his possessions a box containing all his gold pieces.)

Bosses still find ways to protect their privacy and, incidentally, to make invidious comparisons between themselves and those responsible to them. But democratization and its concomitant, the fear of adverse publicity, have drastically changed the style of such exclusions. The current chairman of J. P. Morgan & Company would not dream of sitting in plain sight of the vulgar throng. If he were to try it, in no time at all a Weatherman, a Black Panther, a Nader Raider, or an Episcopal clergyman might walk up to him demanding financing for the social revolution, with a television camera recording the scene for the evening news and posterity. Nor would the chairman of AT&T now venture to keep anyone, not even Jane Fonda, cooling her heels in his anteroom for a fortnight. More devious means are employed nowadays by bosses to exclude the unwanted, whether an employee or an outsider. Courteous secretaries explain in detail how the nabob's many vital functions preclude the possibility of adding a new one. Intriguing if insignificant details of his various appointments are thrown in for the purpose of placating the petitioner with a privileged peek down the corridors of power (for example, "Mr. B. just *has* to see Mrs. Onassis about our beautification program; she's been waiting for two weeks"). To judge by the honey that drips from the secretary's voice as she delivers her dulcet rejection notice, the petitioner, if he wanted to, could probably solace himself by going to bed with her.

In sum, the invidiousness has become gentler in style and equally, or perhaps more, forceful in substance.

Fortune in April, 1980, treated its readers to sketches of those it had selected as the ten "toughest" corporate bosses in the country. One of them, the magazine reported, is known to his subordinates as "Idi" (after the whimsically murderous Uganda dictator Idi Amin), and likes to dress down his peers as well as his subordinates in public. Of another: "Doesn't listen well, so he is frustrating to work for; most glaring trait is his lack of feeling for people." Of another: "Accomplished at belittling people in front of others." Yet another "becomes enamored of someone, but that wears off." And another "demolishes anyone who blows smoke at him." A final entry is described as keeping his subordinates under such surveillance that "they won't go to the bathroom without his permission."

In blunter language, then, the qualities that distinguish these men are arrogance, gratuitous cruelty, self-centeredness, lack of consideration of others, pettiness, fickleness, schoolyard bullying — a catalogue of predatory-invidious traits. Yet they are high among the leaders and the role models for American corporate executives. It is a safe bet that the prestige of the *Fortune* Ten was increased rather than decreased by their listing. One might expect to find (and indeed, one sometimes does find) a certain aristocratic benevolence at the very top of the corporate totem pole, with the dirty work laid off on the drill sergeants of middle management. In these cases, not at all; the top man apparently is glad to keep the dirty work for himself. The glaring suspicion is that he enjoys it. It is easy to imagine that some of these men, in the course of their climb to the top, had to force themselves, against their natures, to cultivate predatory-invidious and to suppress peaceable-savage behavior.

An illuminating facet of behavior in big corporations is the attitude of top-echelon executives toward their dead. Some species of animal, and a few of insect, treat the corpses of their fallen colleagues with what appears to be respect or nostalgic affection. Many others, of course, do not, preferring to eat the corpses littering the heath, or to act as if they were not there. A few years ago, investigating the workings of one of the biggest of American corporations, I had occasion to learn that the executives of that corporation belong with the latter group. Speaking to an executive ranked just below the top level, I alluded to the ideas of a former president (call him Branford), who had died in office a few years earlier, as if those ideas remained a living force within the company. The living executive paused a moment, as if confronted with a notion difficult to grasp. Then he regained his composure, and adopted an attitude of impatience. "But Branford is *dead!*" he said. The subject was closed.

All this is familiar: the corporate organization, being devoted to invidious ideals, is a perfect breeder and nourisher of invidiousness. And the march of democracy has done away with the overlay of aristocratic noblesse oblige at the very top that may formerly have served to some extent as a mitigating factor. Happily for industrial civilization, other concurrent forces have been tugging in the opposite direction. For instance, the massive introduction into office life since the Second World War of new technological devices — computers, copying machines, "word processing" typewriters, and the like — has tended to impersonalize human relations in the office at all levels up to near the top. We must recall that predatory invidiousness is not an impersonal or mechanical but rather a human characteristic — just as human, indeed, as its opposite, peaceable savagery. Machines may be and often are used as instruments of invidiousness (as we saw in the case of the telephone), but no machine is invidious in itself. In the combat between conflicting human tendencies, the machine is neutral. Yet a computer collating and transmitting data may make unnecessary a confusing and perhaps irritating telephone conversation or correspondence, and the distribution of a sheaf of Xerox copies may obviate a meeting where invidiousness would flourish unconfined, as it usually does in meetings. On balance, modern technology has done much more to reduce the occasions for office invidiousness than to increase them.

Another new factor is the increase over recent years in the number of women occupying executive positions. Here the returns are not all in yet. It cannot be said with any degree of confidence that women executives are less prone to invidiousness than men. Indeed, from the accounts of their subordinates one might conclude that some women bosses are capable of behavior that would draw an approving nod from a Lucretia Borgia. S. J. Perelman wrote a fantasy on Fleur Cowles, a woman boss ahead of her time, which he entitled "The Hand That Cradles the Rock." (Perelman was alluding literally to a ring with a huge stone that Mrs. Cowles liked to wear in her office.)

Nevertheless, probably most people who have in recent years worked in offices where executive power has gradually come to be more equally distributed between men and women will agree that the change has been accompanied by a decrease in the raw kind of invidiousness epitomized by the *Fortune* Ten. In the older office, women without power were either decorative (gorgeous

receptionists to impress outsiders) or nourishing (faithful
and supercompetent secretaries to prop up male executives); while the few anomalous women who held formal
power usually devoted themselves to emulating men (feet
up on the desk to flout femininity, or jangling jewelry to
suggest sexual aggressiveness). Nowadays, everything is
a bit more relaxed. The office emotional atmosphere is
more like that of a family — where, to be sure, invidiousness often flourishes, but where power is inclined to
be acquired and used with less reference to sex. (Of
course, it has always been possible for power in a family
to reside in either a man or a woman.) Sexual attraction
and flirtation have a larger part in the new office than they
had in the old one. Indeed, one finds offices where at the
lower and middle executive levels it seems to be the main
topic of conversation, and not in terms that could be
called Aesopian. But the quest for bedmates and the
quest for power have tended to become separate. Formerly, an attractive woman with corporate power was assumed, vulgarly and sometimes accurately, to have
humped her way to it. Although most corporate offices
have by no means become sex-blind in promotion policy,
this assumption is no longer made. Sex is sex, and power
is power; increased emphasis on the bottom line has given
the once-accepted sex-for-power tradeoff a bad name.*

*The question of sex and promotion had its real-life parody-travesty in
1980, when William Agee, divorced, forty-two-year-old chairman of the
huge Bendix Corporation, was suspected of having promoted beautiful, sep-
arated, twenty-nine-year-old Mary Cunningham from executive assistant to
Vice-President for Strategic Planning at least partly on the strength of their
supposed personal relationship. When the rumors began flying, the corporation announced plans for a press conference at which Agee and Cunningham would have "a major announcement" to make. However, as the
hour for the conference approached, it was canceled. A Bendix spokesman

From a Veblenian perspective, the American office is in a state of transition. Male bosses don't write memos in Greek (and couldn't if they tried), while women bosses, if they put their feet up, do it unselfconsciously in jeans rather than defiantly in skirts. Salaried office workers without expectation or hope of major promotions have meanwhile developed a new form of Schweikian passive resistance. Relying largely on their unions to protect their jobs, they just don't show up. Mountains of statistics support the conclusion that "volunteer absenteeism" in offices is running at record levels. In fact, this phenomenon is accused of playing a major role in the recent steep decline in American per-capita productivity. In almost any office building openly conducted elevator conversations can be overheard that reveal the subtleties of thought devoted — surely for the most part on company time — to the matter of excuses that will wash. Illness, of course, leads the list but lacks originality ("I feel a cold coming on"). Status with peers is more efficiently gained with less obvious entries: "I was sold a defective hair dryer and have to go to small-claims court," "The meter reader is coming and I have to let him in," and so on.

This verges on parody — a parody of the largely discredited work ethic. The *Fortune* Ten, even though they head leading companies, are cultural Neanderthals. The big boss of the future, although he will certainly be ruthless, will surely have more style about it. Perhaps he will affect malapropisms, like the sainted Sam Goldwyn, or riding boots, like Michael Korda.

---

said, "We realize we promised a statement. After further discussions this morning, it was determined that there is nothing more that can be said." There, surely, was an instance of sound corporate thinking.

Surely, one way or another, he will have to introduce the note most conspicuously lacking at present in the wielders of office power, the note of irony.

18

Dressing Up

If fashion in clothing is the most sensitive of barometers recording social change in general, clothing itself is the beginning and end of human display, touching on one side the skin of the person and reaching out on the other to announce to all what the person inside the skin is or wishes to be. Just as one's speech is an unceasingly repeated public announcement about background and social standing, so one's clothing is a similar announcement regarding sex, status, wealth, and personality. Moreover, unlike almost all other such announcements except speech, it is made involuntarily. *Whatever* one wears is a statement of personal display — of aggressiveness, or shyness, or authenticity, or a desire to be original, or neatness, or sloppiness, or (one of the strongest statements of all) of being so free of vanity as not to care about clothes.

Small wonder that people obsessed with privacy are apt to be embarrassed by their attire. They do not want to give information about themselves promiscuously. Yet they can't avoid doing so. Everyone knows women who, before setting out for an evening, go back and back, to the closet and the mirror, trying out this, slipping on that, seeking to "get an outfit together." Surely the object, in some cases, is not so much to enhance personal display as to avoid it. What the indecisive one may be seeking is the outfit that will be acceptably attractive while making the minimum personal statement. In theory, going naked would preserve her social anonymity, or at least neutrality, better, because nakedness, while revealing the physical exterior, goes a long way toward concealing the social being. But that method of maintaining privacy is not ordinarily available in social settings, more's the pity.

Clothing then, makes show-offs of us all; it is one of the few forms of conspicuous display that everyone must practice. The waves of stupefying conventionality that periodically sweep over clothing fashion — the gray flannel suits or the sweaters and skirts — must be caused in part by a wish to revolt against involuntary display, to go around, so to speak, sociologically naked. The wearer of such a uniform is saying, in effect, "I'll tell you what I'm really like when I get ready, not before." Similarly, many people's attitudes toward the cost of their clothing show an ambivalence about whether to make economic boasts or not to make them. Eve Merriam offers a nice set of definitions illustrating the parodic language women use about their clothing (the setting is 1960, and the sums mentioned are preinflation 1960 dollars):

> *Basic:* noun, a simple black dress that costs no more than $100.
> *Functional:* adjective, referring to a simple black dress that costs more than $100.
> *Nothing:* noun, a simple black dress that costs more than $200.

Understated: a simple black dress that costs more than $300.

The dresses are all more or less the same apart from quality of cloth and tiny refinements of style, and the words are all more or less synonymous terms of deprecation; but to a listener who knows the price-tag code — and a listener who aspires to worldliness had better know it — the difference in which dress is worn, and which word is used to describe it, is the difference between showing off and not showing off.

There is a larger, related paradox — between the intensely personal quality of clothing and the huge, international, impersonal force, fashion, that has so much influence on what people wear at any particular time. Fashion is as old as clothing, and endless attempts have been made to explain its driving force. The most familiar explanations are the following: that fashions are set by a few influential public figures; that their changes reflect or predict world or national political events; that class competition is responsible; and, finally, that God Himself is in charge. The last is in general disfavor in Paris and on Seventh Avenue, but it may be as good as any of the others. I would venture to add a fifth: that fashion in clothing is popular largely because it enables those who wish to avoid constant conspicuous display insofar as possible to do so by sedulously following what is currently prescribed — that is, to hide a little.

We will hardly be surprised to find Veblen pretty much in the class-competition camp. In a famous chapter of *The Theory of the Leisure Class,* he set forth what he believed to be the first coherent explanation ever offered of the phenomenon of changing fashions in dress. His theory starts with the premise that dress is primarily not the answer to a physical need to keep the body warm but rather to "a 'higher' or spiritual need." Proof: "People go ill-clad in order to appear well-dressed." Specifically, the spiritual need is for "pecuniary decency" — as we know, Veblen's quaint term for the public display of affluence — and it requires that clothing be expensive, inconvenient, free at all times of evidence of dirt or wear, and, above all, obviously unadaptable to productive work of any kind, in order to prove that the wearer has plenty of money and need not do physical work for a living. However, the fulfillment of these requirements invariably leads to clothing that is "intrinsically ugly," because intrinsic beauty — as Veblen understood it, and as we probably do too — is associated with simplicity and usefulness, and ugliness with the tendencies to which he applied his famous phrases "conspicuous consumption" and "conspicuous waste." However, intrinsically ugly though they may be, we find these pecuniarily decent articles of clothing beautiful, because we have been conditioned to confuse expensiveness with beauty: "We readily, and for the most part with utter sincerity, find those things pleasing that are in vogue."

But — and here we approach the heart of the argument — only for a time. Often when the novelty of a given fashion has worn off, people's "abiding aesthetic sense" asserts itself to the point where "aesthetic nausea" sets in. The fashion must then be replaced by a new one — which, of course, must itself meet the standard of pecuniary decency, and so presently becomes aesthetically nauseating in its turn. Thus Veblen sees the fashion cycle as a kind of internal-combustion engine that runs on the fuel (in inexhaustible supply) of human folly. The induction stroke is the need for pecuniary decency; the compression stroke is the creation of a product that meets this need and is accordingly accepted as beautiful; the power stroke is the rise of this product to fashionable status; and the exhaust stroke is the rising gorge of the public as aesthetic nausea sets in, preparing the way for the next cycle.

The system has its ramifications. Women, Veblen insisted, dress primarily not for warmth, or modesty, or even beautification of their bodies, but rather for the purpose of "putting into evidence their master's ability to pay." Thus the high heel, the skirt, the "impracticable bonnet," and above all the corset, do not beautify the wearer, "but the loss suffered on that score is offset by the gain in reputability which comes of her visibly increased expensiveness and infirmity." In particular, infirmity: "the womanliness of women's apparel resolves itself . . . into the more effective hindrance to useful exertion offered by the garments peculiar to women." Who could run a lathe or scrub a floor in high heels, corset, and impracticable bonnet? Nobody; obviously the wearer's husband is rich enough so that she never needs to do either.

The American situation as to clothing sociology stands out from the situation in Europe in that the most striking distinctions in matters of dress are usually between different eras, rather than between different classes in any given era. Where one set of distinctions is chiefly horizontal, the other is chiefly vertical. Even in Colonial times and in the early years of the republic, when American class lines were drawn far more sharply than they are now, each period of North American history is permanently branded with a certain clothing style as its uniform: knickers, silk stockings, and wigs for men in the Colonial period, in dutiful imitation of the mother country; native buckskin in the post-Revolutionary period; conspicuously wasteful overdressing by both sexes in the gilded age after the Civil War; short skirts and silk stockings for *women* in the socially anarchic nineteen-twenties; and so on. (Some even maintain that women's legs suddenly became visible in the twenties as an outcome of technological developments that made silk stockings, previously a luxury item, into one generally available. The newly acquired silks of the many had to be displayed; the resulting display of the legs snugly encased in them was, in this analysis, not so much a function of advancing sexual abandon as a by-product of Veblenian pecuniary decency.)

Nevertheless, the Veblen theory, rather solidly based in class competition, had plenty of relevance in his time. Does it retain that relevance today? Here, as in so many of the areas that we have looked into, we must conclude that the answer is yes and no. The pecuniary decency—aesthetic nausea cycle still plainly operates; observe, for example, the recent wild popularity followed by violent rejection of items like the Nehru jacket for men. Anne Hollander, a writer about clothes chiefly influenced by the artistic tradition rather than the sociological one, wrote recently about what she called the "visual indigestion" brought on by seeing people wearing recently outmoded fashions. The phrase is more than an echo of Veblen's "aesthetic nausea," used in 1899 to describe more or less the same phenomenon. It is almost a synonym; yet Veblen plays no part in Mrs. Hollander's analysis. What Veblen had discovered in 1899 she independently rediscovered in 1978, strongly suggesting that it must still be true.

"Impracticable bonnets" and corsets have disappeared in the interim. Has the motive to which Veblen attributed their popularity disappeared too? The corset as a topic was so irresistible to Veblen that he harped on it like a barroom bore. In *The Theory of The Leisure Class* he wrote that the corset-constricted waistline was to be compared to the feet of Chinese women of the past, deliberately deformed by tightly wound bandages. Both customs, he felt, were "mutilations of unquestioned repulsiveness to the untrained sense, to which a society could become reconciled only through habituation." Half a dozen pages later he was at it again: "The corset is, in economic theory, substantially a mutilation," he insisted, "undergone for the purpose of lowering the subject's vitality and rendering her permanently and obviously unfit for work," and at the same time "impairing the personal attraction of the wearer."

Enough about corsets and mutilation! we want to cry out. Veblen's obsession suggests a traumatically induced nervousness about women's wearing corsets. Still, we may forgive him. Other writers on clothing fashion have shared his obsession, and one of them, James Laver, has gone so far as to argue that the corset is an accurate barometer of economic and social change as regards money and sexual mores. According to Laver's findings, its periodic disappearance from fashion has, throughout history, *always* been accompanied by inflation and an increase in the prevalence of sexual promiscuity. Conversely, tight female waistlines go with tight money, et cetera. A pretty maxim surely, and one certainly borne out by the events of the twentieth century to date. Corsets have disappeared (and so even, in some circles, have brassieres). What has happened meanwhile to currency values and sexual mores is common knowledge. Laver is vindicated. Apparently Veblen, who spoke of corsets as a permanent part of women's lot, is not. But let us consider further. During the period 1900–1980, when corsets were being progressively abandoned, there arose a new and alarming vogue among women. It was for submitting to the surgeon's knife for purely cosmetic reasons. Plastic surgery intended to improve their appearance is now undergone by thousands of Americans, most though not all of them women, each year. It is a most Veblenian procedure. For the payment of a customarily extravagant fee, the usually perfectly healthy "patient" undergoes pain, medical risk, and a period of isolation from society for the sake of eliminating a few hard-earned facial wrinkles. The result in too many cases is not so much a look of restored youth as one of unnatural and disconcerting change, as if from an illness.

Nor is the face the only site of cosmetic surgery. Female breasts are enlarged by the introduction into them of foreign matter, or reduced by the excision of native flesh. Rolls of unwanted fat are cut from bellies and thighs, even though in many cases the same removal could have been accomplished naturally through dieting. Intestines are tampered with surgically to interfere with their capacity for digestion and thereby to decrease the subject's tendency to gain weight. People board jets and fly to distant countries, Brazil in particular, to undergo cosmetic operations — not because the operations are not available nearer home, as is sometimes true in the case of abortion, but because the names of the distant doctors have been spoken by the right people in the right places, and an expensive journey to one of those doctors has become momentarily the pecuniarily decent way to undergo mutilation in beauty's name.

Most of Veblen's strictures about corsets in 1899 apply to cosmetic surgery in 1980. According to Laver's theory, the corset will have to come back eventually, when in the fullness of time the economic conditions cycle back to monetary stringency and the social condition to sexual restrictiveness. In the meantime we may have to conclude that, despite the corset's fall from fashion, Veblen's corset principle is still in force, and the new equivalent of the corset is the plastic surgeon's knife.

Veblen's other prize witness as to women's clothing, high heels, has obviously survived the intervening period (although high heels have been under serious attack from time to time along the way; for instance, in 1920 the Massachusetts Osteopathic Society tried unsuccessfully to have them outlawed by the state legislature on medical grounds). We would like to think that this survival is the result of rational judgment by both men and women, rather than a vindication of Veblen's theory, which posits a society of pretension and faking. The notion that high heels intrinsically increase the attractiveness of female ankles and feet still runs deep in our culture. In such a trendy movie as *The Nude Bomb* (1980), the beautiful female intelligence agent wears her spikes even when she is punching out the male villains — or, rather, especially then. (In movies that strive to make a satirical social comment, it had by that time become almost de rigueur to include a scene in which a lady decks a gentlemen with her tiny but puissant fists.) Most men, myself included, as well as most women, will defend high heels, at least for ceremonial, office, or semiformal wear. If we think about it we have to admit they preposterously decrease the wearer's comfort and her ability to walk, run, or even stand; but we insist that they are intrinsically beauty-enhancing. Are they really? Is there anything wrong aesthetically with feet and ankles in sneakers, flats, or sandals?

Women, as Kennedy Fraser points out, no longer dress to show off their man's money-making skill. On the other hand, "they do not, for the most part, choose to look unattractive to men." Ergo, they like high heels.

Is it not possible that both sexes, in their continuing admiration for this hobbling item of female attire, are showing themselves to be unconscious victims of precisely the folly described by Veblen — a confusion of the fashionable with the beautiful, resulting in a "mutilation of unquestioned repulsiveness . . . to which a society could become reconciled only through habituation"?

The surge of iconoclasm in clothing fashions that accompanied and was part of the social revolution of the nineteen-sixties — love beads and shirts unbuttoned to the navel for men, T-shirts with dirty jokes on them for women, decreased differentiation on account of sex for both — obviously receded in the seventies, but it left its mark. Not only does the sixties scene fit into Veblen's system, it raises that system to new heights of relevance (as they said back then). What could be more intrinsically ugly and, after a certain amount of time, aesthetically nauseating than the flannel suits, trim sweater-and-skirts, and slavishly followed Paris fashions of the fifties? What could provide a more stupefying reversal and change than the "proletarian drag" (term coined by the novelist Harvey Swados) of the sixties? And again, under the aspect of an "abiding aesthetic sense," what could eventually appear more nauseating than a hairy male chest flaunted in a fancy restaurant, or dungarees worn by a woman of fashion to a ball? Veblen wrote the script for dressing in the sixties sixty years ahead of its enactment. What passed for rejection of his fashion theory was actually confirmation of it.

However, in observing fashion change we must not get carried away. We must also do credit to continuity. The people and institutions nearest the American mainstream did not significantly change their clothing habits and requirements during the sixties. On the contrary, they hewed to them more scrupulously than ever, in order to separate themselves as sharply as possible from the hippies and radicals who were threatening the established order. There were still dinner parties (although they became fewer) the invitations to which specified, discreetly but imperiously, "Black Tie." Some men indicated token revolt or self-assertion by wearing to these affairs bow ties that were not black, but rather were red, blue, green, or polka-dot. However, they wore them with tuxedos, as prescribed. The injunction "Black Tie" no longer meant exactly black tie. It meant tuxedos for men and formal dresses, short or long, for women. It had become an abstract code word for conventional formal dress — a warning not to come in an aesthetically nauseating leisure suit. Indeed, the wearing of a tuxedo no longer signifies high social status or aspiration to it. In New York City in the nineteen-sixties, a man felt more comfortable riding the subways wearing a tuxedo than wearing, say, an expensive business suit made by a London tailor. In the latter case, he was taken by the subway throng to be a snob and probably an enemy of the people. In the former, he was taken to be a waiter.

Then there is the case of the familiar jacket-and-tie requirement for everyday wear in settings where it is felt that the standards must not be let down. This is a remarkably persistent small measure of social discipline. As all men except confirmed hippies and radicals know, in summer a jacket in the street or in a room that is not air-conditioned can be remarkably uncomfortable to the wearer, and may be offensive to others in that it quickly gives rise to profuse sweat that may offend their senses of sight and smell. (See Michael Korda's injunction to ambitious executives.) If men's clothing fashion were logical, rather than freighted as it is with symbolism and hidden motives, we might expect the broad informalization of American dress over recent decades to have been accompanied by a summer relaxation of the coat-and-tie rule in offices and in restaurants catering to the well dressed. However, in 1980, and even at the zenith of the sixties (which may actually have come in 1971), only a few high-status American corporations would tolerate open necks for their male executives in either the street or the boardroom, and executives who flouted this rule did so at the risk of their status. As far as office and boardroom were concerned, short-sleeved shirts were emphatically included in the anathema. John T. Molloy, in his best-selling book *Dress for Success,* had put the matter in an appropriately headmasterish way: "You will never, ever, as long as you live, wear a short sleeve shirt for any business purpose, no matter whether you're the office boy or the president of the company." (In mid-1980, *The Wall Street Journal* reported that in Phoenix, Houston, New

Orleans, and southern Florida, a short-sleeved, open-necked shirt called a guayabera was catching on for executive office wear. However, it showed no signs of traveling north.)

As for restaurants and bars with pretentious objectives and clients, in the sixties they adopted, and many preserve, the habit of complying with laws against discriminatory exclusion, and at the same time keeping up the standards, by offering the temporary free loan of jackets and even ties to customers seeking entrance but not wearing those articles. Around 1970 I myself happened to seek entrance to the Bemelmans Bar of the Hotel Carlyle in New York City while in open-necked condition. A waiter, meanwhile barring my way in a civil but decisive manner, offered me the loan of a house tie, and I accepted. The tie he presently brought was of orange and silver material so shiny that it would surely glow in the dark — altogether the most hideous piece of haberdashery I have ever seen. Swallowing my aesthetic nausea, I donned it and entered with my companion; however, after a quick drink I found that wearing it had become intolerable, so I returned it to the waiter and we left. The Bemelmans Bar is known for its subdued and tasteful atmosphere. Perhaps the tie that I was proffered represented a lapse from that standard. I prefer to think that its character was calculated and invidious. Certainly I have learned my lesson as far as the Bemelmans Bar is concerned.

Men in business suits and pulled-up ties appear to those not accustomed to that costume as if they were constricted, tamed to the bit, even prepared for the hangman. Often they do not feel that way. They are no more uncomfortable than are most women wearing high heels, for whom the confidence that their ankles look adorable far outweighs any pinching or hobbling of gait. Indeed, in certain cases it may be that they would be uncomfortable wearing anything else. Richard Nixon, by all accounts a particularly rigid personality, greeted visitors to his San Clemente beach house during his early postpresidential years wearing a jacket and well-knotted tie — hardly traditional beach wear. Indeed, a costume most would rate, in the context, as ridiculous. We may assume he did so because he felt happiest that way. The point Veblen missed in his analysis is the extent to which habituation through fashion can go. Not only can it make clothing that is inherently mutilating and repulsive seem acceptable: it can make it feel comfortable.

19

Dressing Down

We come now to the American blue jeans phenomenon, in many ways a pocket summary of the American style of showing off eighty years after Veblen.

Beyond doubt, the jeans phenomenon is a seismic event in the history of dress, and not only in the United States. Indeed, the habit of wearing jeans is — along with the computer, the copying machine, rock music, polio vaccine, and the hydrogen bomb — one of the major contributions of the United States to the postwar world at large.

Before the nineteen-fifties, jeans were worn, principally in the West and Southwest of the United States, by children, farmers, manual laborers when on the job, and, of course, cowboys. There were isolated exceptions — for example, artists of both sexes took to blue jeans in and around Santa Fe, New Mexico, in the nineteen-twenties and -thirties; around 1940, the male students at Williams College took them up as a mark of differentiation from the chino-wearing snobs of Yale and Princeton; and in the late forties the female students of

Bennington College (not far from Williams) adopted them as a virtual uniform, though only for wear on campus — but it was not until the nineteen-fifties, when James Dean and Marlon Brando wore jeans in movies about youth in revolt against parents and society, when John Wayne wore them in movies about untrammeled heroes in a lawless Old West, and when many schools from coast to coast gave their new symbolism a boost by banning them as inappropriate for classrooms, that jeans acquired the ideological baggage necessary to propel them to national fame.

After that, though, fame came quickly, and it was not long before young Americans — whether to express social dissent, to enjoy comfort, or to emulate their peers — had become so attached to their jeans that some hardly ever took them off. According to a jeans authority, a young man in the North Bronx with a large and indulgent family attained some sort of record by continuously wearing the same pair of jeans, even for bathing and sleeping, for over eight months. Eventually, as all the world knows, the popularity of jeans spread from cowboys and anomic youths to adult Americans of virtually every age and sociopolitical posture, conspicuously including Jimmy Carter when he was a candidate for the presidency. Trucks containing jeans came to rank as one of the three leading targets of hijackers, along with those containing liquor and cigarettes. Estimates of jeans sales in the United States vary wildly, chiefly because the line between jeans and slacks has come to be a fuzzy one. According to the most conservative figures, put out by the leading jeans manufacturer, Levi Strauss & Company, of San Francisco, annual sales of jeans of all kinds in the United States by all manufacturers in 1957 stood at around a hundred and fifty million pairs, while for 1977 they came to over five hundred million, or considerably more than two pairs for every man, woman, and child in the country.

Overseas, jeans had to wait slightly longer for their time to come. American Western movies and the example of American servicemen from the West and Southwest stationed abroad who, as soon as the Second World War ended, changed directly from their service uniforms into blue jeans bought at post exchanges started a fad for them among Europeans in the late nineteen-forties. But the fad remained a small one, partly because of the unavailability of jeans in any quantity; in those days, European customers considered jeans ersatz unless they came from the United States, while United States jeans manufacturers were inclined to be satisfied with a reliable domestic market. Being perennially short of denim, the rough, durable, naturally shrink-and-stretch cotton twill of which basic jeans are made, they were reluctant or unable to undertake overseas expansion.

Gradually, though, denim production in the United States increased, and meanwhile demand for American-made jeans became so overwhelming that in parts of Europe a black market for them developed. American jeans manufacturers began exporting their product in a serious way in the early nineteen-sixties. At first, demand was greatest in Germany, France, England, and the Benelux nations; later it spread to Italy, Spain, and Scandinavia, and eventually to Latin America and the Far East. By 1967, jeans authorities estimate, a hundred and ninety million pairs of jeans were being sold annually outside the United States; of these, all but a small fraction were of local manufacture, and not imports from the United

States, although American-made jeans were still so avidly sought after that some of the local products were blatant counterfeits of the leading American brands, complete with expertly faked labels. In the late nineteen-seventies, estimated jeans sales outside the United States had doubled in a decade, to three hundred and eighty million pairs, of which perhaps a quarter were now made by American firms in plants abroad; the markets in Europe, Mexico, Japan, Australia, and other places had come so close to the saturation point that the fastest-growing jeans market was probably Brazil; Princess Anne, of Great Britain, and Princess Caroline, of Monaco, had been photographed wearing jeans, and King Hussein of Jordan was reported to wear them at home in his palace; the counterfeiting of American brands was a huge international undertaking, which the leading American manufacturers combated with world-ranging security operations. In Russia, authentic American Levi's were a black-market item regularly commanding eighty or more dollars per pair. All in all, it is now beyond doubt that in size and scope the rapid global spread of the habit of wearing blue jeans, however it may be explained, is an event without precedent in the history of human attire. But not without explanation in Veblenian theory.

In no sense and in no particular could blue jeans claim to be new; in fact, the essence of their popularity may be that, in contrast with the characteristic products of fashion, they are not new and do not claim to be. The brand that led the way in sweeping first the United States and then the world — the straight-leg, cotton-denim, copper-riveted jeans made by Levi Strauss and called Levi's — was on sale, with only minor variations from its present-day style, in 1873. The word *denim* is a corruption, originally British, of *serge de Nîmes* — the city of Nîmes, in southern France, having been the place where the fabric was traditionally produced; the earliest reference to *denim* in the *Oxford English Dictionary* is dated 1695. The same source traces the term *jean* back to 1567, identifying it as deriving from *Genoese* and as having originally meant a twilled cotton cloth made in Genoa. The indigo dye that gives blue jeans their characteristic color and tendency to fade is synthetic now, but its prototype, natural dye prepared from the leaves of various plants, has played a rich role in world clothing history, going back to the earliest recorded times.

However, it is unlikely that the hundreds of millions who took up blue jeans in the nineteen-fifties and -sixties were responding to an atavistic urge for denim or for indigo. More plausibly — in the United States, at least — they were to one extent or another making a small, intensely personal, apparently harmless, and surely only partly conscious protest against the sense of powerlessness, impersonality, and regimentation that descended on the country at the time when space vehicles, pesticides, the hydrogen bomb, urban sprawl, and the computer were comparatively new, and when organizations seemed on the way to taking permanent charge of American life, not merely American work, in most places and at nearly all economic levels. We have remarked that impersonality and regimentation infiltrated the clothing styles of the nineteen-fifties. Even schoolchildren — other than those in a few big-city progressive schools, which were regarded in most quarters as somewhere between harmlessly aberrant and downright subversive — were required by parents and school authorities to dress

in uniform, often literally. The importance of the requirements, and the anxiety inspired by the possibility of their
being defied, is forcefully suggested by the situation in
Wisconsin, where for a number of years boys in both public and private schools were prohibited from wearing blue
jeans in school, with the single exception of certifiable
members of farm families, who could presumably wear
jeans without meaning anything by it.

In a whole galaxy of ways jeans conformed to, and
exemplified with almost magical precision, the new view
of American life that began emerging among young
Americans of the late nineteen-fifties and the early nineteen-sixties. Jeans' celebrated durability was a challenge
to a society in which planned obsolescence, epitomized
by the automobile industry's annual change of models,
had (whether the jeans wearers knew it or not) come to be
the mainspring of the national economy. Jeans' association with physical labor confronted the trend of a society
in which a constantly larger percentage of the work force
was in offices and a smaller percentage in factories and
on farms. Jeans' proletarian associations by implication
criticized the pretensions of the upwardly mobile at a moment of great national upward mobility, and jeans' air of
genuineness similarly criticized the artificiality of a society becoming ever more artificial. Beyond all that,
jeans lent themselves naturally to the deeper, more personal feelings of the children of American affluence. It
came to be dogma among many of those children that their
parents' generation had been and was too rigid in defining
sex roles, insisting with a certain hysteria on stereotyped
differences between boys and girls in such matters as
sports, social activities, and clothing. Where Brooks
Brothers and Peck & Peck catered to the stereotypes,

blue jeans could be worn with equal comfort, physical and psychic, by both sexes. Finally, jeans had a special propensity for shrinking and stretching as they were washed and worn. (That is, the original jeans had, and the original type still has, but now that the popularity of jeans has long since passed from the realm of connoisseurs to that of a mass public a huge majority of the pairs sold are preshrunk.) This propensity made it possible for a pair, sufficiently conditioned, to end up fitting the wearer with a conformity to his or her anatomical idiosyncrasies that could not be matched by the handiwork of the most expert custom tailor. Natural means accomplished what technical proficiency could not; the jeans wearer, in a world of intractable objects that could not be shaped, at last had an object — if only a pair of pants — that would shape itself to his or her measure, rather than he or she to its.

Over the years after jeans' original flowering in the nineteen-fifties their symbolism in the United States evolved. In the late nineteen-sixties, they went through a brief period of identification with hippies, the drug subculture, and opposition to the Vietnam War; in the early nineteen-seventies, as they were taken up more and more by older people, they came to stand to some extent for a search for the Fountain of Youth (youth, it is interesting to note, of a sort very different from what the middle-aged wearers had themselves experienced); and in the late seventies, in a polar reversal of their connotations of twenty years earlier, jeans became an important fashion item, purveyed by Yves Saint-Laurent, Geoffrey Beene, Oscar de la Renta, Calvin Klein, Gloria Vanderbilt, and the like, at prices that would shock a cowboy. Of that more later.

Meanwhile, pundits were having their licks at figuring out what it all meant. The explanations that they came up with were essentially three: that jeans-wearing stood for a new and humanized American consciousness; that it symbolized political and social revolt; and that it reflected the achievement, at long last, of the age-old American dream of classlessness. As follows:

1. Charles Reich in *The Greening of America* (1970) made much of blue jeans as one of the hallmarks —along with rock and folk music, community living, psychedelic drugs, unhomogenized peanut butter, and the expression, "Oh, wow!" — of a new American state of mind that he designated as Consciousness III: adherence to "the sensual beauty of a creative, loving, unrepressed life," which he saw as having arisen "out of the strong soil of the American corporate state."

2. The Canadian philosopher Marshall McLuhan summed up the second hypothesis when he said in 1973, "Jeans represent a ripoff and a rage against the Establishment."

3. The American-dream position was summarized in 1978 by Arthur Asa Berger, a professor at San Francisco State University. He wrote, "Denim's 'rise' in the world is very much a part of the so-called American Dream, which says that anyone can rise in the world if he has enough will-power and a bit of luck. Denim is one more immigrant . . . which has made good in America." That is to say, denim is squarely in the American tradition rather than in confrontation with it. And denim's "cultural message" is the encouraging one that "work and play have lost their separate identities and are no longer polar opposites." Moreover, denim has contributed to the breaking down of class distinctions: "The professors look

like janitors — and quite often the janitors look like professors." More often than not, "denimization reflects an attempt to escape from one's family and class history" — precisely the possibility that the American dream promised in the first place.

On consideration, none of these explanations will quite do. The trouble with Consciousness III is that it has turned out to have been a fad itself — a pipe dream, the product of a momentary euphoria, inevitably attractive only until the passage of time (and not much time) revealed it as hopelessly romantic and utopian. Between 1970 and 1980, community living, "Oh, wow!" psychedelic drugs, and the sensual beauty of a creative life all lost ground sharply — rock music and unhomogenized peanut butter held firm and closed mixed — while jeans continued to soar in national popularity. It would appear they have something going for them other than conduciveness to love and sensuality.

The Establishment ripoff theory will not stand even cursory examination. Jeans merchants contend that while jeans did to some extent represent that early in their glory days in the United States, and probably in Canada, too, they soon ceased doing so; moreover, such connotations were never strongly attached to them in Europe, Australia, or the Far East, and in Latin America were attached to them hardly at all. One can only feel that McLuhan — understandably, since he was apparently called upon to give a comment on the telephone, with no time for reflection — missed a chance to use the worldwide proliferation of jeans-wearing as evidence in support of his celebrated notion, introduced in *Understanding Media* in 1964, of the modern world as a "global village" brought into being chiefly by television. Before jeans — and before television — many villages, nations, and even cultures had often adopted clothing fashions more or less unanimously; the whole world had conspicuously never done so.

The "one more immigrant" position — that jeans-wearing is a traditional American phenomenon and not a break with the past at all — is appealing but inadequate. If jeans serve to fulfill specifically American ideals, why are they so popular in Hong Kong, Tenerife, and Patagonia? So far as the jeans fad is concerned, denim, on balance, is far more an American emigrant than immigrant.

Therefore let us summon Veblen from the bullpen — Veblen, who lived when jeans were still work clothes, and who may well have worn Levi's quite innocent of social implications in his nineteenth-century youth on his father's Wisconsin farm. Putting the jeans phenomenon in a test tube with Veblen's theory of clothing fashion, we immediately find a violent reaction taking place. Right at the start we find, in fact, what appears to be a neat and definitive refutation of the theory. As follows:

Veblen's explanation of fashion	*Blue jeans 1965*
Must be wastefully expensive	Characteristically inexpensive
Must be inconvenient	Quintessentially convenient
Must be unadaptable to physical work; should hinder any useful exertion	Quintessentially adaptable to work; no hindrance

| Must be uncomfortable, preferably painful | Quintessentially comfortable* |
| Must be worn free of dirt or wear | Most prized when dirty, worn, and faded |

Here, on its face, seems to be the irrefutable *contra-Veblen* — the evidence that either his theory of fashion had been wrong all along or that it had, with the passage of time, become wrong. But something else was going on under the surface, and not far under. In truth, from its very start the postwar explosion of jeans-wearing was not quite so peaceable-savage as its devotees wanted it to appear. The new jeans wearers of the fifties were seldom entirely simple-hearted. They wanted to put other people down — squares, conservatives, school authorities, defenders of corporations, parents, or a combination of these. Stated another way, they wanted to put down the remnants of Veblen's "leisure class," which over the years had ceased to be a class at all and had become a national majority. And in doing so, of course, they were indulging in that classic Veblenian practice, invidiousness.

As the jeans phenomenon matured, and jeans-wearing gradually changed from an act of revolt to one of conformity, *not* wearing them tended to become, in certain

---

*However, a signal instance of Levi's as a momentarily *un*comfortable garment is enshrined in the corporate history of Levi Strauss & Company. In 1933, Walter Haas, Sr., then president of the company, was camping in the Sierra Nevada near Mt. Whitney when he crouched close to a campfire, causing the crotch rivet of his Levi's — a feature of Levi's right from the beginning — to become uncomfortably hot. Haas mentioned his complaint to some professional wranglers who were in the party, and they earnestly and unanimously declared that they had often had the same trouble. Haas, astonished that no one had ever mentioned the problem to him before, decided then and there that the crotch rivet had to go, and, by vote at the next meeting of the board of directors, it went.

circles, an act of revolt subject to potential censure. To invidiousness was thus added that other Veblenian trait, emulation. The introduction in the later nineteen-seventies of designer-name jeans as items of fashion represented the last stage of the transformation. Instead of a symbol of disdain for competitive display, jeans-wearing became competitive display itself. Meanwhile, the industrial situation provided a final twist of irony. Jeans — even "status" jeans designed to sell for twice or three times as much as the original product — happen to be cheaper to produce than other forms of pants, since the cut of the garment requires about one-third fewer labor operations. Here, then, was a high-priced, much-in-demand fashion product that could be produced on the cheap. Small wonder that a flood of quick-buck operators rushed into the business, and jeans-making suddenly became the momentary mecca of the predatory-invidious, Veblenian American entrepreneur.

It is time for a new chart.

Veblen's explanation of fashion	*"Status" blue jeans 1980*
Must be wastefully expensive	Wastefully expensive
Must signify invidious comparison to others	Signify invidious comparison
Must be worn in emulation of others	Worn in emulation
Must not be associated with physical work	No longer associated with physical work
Must be worn free of dirt or wear	Most prized now when worn clean and new

In fifteen years, the social overtones of jeans-wearing had undergone a polar reversal. Belatedly, Veblen had his revenge. And the broad change in the American style of competitive display since 1900 — the change from straightforward display of money to more complex and sophisticated forms of showing off style, acquired sense of taste, and playful irony, which we have seen exemplified in different ways as regards sports, eating, drinking, class aspirations, office manners, and so on — had found in the jeans phenomenon its symbolic event.

20

Life Parodies

Parody as a form of competitive display, a ploy in the game of life, has become pervasive in our time. In a few instances, isolated but perhaps prophetic, it has gone farther than that. It has surpassed the role of technique or style in life to become nothing less than life's substance. A few highly successful and visible lives in our time do not just use parody; they *are* parody.

I do not speak of show business, in which parody is a studied art form; a Woody Allen or a Hermione Gingold works in a tradition as old as the theater itself. The professional parodist may *appear* to lead a life of parody because, unless we happen to be his or her friend, we see him or her only onstage, or else via the quasistage of fan literature in its many forms (gossip columns, "people" magazines, TV interview shows). But the appearance is almost certainly an illusion. Art is not life; a performer's stage personality is seldom real, much as we may wish to think that it is. The clowns of *I Pagliacci* lead lives of desperation. Marilyn Monroe, America's official sex symbol for a few memorable years, exquisitely parodied that role onstage — and it was the parody rather than the sex that set her apart, that gave her a touch of greatness, as had been the case a generation earlier with Mae West. Meanwhile, when she married first the most famous of ballplayers and then the brainiest of playwrights, she seemed to be living the parody. But we know now what at the time we merely sensed — that she was not. Her personal life was not a takeoff but a tragedy.

(As a footnote on parody in show business, it is worth noting that it sometimes appears to be antithetical to commercial success. In the early postwar years Henry Morgan, a talented young comic radio monologuist, took the daring step of doing parody commercials with considerable mordant bite, in defiance of the product manufacturers who were paying him to push their goods. The manufacturers dropped Morgan. Later he achieved his pinnacle of fame as a regular panelist on the television show *I've Got a Secret* — no longer a parodist with bite, but just another bland, self-serving television jokester.)

For life parodies we must look outside show business. The life parodist is a professional in some other field that calls for a degree of public performance, such as politics, religion, or the literary life — a performer, certainly, but one whose stage is life itself. Some, of course, merely dabble in life parody; I think of the railroad president's son and former Harvard psychologist Richard Alpert, who, when he became a professional guru, chose to adopt the burlesque-show name Ram Dass. But others go the whole way, becoming, in effect, parodists for a living. Apparently they are something new — pioneers in a profession only recently made possible by a cultural climate so receptive to parody that the mountebank component in such a person is no longer a liability to be concealed, but has become an asset to be flaunted.

Those who adopt parody as a way of life seem to do so mostly by accident, without conscious intention at least in the early stages; later, having discovered an asset, they may become self-conscious about it to one degree or another. Certainly nothing could have been further than theatrical performance from the mind of young Bernard Cornfeld in the nineteen-forties, when he was living in Brooklyn as the son of intellectual middle-class European-born parents, overcoming a speech defect, attending Brooklyn College, espousing Norman Thomas Socialism, and becoming a social worker like many a serious-minded Brooklyn Jewish boy of the time. True enough, a predilection for extravagant mischief, and a portent of escapades to come, may be said to have appeared when he managed to accumulate five thousand dollars' worth of unpaid New York City parking tickets (if we may credit the account of a later business associate). But Cornfeld was well within the canon of the American success ethic when, just before turning thirty, he moved to Paris and opened up a business selling American mutual funds to Americans in Europe under the company name of Investors Overseas Services.

Specifically, this move represented a conventional exercise in the time-honored entrepreneurial practices of loophole-spotting and opportunity-grabbing. For one thing, mutual funds were then the hottest novelty in the American securities markets, and Europe was then saturated with American servicemen and their families with plenty of hard currency, who in the normal course had little opportunity, or temptation, to buy mutual funds.

For another thing, the reach of the Securities and Exchange Commission, which regulated the activities of the
mutual-fund market in the United States, extended beyond the national borders only inefficiently when at all.
Cornfeld's small but vigorous operation did not suit the
French authorities, however, and it was banished from
Paris in 1958, only to turn up in Geneva. There it ex-
panded hugely — its principal new customers being not
United States servicemen but rather the rich in soft-cur-
rency countries like Brazil and Italy, who used Cornfeld's
American mutual funds as a way of getting their money
out of their own sinking currencies and into hard dollars.
Cornfeld had scored by mistake. However, such expa-
triation of capital was almost always illegal under local
currency regulations, and consequently the Cornfeld operation kept getting thrown out of various countries, only
to pop up soon afterward in others. Still it kept growing;
by the end of the nineteen-sixties it managed two and a
half billion dollars, had twenty thousand employees in
more than one hundred countries, and was recognized as
one of the more important as well as one of the more baroque institutions of the financial world.

Along the way, Cornfeld and his organization had
evolved a characteristic style. That style — surely in
part a self-serving effort to distract attention from doubt-
fully legal activities, and in part a show-off response to
being in the media limelight — was parody of conventional business actions and utterances. More or less public, and in any case widely quoted, statements of I.O.S.
people began to sound like musical-comedy one-liners.
"We observe the letter of the law — no more, no less,"
declared Cornfeld's right-hand man, a Harvard-trained
lawyer named Ed Cowett. The chief executives of Ford

Motor Company or Citibank might or might not *think* that line; they would assuredly never utter it in public. I.O.S. had become the id of American enterprise. In an internal I.O.S. memo that later became public, Cowett wrote, "I can ask no more than that each person do his part to cutting down the extent of our obvious violations." This time he was speaking, of course, of violations of the letter of law. The most famous one-liner of Cornfeld himself — or "Bernie," as he was called universally in his organization and usually in the press — was his favorite question to prospective salesmen, which became the title of the biography written of him by Godfrey Hodgson, Bruce Page, and Charles Raw: "Do you sincerely want to be rich?" (The biographers, either solemnly seeking to explain this fine parodic line or bravely seeking to top it, wrote of it, "This was a brilliant reading by Cornfeld from Adler and the theory of goals.")

The solemnity, self-righteousness, hypocrisy, and tongue-tied formality of most business rhetoric was obviously ripe for parody, and Cornfeld and his crew were ready to fill that gap. As previously noted, this was not entirely a matter of art for art's sake. If the world could be made to laugh with them, it would be less inclined to censure them. Parody could be made to serve the bottom line. When Cornfeld hired James Roosevelt as a "father figure" to the organization, and followed up this coup by bringing in the former vice-chancellor of West Germany, he was both parodying the stuffy habit of American corporations of signing up retired military brass and buying respectability himself. A similar self-servingness obtained in the matter of the worldwide publicization — encouraged by Cornfeld as soon as he realized what a good thing he had hit upon — of his parody-hedonist "way of life." Bernie never smoked or drank alcohol; those starchy, self-destructive Protestant gestures toward relaxation were left to conventional businessmen, engaged as they so notoriously were in perpetuating the age-old association between capitalism and Calvinistic theology. Instead, Bernie drank Cokes, and kept Villa Elma, his mansion in Geneva, which had been built by Napoleon for Josephine — Bernie also maintained for his own use a castle in France, a town house in London, an apartment in Paris, and a brownstone in Manhattan — full of a constantly changing chorus line of miniskirted "protégées," numbering a dozen or more at any given time, and coming and going at all hours of the day and night. A girl who worked for I.O.S. and went to Cornfeld's parties (or rather, since it seems to have been continuous, party) later described the group that frequented Villa Elma as "Bernie's great big happy family."

All this was heady stuff for the world of profit and loss. Playboy Clubs with their coy bunnies seemed by comparison timid and inhibited in their toe-in-the-water approach to hedonism. Capitalism and Calvinism seemed at last to be getting a divorce in Geneva. Cornfeld, realizing from the press notices that by doing what came naturally he had scored a publicity hit, went into the myth-making business. The former middle-class Brooklyn social worker became now the "poor, immigrant" Brooklyn social worker. The standard Cornfeld promise to new salesmen came to be all the girls they wanted as a fringe benefit; and so on. By 1970, Cornfeld and his associates were conducting at Villa Elma a full-scale real-life musical comedy, the script all written, the cast complete, virtually ready to go on Broadway. "Bernie!" it would have been called, if anyone had been bold enough to defy the libel and privacy laws by staging it. In it — as the reality was described by a former I.O.S. man named Bert Cantor — beautiful girls would wander in and out of the unlocked door of the villa; one of Bernie's pet ocelots would knock over a vase of roses, then placidly urinate in a silver bowl of salted almonds; supper, American style (southern fried chicken, chocolate sundaes) would be served long after midnight, and then everyone would repair to Bernie's bedroom to while away the small hours watching a movie on videotape while Bernie and one of his protégées (fully clothed) squirmed together under the bedcovers. Thus the world would learn the new style of big international business; and just in case anyone thought things were going too far, and a homey touch was in order, there was always Sophie, Bernie's mother, who lived in the Villa Elma and stubbornly insisted on going to bed early. If the merrymaking below got too loud and disturbed her, she would bang on the marble floor for quiet.

Then came the real-life last act. Simultaneously with I.O.S.'s rise to its position as the Venusberg of commerce (around one hundred thousand dollars went for the 1969 Christmas party), the regulatory authorities in the United States finally began to close in on it, and financial desperation brought about by a plunging stock market led to disastrous investments. Some seventy-five million dollars went down the drain in six months, and in May, 1970, with I.O.S. on the brink of bankruptcy, Cornfeld was expelled from its management and accused of having brought on its downfall. In the last scene, Venusberg has changed into Hell, where Bernie and his former "happy family" gnash their teeth and shout imprecations at each other: "Kickback expert!" "Incompetent!" "Shmuck!"

And worst of all: "Lousy lover!" Even in real-life catastrophe, then, the tone of parody is maintained. The last scene of "Bernie!" is a parody of conventional morality as much as its early scenes are. The show ends up *Faust* done as a sophomore put-on.

Finally, the show's reviews, which come in the form of Bernie's trial in Geneva in the autumn of 1979, ten years after the event, on charges of having defrauded some of I. O. S.'s employees, who had bought stock that subsequently became nearly worthless. Long before the trial, Cornfeld had spent eleven months in custody in a Geneva jail; he had finally been released after posting three million dollars' bail. He subsequently pledged all of the bail money to disgruntled former employees, to be paid after his trial. (An odd provision of his agreement with them seems to have been that the pledge might become null and void if he should at any time take a notion to jump bail.) Came the trial, and the key witnesses against Cornfeld turned out to have changed their minds and not to be disgruntled anymore; one after the other, they testified that as far as they knew, Bernie had done nothing wrong. Thus stymied, the state prosecutor did not even ask the jury for a Guilty verdict. The jury returned a Not Guilty one in less than an hour. After the trial judge had declared the proceedings to be "a circus and a farce," everybody went home — the reluctant witnesses for the prosecution taking with them their respective shares of the three-million-dollar bail pie, and Bernie — who had somehow escaped from the whole affair with several million dollars of his own — to his new mansion in (where else?) California.

So the reviews were unanimous. "Bernie!" had been a hit show, and Bernie himself was not a scoundrel but a kind of hero. Life parody seemed to have won its first great public victory.

Action in the political arena has always served as a barometer of our national styles, and indeed, in recent years when television has come to play such an overmastering role in the political process, it has sometimes appeared that style is the real subject of politics. However, it is not the most sensitive of barometers. A political candidate who wants to win must appeal to the broad center. No true avant-garde can be a majority, and therefore avante-garde ideas and attitudes tend to get screened out of political activity. When a new current is running in our national life, politics will tend to be one of the last places where it is reflected.

Nevertheless, a bit shyly and tentatively, parody as a style of life has crept into American politics. The late Everett McKinley Dirksen regularly used to parody overblown political rhetoric in his public discourses, in a time well before parody display had gained a national foothold. The reason this was not a political mistake is simple. Dirksen's constituents missed the parody (which was surely more instinctive than calculated in any case), and took his bombast straight. If they had suspected parody, they would have been horrified. Dirksen's joke remained secret to all but a minority, and that minority was never going to vote for him anyhow.

Now, when voters everywhere have learned to recognize parody when they see or hear it, a few important politicians have taken to using it deliberately and with calculation. New York Mayor Edward Koch quite evidently believes that he endears himself to New Yorkers by adopting a style that parodies the Catskill-resort Jewish comic style. In a far more heart-of-America setting, Senator Howard Baker of Tennessee (Dirksen's son-in-law) sometimes risks a bit of irony in his political style, even though, in contrast to Koch, he is a Middle American Republican. James Reston reported in *The New York Times* early in 1980 that Baker, while campaigning for the Republican presidential nomination, had been boasting of being the inventor of "dishwasher fish" — "one of the really innovative culinary achievements of the electronic age," Reston called it. According to Reston, "Baker figured out that if you put filets of sole or even catfish in a double wrapper of thick aluminum foil, with a little lemon, butter, and a bay leaf, and placed them on the upper rack of your dishwasher, and ran it through one cycle, you would come out with one of the rare delicacies of the age." This was travesty, first cousin to parody, and surely the cousin most likely to reside in the Ozark Mountains of Tennessee. On the irony scale, a Middle American Republican had thus gone well beyond, say, the aristocratic, quintessentially northeastern Franklin D. Roosevelt, with his heavy-handed quips about his dog Fala. Thus had the national temper changed. (Still, it ought to be noted that Baker, ignominiously defeated in a series of primaries, dropped out of the presidential race shortly after boasting about dishwasher fish.)

The preeminent life parodist among American political figures up to now is certainly Edmund G. (Jerry) Brown of California. Brown seems to have discovered very early in his political career — which reached its peak to date with his election as governor of California in 1975 — that his constituents liked him to parody con-

ventional political styles, and would reward him for doing
so by voting for him. In his successful gubernatorial campaign, he announced, "I am going to starve the schools
financially until I get some educational reforms." Asked
what reforms, he replied blandly, "I don't know yet."
Well known to be a Catholic who had once trained for the
Jesuit priesthood, he repeatedly went out of his way to
announce and demonstrate a special interest in Zen
Buddhism, not a religion previously thought to have a
large constituency in the United States. ("Catholicism,"
he explained, by way of resolving any implied conflict,
"is really quite similar to Zen, in a way.") With considerably more iconoclasm, he announced that among his
political idols were Ho Chi Minh and Mao.

In office, besides spurning the governor's mansion
in Sacramento for an apartment of his own (where he insisted that the building's water be heated by a solar plant
that, the other tenants complained, didn't get it hot
enough), he would maintain no official schedule, preferring to keep his days "free-form." He banned the use of
such standard bureaucratic words as *agenda, data, systems analysis, expertise,* and *redevelopment,* and kept uttering such unusual gubernatorial pronouncements as
"Life just is. You have to flow with it. Give yourself to the
moment. Let it happen." If a President of the United
States were to say that about, say, relations with the Rus-
sians, there might be a national rush for the hills. In
claiming as among his political idols two hard-line Communist leaders, one of whose nations was then at war with
the United States, Brown certainly scored a political first.
As to political unorthodoxy, however, he may have
topped even that a couple of years later when he made an

elaborately publicized trip abroad in the company of a woman not his wife, the singer Linda Ronstadt. The traditional American politician would probably rather have been photographed walking out of Fort Knox naked and carrying an armload of gold bars.

Certainly, the key to the success of Brown's style was and remains its venue. California — land of Esalen and Jacuzzi — and he were a match. Californians could wave Brown at the rest of the country like a flag. He certified their difference, their unique freedom from cant and convention. A poll taken a few months after he had been elected governor showed that only 7 percent of California voters disapproved of his "performance," and when he came up for reelection in 1978, it was no contest. That is, life parody as a political style had captured California. But a larger question remained. How did the rest of the country like Brown? How would life parody play in Peoria?

In the 1976 presidential primaries, it played pretty well. Brown won the Maryland Democratic primary, with 49 percent of the vote to Jimmy Carter's 37 percent. In Oregon, Brown racked up one hundred thousand write-in votes, and beat Carter again. He knocked off Carter a third time, less surprisingly, in his own state. But after Carter had won in Ohio, Brown never had a chance for the nomination, and at the Democratic national convention in New York City, when he offered to turn over his three hundred-odd delegate votes to Carter to make the nomination unanimous, Carter snubbed Brown and life parody by refusing to accept the votes.

What happened in the 1976 Brown presidential campaign is clear in retrospect. The voters outside California who made him momentarily a prime prospect, if not for a time actually the front runner, simply did not know the man they were voting for very well. On the basis of insufficient evidence and wishful thinking, they mistook him for a clean-limbed new traditional liberal in the Adlai Stevenson–John Kennedy mold. When they got to know him a little better — his humble apartment, free-form days, admiration for Ho and Mao, Linda, Zen — they decided he was "flaky" and stopped voting for him. American presidential politics wasn't ready quite yet for life parody as a potential presidential style. In Peoria, it still closed on Saturday night. Brown himself, a prudent politician at bottom, apparently recognized this fact a couple of years later when, suddenly offered a chance to visit China, he declined with the explanation that a sudden trip there "would be too flaky, I've got to watch that. All this Zen stuff — and then flying to China for the day . . ."

However, despite such strategic retreats the returns are not all in yet, and it may not be too long before Jerry Brown or some other political life parodist winds up in the White House. By slow degrees, irony is ascendant in the land, and may soon end up politically in charge.

Perhaps the model of life parody in current United States culture is the writer and lecturer George Ames Plimpton. As everyone must know, Plimpton has achieved celebrity as a parodist of the accomplished in many fields — taking a turn, by advance arrangement, as a pitcher for the New York Yankees, a quarterback for the Detroit Lions, a competitor against champions at golf, a boxer against Archie Moore, an instrumentalist in the

New York Philharmonic, and so on. Some of the books that he has written about these exploits have been commercially successful, but the real basis of his celebrity has been the more popular media, television and the lecture platform. By way of them, he has succeeded in endearing himself, and parody itself, to Everyman.

Plimpton himself is not exactly Everyman. The son of a distinguished New York lawyer and diplomat, he graduated from Harvard, took a master's degree at Cambridge, and shortly thereafter, like a serious privileged young man with literary inclinations, helped found a literary periodical, *The Paris Review*, of which — unknown, surely, to all but a tiny fraction of latter-day Plimpton fans — he is still editor. After a spell of career floundering, aged thirty-four he published *Out of My League*, a ruefully comic account of his fling on the mound for the Yankees, and was on his way. He had discovered a life of parody.

Plimpton's basic "act" — based as good parody must be on a delicate balance between irony and hero-worship — is only the visible top of a monolithic berg of personal parody display. A born life parodist, he clearly does not have to work at it intellectually; rather, it comes naturally, perhaps instinctively, to him. For example, by way of a hobby he is an expert on and an enthusiastic exhibitor of fireworks. In American cultural iconography fireworks represent naive patriotism, unguarded enthusiasm, simpleminded spectacle — everything a well-bred northeastern liberal intellectual might conventionally be expected to regard with distaste or disdain. A strain of self-parody crops up in all of Plimpton's capers; in this one, it is dominant. Again, it is beyond question that Plimpton is a good enough writer to have achieved reputation and ample fortune as a writer pure and simple. If we study his style we have no trouble determining why he was not content to do that. It would have been too close to what might logically have been expected of him; even if what he wrote was categorically parody, writing for a living would not have been a *life* of parody.

A striking and illuminating bit of Plimptoniana is contained in the fact that from time to time in recent years he has lent his voice and presence to television and radio commercials, principally for a New York City savings bank and an international shipping line. (In the latter case, he went so far as to allow himself to be used as bait, offering the opportunity to meet him on a cruise as an inducement to people to sign up for it.) Instantly and predictably, a chorus went up from Plimpton's friends and acquaintances: "What an outrage, George shilling for commercial enterprises on the mass media. This time he's gone too far. He'll do anything for money." While it is hard to believe that Plimpton did the shilling in a calculated effort to elicit this reaction, it is equally hard to believe that he was seriously disturbed by it. Doubtless it is true, as Plimpton has been quoted as saying, that he did indeed do it for the money; after all, he has extravagant tastes. But surely that is only a partial explanation. Somewhere deep down, perhaps in the Plimpton unconscious, one suspects there might be found the origin of a mischievous impulse to revel in what his own "set" would consider farthest beyond the pale, the most blatant and deliberate of affronts to their mandarin taste and manners. Similarly, in the world of pop art, Andy Warhol's soup cans, Claes Oldenburg's glazed dishes of junk food, and Roy Lichtenstein's huge comic strips seemed to represent mischievous exploitation of what those artists' conventional admirers held in greatest disrepute — although the artists, like Plimpton with his commercials, were always careful to insist that parody was the farthest thing from their minds.

That Plimpton's parody display arises more out of instinct than out of calculation is further attested to by the fact that it shows up so seamlessly in the small details of his life. His speech accent is New England boarding school in the extreme, yet never — not in gossiping with Muhammed Ali or consorting with the Lions in the locker room — does he deign to suppress it, after the fashion of the democratic declassers described in Chapter 5. Nor, on the other hand, does he exaggerate it. He simply speaks in the way that comes naturally to him, which happens to emerge as both a self-parody and a self-advertisement. He dresses ultraconservatively like a lawyer or banker, not dowdily like the popular idea of a writer nor flashily like the popular idea of a celebrity. Unlike the routine celebrity, he lists his address and telephone number in the Manhattan directory, and often answers his phone himself. All of these details add up to a consistent life-parody pattern: a conventional, approachable, unpretentious private style set off against a systematic and seemingly innate propensity for showing off in public.

Certainly there is about Plimpton's career a certain whiff of the ancient phenomenon of *le roi s'amuse* — inherited privilege providing both the material resources and the inner self-confidence to enable a life of elaborate jokes executed in the public eye. But Plimpton is also part of something new. In a democratic state with progressive income taxes and an ironic view of privilege, even a Plimpton has to make his own way to fame. For a king to amuse himself now, he must first invent himself a king. Life parody is *le roi s'amuse* adapted for democracy. Plimpton's career shows that it can be made to pay off, at least outside politics.

Parody display is here; it is the new form of showing off in America. Its ultimate manifestation, life parody, is still struggling to be born. Most current approaches to life parody end up stillbirths. In addition to Ram Dass, Dirksen, and Koch, one thinks of the sociopolitical "crazies" of the sixties: the two well-bred ladies fleeing their bomb-factory townhouse on Eleventh Street, stripped bare like Duchamp's bride by their botched bomb (and the three others who died for parody); and in particular, Abbie Hoffman, who by the physically peaceable but culturally inflammatory act of throwing dollar bills on the Stock Exchange floor caused the Exchange to take the drastic step of separating the public gallery from the trading floor with bullet-proof glass, and who later, while living under a pseudonym as a fugitive from justice, managed to get compliments from government officials and a United States Senator on his environmental work. (He had not even been disguised, except as the male part of Mr. and Mrs. A. H. Hoffman, when he had contrived, or claimed he had, to get an embossed message of congratulations on the birth of his son from President and Mrs. Richard Nixon.) But the Hoffman life parody is tainted: it comes off as too close to calculated self-advertisement for the benefit of the television cameras, and thus fails to project a strong enough impression of art for art's sake, as even Bernie Cornfeld's did. This flaw is notably absent in the life parody of that rising figure on the American social stage, the homosexual drag queen, whose parody is almost pure, disinterested art; but so far no single towering presence in this genre has arisen to shock and enlighten the bourgeois. As of now, Cornfeld, Brown, and Plimpton must stand as the pioneers of American life parody.

It is notable that there is as yet no wholly successful female life parodist. Bella Abzug, as a member of Congress from New York in the early nineteen-sixties, made a game try at becoming the first female life parodist in American politics (picture hats and cuss words in the House of Representatives). In so doing, she broke new social ground. But eventually her colleagues and constituents alike tired of her act and hooted it down much more decisively, and derisively, than they hooted down Jerry Brown's. She was ahead of her time. More recently, Dixy Lee Ray, elected the first woman governor of the State of Washington in 1977, carried on the work begun by Abzug, arguing while in office that nuclear power is no more dangerous to the public than a broken bottle on the sidewalk is to a child's foot, and naming a litter of piglets on her farm after members of the Capitol press corps. In another field, the writer Erica Jong has shown early foot as a life parodist.

If these acts have not quite succeeded, an explanation readily suggests itself. A prerequisite for parody of any kind is the self-confidence that allows the parodist to feel superior enough to the subject to make sport of it. Except in a limited number of callings, such as show business, women in American society have until recently not been allowed to feel such self-confidence with regard to it. Our famous public women, from Susan Anthony to Eleanor Roosevelt, have seldom been strong on irony or humor. They have made their mark through moral force directly applied. As to life parody, American women may now be about where American men were a generation ago.

Life parody is on its way to becoming a settled form of American competitive display. Perhaps it is the most advanced post-Veblen form, the cutting edge of a new national style. (The only life parodists of Veblen's time who come to mind are that period's celebrated confidence men, who, of course, were outlaws.) The thought of a future nation full of Cornfelds, Browns, and Plimptons may be an intimidating one, but is not such an implausible one.

It is, at any rate, bemusing to think of the bright promises of life parody and parody display in the nineteen-eighties or -nineties: the black female senator who is a former cosmonaut; the Nobel Prize–winning courtesan whose citation credits her with having "restored the sex act to the realm of laughter"; the arthritic, ninety-eight-pound, eighty-five-year-old football coach indicted for the on-field maiming of the three-hundred-and-thirty-five-pound, All-American linebacker "Muscles" McGonigan; the lawn company advertising seeds of the newly introduced all-purpose lawn plant, *Cannabis sativa;* the new fad for having rabbit's fur implanted in one's head; the Bell System's new telephone appliance that at the push of a button can momentarily and harmlessly paralyze the tongue of the person on the other end of the line; the vintage outhouse, unpainted and with crescent-moon window slot, offered for sale at one million dollars.

But this falls short; like the poems and the jokes of the future, its methods of showing off are unpredictable.

They must surprise us as they come, and they will. Surely, the great days lie ahead. Anyone who bets against the future of parody display and life parody in America is betting against a sure thing.

21

The Prophet

Veblen was born in 1857 on a frontier farm in Wisconsin, the fourth of what would eventually be twelve children of Thomas Anderson and Kari Bunde Veblen, Norwegian immigrants. His father was a master carpenter turned farmer, with a philosophical turn of mind and a profound skepticism about the nominal religiosity and the passionate respect for business enterprise that permeated American life at the time. Thomas Veblen eventually became a leading farmer in Wisconsin and later in Minnesota, but not until he had suffered the consequences of being a Norwegian immigrant in an area dominated economically by transplanted New Englanders. He was forced off his first land claim by Yankee traders — much as, back in the old country, *his* father had been tricked out of his farm by city men, and his wife's father, forced to sell his farm to meet the fees of lawyers, had died disconsolate at the age of thirty-five, leaving his daughter Kari an orphan. In Wisconsin, a similar running battle between farmers and entrepreneurs went on. "The Yankees," said one of Thomas Veblen's fellow Norwegians there, "know how to introduce a certain appearance of law and order into a practice which is the direct opposite of law and order." We need look no farther to find the source of Thorstein Veblen's notion of the Anglo-Saxon as predatory barbarian.

In reaction, the Veblens turned to their own heritage. Although Thomas and Kari Veblen spoke English, Norwegian was the language of their household, and they even hired a scholarly Norwegian to train their children in Norse grammar and literature.

Thorstein Veblen as a boy showed a satirical strain that, even though its edge was blunted by an air of indolent good nature, made him somewhat feared and not much liked by his schoolmates. At seventeen, he went to little Carleton College, in Northfield, Minnesota. Thomas Veblen was the only farmer in his community who insisted on sending his children of both sexes to college. A man of unusual qualities, he aroused in his fourth son intensely ambivalent feelings — respect for his reflectiveness and integrity, resentment of his iron peasant authority. Some scholars have proposed that ambivalence as the lifelong key to Thorstein Veblen's curious character.

Carleton College in the eighteen-seventies was a place where a faculty of New England Congregationalists earnestly went about the missionary duty of inculcating into the children of the frontier the then-reigning American philosophy of moral utilitarianism. Industry and frugality under God; knowledge acquired for the categorical purpose of learning to acquire wealth; trust that the moral character of business leaders insures the fairness of society — such were the principles taught at Carleton. As a student there, young Veblen, bolstered by his father's skepticism, became a campus iconoclast. He earned a reputation for being sneering and supercilious, though still concurrently lazy and good-natured. At well-chosen intervals he administered shocks to faculty and students with declamations on such elaborately outrageous themes as "A Plea for Cannibalism" and — perhaps, by the lights of Carleton, even worse — "An Apology for a Toper." At the same time, he betrayed an Establishment strain by taking up with Ellen Rolfe, a fellow student who was niece to the college's president and daughter to one of the Midwest's leading businessmen. Bright, highly intellectual, and rather neurotic, Ellen was as much a misfit as Thorstein. At college parties they would sit solemnly talking only to each other.

By the spring of 1880, when Veblen was to graduate, he had cut a figure at Carleton and in the town of Northfield. Most of the faculty looked upon him with hostility, but conceded him good grades. Veblen's biographer Dorfman writes: "His public oration for graduation was a spectacular performance. Instead of choosing the usual kind of topic, such as 'The Duty of a Christian Scholar,' Veblen spoke on 'Mill's Examination of Hamilton's Philosophy of the Conditioned.' The task of expounding one of the greatest English philosophical works did not disturb him. He discussed the mathematical points as if he were a master of the subject." The local Northfield newspaper reported afterward, "Veblen, son of Thor, in spite of the heat, hammered away with blow after blow, and with no mean skill, at a subject the bare name of which was almost an overdose for the average reader. . . . He held that the case of Mill versus Hamilton was clearly one of *non sequitur*." Pretty good for a country newspaper, thus to recognize, by ironic indirection, the exceptional mental quality of a misfit immigrant youth. But another judgment, more categorical and with an astuteness of its own, was uttered about the same performance by the youth's instructor in mathematics. In the Congregational church where the graduation ceremony took place, the instructor happened to sit next to Andrew Veblen, brother of the orator; and as the orator's hammer-blows fell one by one from the lectern, the instructor turned to the brother and confided, "Thorstein is a fraud."

Veblen's life over the next decade and a half oddly suggests that of many young Americans of more recent times. It was, to all appearances, a life of prolonging formal education for the sake of indulging indolence. Following graduation from Carleton, he taught for a short time at a private school in Madison, Wisconsin, and then went to Johns Hopkins in Baltimore to work for an advanced degree in philosophy. Quartered there with a family of impoverished mid-South gentlefolk, he had his first opportunity to observe at first hand the exaggerated leisure-class manners of people for whom manners were the sole remaining credential of membership in the leisure class. But not for long. Lonely, homesick, and short of funds, Veblen left Johns Hopkins before the end of his first term there, and moved to Yale, where he was to live and study for the next two and a half years.

Veblen at Yale was known for what Dorfman called "an air of intellectual preeminence and Olympian aloofness." "He was not an attractive or polished man in character or carriage," one of his associates said later, and described him as interested in life "as an enticing object of study" but one "for which he had no responsibility." The atmosphere at Yale, which was emphatically New

England Christian, certainly gave him occasion to form his opinions of the role of "devout observances" in American life. Moreover, almost the entire Yale community at the time, students and faculty alike, came from well-to-do backgrounds quite unlike Veblen's, and their conduct surely constituted an excellent sample of leisure-class manners and attitudes. Intercollegiate football, still in its infancy, and in the process of evolving out of soccer and rugby — the first intercollegiate "football" game, between Rutgers and Princeton, had been played only a little more than a decade earlier — was at Yale in Veblen's time just becoming the overwhelming undergraduate preoccupation and status icon that it would be by around 1900, and at many American colleges has remained ever since. Somewhat the same feelings attached to baseball. "The Base Ball game between Yale and Harvard took place the other day — Yale was beaten, as you may have heard," Veblen wrote to a friend from Johns Hopkins in June 1882. "It has been some surprise to me to see how kindly the puritan of today takes to baseball and circuses. I noticed a Prof. from the Theological Seminary at the Baseball game. Athletics . . . is decidedly the most characteristic virtue of Yale . . . and I am afraid it covers a multitude of sins." We may safely infer that those sins included what even then Veblen may have been formulating into his baroque phrase "an exercise for dexterity and for the emulative ferocity and astuteness characteristic of predatory life."

At the same time, let us note that, along with the Prof. from the Seminary and others, *Veblen* was present at the big game; not only that, he cared enough about the outcome to report it to his friend. He was, after all, not a drinking and sporting undergraduate preparing himself for a life in the predatory commercial world, but part of a separate world, the cloistered intellectual ghetto of the graduate school. Nevertheless, some secret part of him yearned to be a real Yale man. Proud as he was of his Norwegian roots, much as he gloried in his differentness, he was already preoccupied with the characteristics of the all-American, Anglo-Saxon "leisure class." Meanwhile, the intellectual lessons he was learning at Yale fitted — or were forced by the strength of his own intellect to fit — what he was learning by watching from a distance at ball games and drinking parties. His most influential instructor, the nationally known social philosopher William Graham Sumner, was the leading American apostle of Herbert Spencer and the philosophy of Social Darwinism, which placed the highest ethical value on survival in the competitive business jungle through drive, hard work, and natural talent. Sumner at Yale was half a maverick, half a conformist. He differed with the institution's accepted view of the primacy of religious faith (and indeed, he was a force toward secularization of the Yale curriculum); but on the matter of the propriety and righteousness of worldly success, he stood shoulder to shoulder with his orthodox colleagues. Between Sumner and his student, Veblen, there grew up a considerable and complex relationship. In Sumner, Veblen found both a stimulating teacher and a target for later satire. Never named in *The Theory of the Leisure Class*, he stalks through its pages in two contrasting roles. One role is as the source of the elaborately "scientific" habit of thought on which the book is based. The other is as a living epitome of Gilded Age thought about American economic and social life, the ultimate philosophical apologist for the predatory-invidious way of life.

In 1884 Veblen got his Ph.D. from Yale in philosophy and political economy, with the fulsome blessings of
both Sumner and the university's president, dear, jowly,
pious old Noah Porter, who disliked Veblen's opinions
but recognized his intellectual ability. Armed with their
impressive letters of recommendation, he set out, at
twenty-seven, to find an academic job. This effort resulted in disastrous failure, partly because Veblen was
an exceptionally listless and unaggressive job-hunter,
and partly because, in the cultural and religious climate
of the time, no institution was prepared to take a chance
on a "Norskie" who was suspected of being an agnostic.
Thus began an extended period that one commentator,
with Veblenian irony, has referred to as his "premature
retirement."

He went home to Minnesota. One of his brothers
said testily, "He read and loafed, and the next day he
loafed and read. . . . I must admit that I got somewhat
disgusted." He was often sick — or, as his relatives suspected, often pretended to be. Sometimes he camped out
in the woods alone for days at a time. Sometimes he invented agricultural implements — only to find that they
had already been not only invented, but patented. In
1886, by which time the patience of his diligent family
was sorely tried, he became engaged to Ellen Rolfe, a
step that seemed to be right in character, since her family's modest income would presumably make it possible
for him to prolong his loafing indefinitely. The two were
married in 1888, against the vocal reluctance of both
families, and settled down to live on the Rolfe farm in
Stacyville, Iowa. Veblen's father-in-law gamely tried to
get him a job as an economist with the Santa Fe Railroad;
when that effort failed, Veblen, with his wife as company

now, resumed loafing and reading, which occupied them most of the time for three more years. At last, prodded by his brother Andrew, he went in 1891 to Cornell University to be a graduate student again.

Veblen now seemed well on his way to becoming a settled member of a sort of "leisure class" quite different from the one he would describe in print, but far from unknown in either his times or ours — an academic bum supported by his wife. But at Cornell he finally caught fire, ignited, it seems, by J. Laurence Laughlin, head of the department of economics there. Veblen and Laughlin were a comical pair. The latter was distinguished in his profession, thoroughly *reçu,* and so conservative that he suspected the cautious and conservative American Economic Association of socialistic leanings. The former was a wild-eyed nobody who *really* had socialistic leanings. Nevertheless, a spark was struck between them when Veblen, unknown and unannounced, appeared in Laughlin's office wearing a coonskin cap, and stated in a sententious way, "I am Thorstein Veblen." Evidently charmed, Laughlin made Veblen his protégé. He wangled him a special fellowship at Cornell, and a year later, when Laughlin was appointed head of economics at the University of Chicago, he arranged for Veblen to come along as a "fellow" at a salary of $520 per year. At thirty-five, Veblen finally had his first real job.

At Chicago — where he was slowly promoted from fellow to reader, from reader to tutor, and from tutor to instructor — he began to make a kind of name for himself. He did most of the editing of the Chicago-based *Journal of Political Economy,* and began publishing articles of his own in it and elsewhere. Some of these essays foreshadowed the ideas in *The Theory of the Leisure Class.*

As a teacher given to mumbling incomprehensibly in a barely audible monotone, and to showing little interest in his students unless they were nubile young women, he began to develop the reputation of being a pedagogical disaster that would dog him, and help keep his income at near subsistence level, all his life. Above all, at Chicago he gradually acquired from his distinguished faculty colleagues there — among them Jacques Loeb, Lloyd Morgan, Franz Boas, Charles Closson, and John Dewey — various of the disparate ideas that would serve as the building blocks of the system to be expounded in *The Theory*. From Closson, who was an instructor in mathematics but had an amateur's interest in anthropology and sociology, he picked up the notion (derived by Closson from European sources) of a close connection between social progress and ethnic stock, and in particular, of the superiority in a competitive environment of the northern European "dolichocephalic blond." This idea — with the polarity of values reversed, as in the case of Veblen's treatment of Sumner's ideas on economics — went into *The Theory* practically intact. Above all, he learned from Franz Boas about the Kwakiutl potlatch.

So at the Rockefeller-sponsored University of Chicago — where unrebellious students dutifully chanted

John D. Rockefeller, wonderful man is he,
Gives all his spare change to the U. of C.

— Veblen hatched the book that, if it did not exactly destroy the class epitomized by John D. Rockefeller, changed forever America's view of that class and indeed its view of our domestic manners in general. By the end of 1895, Veblen was spending an hour or two a day on his book; as he wrote to one of his devoted female former students, "I . . . have to neglect the class work in order to do that." Other evidence amply suggests that no pretext was needed for him to neglect the class work. Perhaps what Veblen was now neglecting for a change was the female students. Four years later, in 1899 — not without the publisher's requirement that Veblen put up a financial guarantee against losses on it — *The Theory of the Leisure Class* was published.

Although no popular bestseller then or ever, the book was an immediate sensation in academic and intellectual circles. Orthodox economists denounced it in the journals (including Veblen's own *Journal of Political Economy*) as vicious, subversive, unsophisticated, unsupported by facts — the sort of amateur effort that gives sociology a bad name. The subjects of its satire — the strivers of the leisure class, masters of the show-off and the putdown — ignored it as they habitually ignored all serious books. There is no evidence that Chicago's patron John D. Rockefeller ever heard of it, much less read it. But it was highly praised by the leading sociologist Lester Ward in *The American Journal of Sociology* and by the avuncular panjandrum of popular literature William Dean Howells in *Literature*. It was wildly acclaimed by political radicals (although Veblen, then as always, despised them for the rigidity of their thinking), and overnight its quaint phrases began to be heard on university campuses. Veblen ever thereafter would be known in academic circles as a man of substance, the author of *The Theory of the Leisure Class*.

That his fame did not spell academic success is easily attributable to two factors — the quality of his teaching, and the irregularity of his personal life. As to the former, although Veblen earned a bare living as a teacher for almost forty years, for all but a few brilliant students he was surely one of the most disastrous academic time-servers who ever put an American classroom to sleep. At Chicago he droned on in a low monotone ("into his lap," said one student), sometimes seeming to be half asleep himself, gave no examinations to avoid the necessity of correcting and grading them, and awarded every student a C, presumably to avoid both invidiousness and personal effort. To dodge a heavy teaching load, he discouraged prospective students by telling them that as prerequisites he required knowledge of French, German, philosophy, psychology, and other hard subjects. When a student would surprise him with a clever question, he would reply, "I don't know; I'm not bothered that way." Later, at the University of Missouri, his office visiting hours, originally ten to eleven three days a week, progressively contracted until at last they were from ten until five minutes past ten on Mondays only. Nor did the situation improve late in his life, when he was teaching at the New School for Social Research in New York City. Drawn by his reputation, which by then had assumed enormous proportions, students would pack his classroom at the start of the term, but as the term wore on, attendance would dwindle to a diehard handful. If American businessmen, as Veblen maintained in one of his books, were engaged in systematic sabotage of the industrial process, he himself, over a lifetime of what passed for teaching, seemed to be engaged in systematic sabotage of academic instruction.

However — the values of university administrators being what they were — he undoubtedly damaged his career more with sexual escapades than he did with bad teaching. In our times, reports are that at certain institutions it means marks against a young professor if he does *not* go to bed with women students. In Veblen's time the reverse was emphatically true. Indolent, habitually unkempt, and bookish, he was no Don Juan. Like the toadfish, he was ugly and sedentary, and attracted females by songs (in his case, lectures). A certain type of woman student was mad about him. They chased *him,* and he did not run. "What is one to do if the woman moves in on you?" he once said to an exasperated friend in explanation of a new peccadillo — and, not incidentally, in a lamentable lapse from the rigor of thought that he required of himself in his writing.

Early in his marriage, Veblen told Ellen that he did not want children because he was not the proper sort of man for a father. She seems to have acceded to this high-handed decree (although there is some evidence that she may have been physically unable to give birth). Beginning in 1895, she took to leaving him at intervals — now to live on a farm in Idaho, now in a cabin in Oregon — but always hoping for a reconciliation, and, for a time, always eventually getting one. But there was a streak of cruelty in Veblen; during their periods together, he would leave letters from his lovers lying around the house. In 1906 he left the University of Chicago under a two-headed cloud of official disapproval, partly of his unpopular views and partly of his sexual habits. Friends got him an appointment at Stanford, in Palo Alto, California, and for a time he lived there with Ellen. That lasted three years; then a woman "moved in," there was a public scandal, and Veblen was fired again. "The president doesn't approve of my domestic arrangements. Nor do I," he remarked, with at least a show of rue. Heroic efforts by his friends resulted in 1911 in a faculty appointment at the University of Missouri, at a cut in annual salary from $3,000 to $1,920. The same year, in response to his constant urging, Ellen divorced him. "What a horrible rupture divorce is! Incredible!" she wrote. "Mr. Veblen, though his part of the bargain is to furnish me with $25 a month, probably will not do it." All the evidence suggests that he never did; in his defense it can be said that he needed the money more than she did.

In 1914 he married Anne Fessenden Bradley, a divorcée with two daughters of her own, whom he had known in Chicago and California. The new Mrs. Veblen was an avid housekeeper and an emotional, humorless radical. She did Veblen's typing, washed his laundry, and preserved absolute quiet in the house for the benefit of his work. She brought up her daughters in accordance with a literal interpretation of *The Theory of the Leisure Class* — to their acute embarrassment when they were forced, for example, to wear long dresses when the fashion was for short ones. In 1918 she suffered what seems to have been a schizophrenic breakdown, and in 1920 she died. Ellen Rolfe Veblen lived until 1926, periodically writing letters to Veblen in which she tried to convert him to theosophy, still believing foolishly that he would come back to her. It is one of the many disturbing facts of Veblen's life that this early champion of women's rights, this exposer of the iniquities and absurdities of male domination, by all accounts was in his own relations with women at least an average-insensitive male chauvinist.

Meanwhile, he was bringing out more books, almost always partly on a "vanity" basis — that is, with a small cash subsidy paid by him to the publisher to help protect the latter against loss. *The Theory of Business Enterprise* (1904) is Veblen's head-on assault on the American business system: its most durable idea is the contrast insisted on in it between "industrial" work — making something with hands or machines — and "pecuniary" work — financial manipulation by owners and managers, who Veblen was sure were bent on sabotaging industrial work in pursuit of their own enrichment. In 1914, after a long hiatus, came *The Instinct of Workmanship*. This was a book-length enlargement on the idea, introduced in *The Theory of the Leisure Class*, that the human makeup includes an innate drive toward useful work that is always in tension with the opposing drive toward wasteful competitive display for the purpose of gaining status. To some extent, *The Instinct of Workmanship* constitutes a revision of *The Leisure Class*. In the later book, he still insisted that the "pecuniary culture" is conducive to shoddy work. However, he now conceded that over the intervening years — the period, we may note, of Theodore Roosevelt's trust-busting and other national reforms of predatory business practices — the instinct of workmanship had gained ground at the expense of "the predatory scheme of life." Even among the self-made rich, Veblen now found a growing conviction that "peaceable diligence and thrift are meritorious traits." At the same time, though, the instinct of workmanship was being "contaminated" by the pecuniary culture; for example, that archetype of invidiousness, the "captain of industry," had now come to be widely regarded as, in his own way, a skillful craftsman himself. All in all, not exactly a recantation, but certainly a shading, an admission that in 1899 he might have gone too far. *The Instinct of Workmanhip* — which Veblen always insisted was his best book — is more temperate and balanced than *The Theory of the Leisure Class*. It is also dense, clumsy, over-theoretical, and entirely lacking in the mordant wit that is close to being the essence of *The Theory*. Put another way, it misses being what that first, long-pent effusion managed to be — a work of genius, the apt expression of an idea whose time had come.

Veblen's last decade was spent mostly in New York City. Having left Missouri with no particular regrets on either side, he worked briefly in Washington for the Food Administration at the end of the First World War — his notions on administering food were not generally well received in bureaucratic circles — and then went to New York, where for about a year he was a writer and editor for the intellectual magazine *The Dial*. Then he joined the faculty of the progressive New School for Social Research, and lectured there, to ever-vanishing classes, until 1926, three years before his death. Suddenly prolific, between 1915 and 1925 he brought out eight books. None of them is particularly memorable. In three of them, he hammered away at the captains of industry in a fairly routine way — how they grind down the common man, how they own and control land and enterprises from distant locations, how as trustees they put their philistine touch on colleges and universities. *The Engineers and the Price System* dubiously put forward the engineer, apostle of efficiency, as the potential savior of modern society. Two other books departed entirely from American social and economic theory to discuss world political affairs — the menace of "Imperial Germany," and the peace settlement after the First World War. Veblen's last book was a translation from the Icelandic of *The Laxdaela Saga*. And so, in a way, he came full circle, for *The Theory of the Leisure Class* had been a sort of saga: surely it is not by

accident, but out of the memory of the Norse sagas read
to Veblen in the frontier farmhouse in his childhood, that
that book's rolling, polysyllabic style is built on words
containing the dactyls so beloved of saga writers — *industrial, invidious, decency, barbarian, conspicuous,
peaceable, vicarious, efficiency*. Veblen late in life took to
deprecating his early masterpiece — he once referred to
it as "that chestnut" — but we need not take him too
seriously; no writer of many books cares to be identified
with and remembered for just one. He knew in his heart
that the book was true, and that in its time its ideas had
been new.

After the first reviews and the initial flush of noto-
riety, the reputation of *The Theory of the Leisure Class*
settled into a cycle that mostly coincided with the ups and
downs of liberal and progressive thought nationwide. In
the first years of the new century its vocabulary and core
ideas became firmly established in the idiom of social
criticism, but Veblen remained all but unknown outside
the little world of academia and urban intellectuals. After
the publication in 1904 of *The Theory of Business Enterprise*, the suspicion spread in those circles that Veblen
was a Marxist, and Marxists themselves eagerly claimed
him as one of them. Veblen reacted, in a lecture to Harvard students in 1906, by elaborately disassociating himself from Marx on technical economic grounds. "The
Marxian system is not only not tenable, it is not even
intelligible," he roundly declared. But his real reasons
for wanting to put a lot of space between him and Marx
were more than technical. In contrast to Marx, Veblen
did not idealize the common man, or trust him, or even
feel particularly sympathetic to him. His specialty was
describing and criticizing the upper reaches of existing

society, not proposing schemes for its reform. Besides, he was a loner, not prone to joining movements, political or other. Having constructed his own theory, he was in no mood to endorse somebody else's.

By 1912, *The Theory of the Leisure Class* was popular enough to merit a new, cheaper edition designed to reach a wider audience, and during the later teen years, while radical criticism of American society was building up to a small crescendo, Veblen to an influential minority became something of a hero. Maxwell Anderson in 1919 quoted a friend of his as saying that Veblen's thinking "permeates the atmosphere." Mencken in his famous 1919 essay — the one we have encountered in connection with the matter of lawns and the consequences of passing astern of a cow — fulsomely described the situation:

> Everyone of intellectual pretensions read his works. Veblenism was shining in full brilliance. There were Veblenists, Veblen clubs, Veblen remedies for the sorrows of the world. There were even, in Chicago, Veblen Girls — perhaps Gibson girls grown middle-aged and despairing. . . . All of a sudden, Siss! Boom! Ah! . . . rah, rah, rah for Prof. Dr. Thorstein Veblen!

The scapegrace professor holding his two-thousand-dollar job by the skin of his teeth and earning a few hundred dollars a year more from book royalties must have been surprised to read of his great eminence in the land.

Mencken's attack remains the heaviest, if not the most accurate, broadside ever directed at *The Theory of the Leisure Class*. "A geyser of pishposh"; "chiefly a mass of platitudes"; "a cent's worth of information wrapped in a bale of polysyllables"; "intolerably flapdoodlish phrases"; "gnarled sentences like a bull trapped by barbed wire"; "inane debasement of scientific curiosity to the level of mob gaping"; "almost unbelievable tediousness and flatulence"; "unprecedented talent for saying nothing in an august and heroic manner"; "downright hoggishness": such were some of the myriad jagged missiles that made up Mencken's barrage. Whether it was by the barrage or by the conservative turn that the United States took after the war, Veblen's reputation was hurt by something. Through the complacent nineteen-twenties, he was little read or mentioned except by orthodox economists, who ritually denounced or ridiculed him. Another turnabout came after the 1929 crash, when he was posthumously hailed as the prophet who had foretold it (although in fact he hadn't), and his ideas about engineers became the basis of the briefly popular movement called Technocracy. Liberal writers took him up. John Chamberlain in *Farewell to Reform* (1932) wrote that he "now shines like a star of the first magnitude" (his candlepower had apparently increased since Mencken's piece); John Dos Passos in *The Big Money* (1936) favored him with a worshipful profile; and Malcolm Cowley, in a 1938 poll of leading American intellectuals as to which writers had had the greatest effect on their thinking, found that Veblen led the list by a wide margin.

And the post–World War II period? Yet another turnaround, and, comparatively speaking, another dead time for Veblen's reputation. The sociologist David Riesman psychoanalyzed him, generally sympathetically, in *Thorstein Veblen, a Critical Interpretation* (1953). Robert Heilbroner put him among the leading economists of world history in his enormously popular *Worldly Philosophers* (1953). And John Kenneth Galbraith, always a Veblenian, wrote in a 1973 introduction to a new edition of *The Theory of the Leisure Class* that "no one who has read the book ever again sees the consumption of goods in the same light," and that the book is "wonderfully relevant to modern affluence." A new and thoughtful biography of Veblen by John P. Diggins appeared in 1978.

Otherwise, in recent years there has been little comment or interest in Veblen or his ideas. This is not to say that the ideas are dead. On the contrary. Who these days — whether or not he has ever so much as heard of Thorstein Veblen — gets through a lifetime, or even a year, without thinking of "conspicuous consumption" or "conspicuous waste"? *The Theory of the Leisure Class* is bought so seldom that it barely stays in print, but while neglecting the work we have paid its author the ultimate compliment of taking his thought for granted.

In 1926, almost seventy, tired of teaching, and with no new ideas to put into writing, Veblen left New York to live in the mountains near Palo Alto, in a cabin that he had owned since his Stanford days. There he spent his last three years, a strange, lonely old man, not exactly embittered, but hardly benign, either — a kind of embodiment of his ideal, the peaceable savage, gone askew to the edge of madness.

An illuminating episode six years earlier, involving the California cabin, prefigured this askewness, and also pointed to how directly Veblen's writing came out of his life experiences. Veblen believed that he had been deprived of the cabin's ownership through the trickery of local real-estate operators, as a result of which title to it had fallen to an absentee "owner" — much as his father and grandfather had been done out of their land years earlier. It must have seemed to him that the predatory invidiousness of the leisure class fell on the successive generations of Veblens as the ancient curse had fallen on the house of Atreus in Greek mythology. In the summer of 1920 Veblen, revisiting California, arrived at the cabin by automobile in the company of several friends. Dorfman describes the scene: "He took a hatchet and methodically broke the windows, going at the matter with a dull intensity that was like madness, the intensity of a physically lazy person roused into sudden activity by anger. If there were to be any disputes about the ownership, he intended to make the place thoroughly uninhabitable for all concerned. . . . Most of the group were acutely embarrassed. In time they got themselves back into the car, and in a brave effort to return to normal behavior someone asked, 'And what is going to be the title of your next book, Dr. Veblen?' '*Absentee Ownership*,' he answered, and said nothing more . . . until three years later when the title of *Absentee Ownership* was actually announced." And now the tragicomic irony of the episode: Veblen had been wrong; as he soon learned, he had not lost title to the cabin at all. It was still legally his. The absentee owner who had despoiled it was Thorstein Veblen. The peaceable savage, thinking he was holding his own against predatory invidiousness, had become a parody of predatory invidiousness himself.

Much the same irony attended those last three years. At the cabin, now restored to habitability, and at another modest house in a poor section of Palo Alto, he lived alone, passing the time reading current novels and gossiping with neighbors. He built himself an outdoor chair from which to admire the surrounding view. Nature was left undisturbed; weeds and grass grew uncut, wood rats freely entered the larder, and cats and skunks brushed against his legs. When someone asked whether he was the author of *The Theory of the Leisure Class*, he replied, "If I am, it has been a long time ago, and I promise never to do it again." When an unscrupulous neighbor, thinking Veblen was away, brazenly stole some lumber and drainpipes from his property, he sat smiling and watching from ambush behind a clump of bushes, not intervening. Unwilling or unable to defend himself against a real wrong, on other occasions he exploded into cruelty without cause. On a walk in the woods one day, he found a hornets' nest. Shortly thereafter, coming upon a farmer with an empty sack, he asked to borrow the sack awhile. Returning to the nest, he put the hornets in the sack, then took it back to the farmer and returned it to him saying, "Thank you." It may be noted that motiveless malignity had had no part in the makeup of the peaceable savage as Veblen had described him.

Something had gone wrong, and perhaps it was that Veblen in his old age was learning, to his disillusionment, that the peaceable savage, being an ideal, does not exist — that in every person, even in Thorstein Veblen, it is at best a tendency to be encouraged, ever contending with an equally strong opposite tendency, as, in the realm of morals, good wrestles with evil. The best one could hope for, perhaps, was to fake it, to honor the ideal by *seeming* to be peaceable-savage. At a meeting of the American Economic Association several years earlier — the organization whose presidency, belatedly offered to him, Veblen had refused because "they didn't offer it to me when I needed it" — Veblen had stood leaning insouciantly against a wall, wearing a highly conspicuous red scarf. Joseph Schumpeter had seen him there, and had commented later that Veblen was almost a common *poseur,* and little better than a charlatan.

From the Carleton mathematics professor's "Thorstein is a fraud" of the young man, then, to a great economist's "little better than a charlatan" of the old one. If Veblen was always part fraud and charlatan, his were the fraudulence and charlatanism of one who sees through the surface of the life around him, and adopts fraudulence and charlatanism as a defense of his vulnerable person against the truth he sees. He belongs among the American eccentrics — Ford, Edison, John Brown come to mind — who changed our lives, but never learned to live their own.

22

The Prophecy Revised

1. In status competition, display of wealth evolves into display of style.

2. The most effective status-seeking style is mockery of status seeking.

On the main street of a summer resort lined with meticulously restored or copied Early American buildings, many of them containing antique shops and natural-food emporiums, and one of them discreetly offering mechanical aids to sexual delight, a young woman and her eleven-year-old daughter both wear, above their jeans, T-shirts bearing messages. The mother's T-shirt says "DRACULA" and the child's says "IMPERFECT IDENTIFICATION." Both messages have slightly macabre associations. The couple are darling enough in their sweet persons, so that a dash of bitters is needed. The twist, necessary to make the cocktail perfect, is that the mother and daughter seem to be wearing each other's shirts.

At Caesar's Palace, in Las Vegas, in 1979, one is greeted at the entrance by a monumental, twice-life-size statue of the heavyweight champion Joe Louis thirty-five or forty years earlier, when he was in his fighting prime. Beside the huge legs of the colossus sits the living Joe Louis, an amiable but pathetic man in a wheelchair.

In Los Angeles, possession of a Russian wolfhound is thought to show good taste and flair, and thereby to confer status. For those with the desire to attain these benefits but not the inclination to possess a Russian wolfhound, dogs of that breed could in 1979 be rented for a modest $100 per week.

The junior executive, at home with his female roommate at their two-income condominium, is entertaining a few friends. Out of mutual respect and affection, nobody wears shoes. A few guiltily puff on a cigarette ("It's gross, but . . . "). Nobody is doing anything as gross as smoking marijuana. Public displays of sex or affection are out; nobody touches much, and especially one doesn't touch one's bedmate. On balance, it is a more relaxed, and therefore more attractive, group than one in comparable circumstances would have been in 1900, when everyone would have been showing off dress and breeding, or in 1925, when everyone would have been showing off unconventionality, or in 1950, when everyone would have been showing off ability to assimilate martinis.

However, the host is showing off wine knowledge. He is displaying the bottle that he proposes to serve, turning it respectfully, and discoursing on its subtle virtues. (It may acceptably come from California.) In his relaxed way, he is a wine snob, of the new at-home variety as opposed to the old public-restaurant variety. There are few of the latter left — the macho restaurant host going through a haggle with the sommelier as long, intricate, and stylized as a matador's haggle with a bull. True enough, *The New York Times* has recently explained how to send back a bottle in a restaurant. ("To be polite and indicate how carefully I am making my decision, I may ask for a second taste, and sometimes I suggest that others at my table be given samples. By now the wine steward knows something is wrong, and it is time to suggest that he taste the wine himself. In so doing, I have begun shifting the decision to the restaurant and creating the opportunity to save face. . . . I suggest that the proprietor be given a taste. . . . To help him make the right decision, I may ask, 'Would you serve that wine in your own house on a special occasion?' . . . He decides to take the bottle back and recommend another. . . . I congratulate him on a wise choice.") But all that has become a bit wearying and complicated in the context of breezy contemporary manners, particularly the elaborate denial of class distinctions — the matador showing that he considers the bull his equal by being courteous. Besides, very few restaurants *have* wine stewards any more, and those that do sometimes have them principally to indulge customers who like to bully wine stewards.

The wine snob now operates at home. Our host — hawk-shaped bottle opener poised in the air — is regaling the group with a tale about a bottle that his father gave him that has now become so valuable that it would be outrageously wasteful to drink it. For now, this bottle is quite adequate. It cost less than five dollars. It is more than adequate. (Everyone is panting with thirst by now.) In fact, it is — pop! — a real find.

Autre temps, autre moeurs. As we have seen all along the way, some things have changed since Veblen's time.

None of these vignettes of contemporary American manners has much of anything to do with pecuniary decency, conspicuous consumption, vicarious consumption, or industrial exemption. However, they have very much to do with competitive display — display now not so much of being in the chips as of being in the know. As a concomitant, they have to do with invidiousness, and quite possibly with predatory barbarism.

Manners and customs change, but competitive display, in one mode or another, seems to go on. (And not only in the United States. In Brazil in the summer of 1980, Pope John Paul II called for a society "free of showy manipulation." It would appear that there is no such thing.) If we may risk a comparison between social and natural science, competitive display seems to be a permanently fixed quantity, like energy in the universe. Whence comes it? What are its psychological origins?

Veblen thought that they were in the social need to achieve or announce superiority to others. The brilliant and original contemporary anthropologist Lionel Tiger, whom we have encountered as the prophet of male bonding, has quite another explanation. In his recent book *Optimism,* Tiger proposes competitive display as an expression of innocent hope. Such optimism, he insists, is a human imperative, biologically stimulated by "norepinephrine in the brain"; an illusion, but a benign one, necessary to make life bearable in a world of which an objective view would produce despair.

Without saying that he intends to refute Veblen — indeed, without mentioning Veblen at all — Tiger refers specifically to several of the key Veblenian phenomena and treats them as manifestations of optimism. Conspicuous consumption, he says, is "the pathology of prosperity" — a pathology not of surly self-serving but of manic high spirits. One goes on a public spending spree not to gain social advantage but just for the pleasure of feeling expansive. Even invidiousness itself, in Tiger's view, is a component of the "optimistic syndrome." Fierce competitiveness, whether in sport, business, or social life, arises out of euphoria: "Contest is to optimism what flirtation is to love." The wish for plastic surgery arises not out of vanity or slavishness to fashion but rather out of the need to become, or at least to *feel,* sexually attractive and therefore potentially procreative; like sexual attraction itself, it serves to raise human hopes. We show off, that is, not to make others feel bad, but to make ourselves feel good.

This is a philosophy both cheering and depressing. If showing off is merely an automatic, involuntary response to chemical signals from the body, necessary to sustain life, we cannot condemn it. We can only give thanks for the clever adaptive mechanism — a gift from God or evolution — that makes it possible. On the other hand, if it is only a response to biological necessity and not a product of free choice, we can't applaud it, either. It has no moral aspect at all.

Perhaps even worse, we can't laugh at it. Pathology isn't funny — not even useful and necessary pathology. To be able to laugh at human foibles, we have to believe that they come about not because of substances in the brain but out of human foolishness that could be eliminated or controlled by acts of will. And the vast enjoyment that we derive from contemplating human foolishness — in others and even, by an effort of will, in ourselves — is one of the saving rewards of life. It may even be optimism.

So let us grant Tiger his due, and agree that much showing off in America — from Henry Clay Frick figuring out at first glance that the Vanderbilt mansion cost a thousand dollars a day to maintain to the eager customers of Gloria Vanderbilt et al. persuading themselves that work pants are ideal party wear — has in it an element of the grimly determined, of the biologically useful. But let us insist that that is not the whole story. Let us insist that, if they seriously wanted to try, and without throwing themselves into a permanent funk of pessimism, Frick could have remarked on the appearance of the earlier Vanderbilt product before he calculated the upkeep, or the fashion-jeans customers asked themselves whether wearing the later Vanderbilt product to parties isn't really pretty funny. As, in fact, it is.

We may close with the automobile. Through most of its commercial life, which almost coincides with the years since *The Theory of the Leisure Class,* it has been a primary object of competitive display. Indeed, its career in that role has become so familiar, and has been so much commented on, as to call for only glancing comment in these pages. Still, that career may serve as a summary of what has happened to conspicuous display in America since Veblen. Early in the century the automobile was, in Woodrow Wilson's words, "a picture of the arrogance of wealth." In the nineteen-twenties it became the symbol of achieved status, the badge of the arriviste. In the nineteen-fifties it became first the necessary proof of middle-class standing, and then, by gradual refinement, the insigne of precise rank *within* the middle class.

And now, at last, it shows signs of shedding largely or entirely any place at all as a class or status identification tag, and becoming — a means of transportation. It took a geopolitical upheaval, the gasoline shortage, to bring about this epochal social change. But it also took something else: a changing national mood, an emerging new national style. David Riesman said of the growing popularity of small, unpretentious cars, "Showiness has been so long satirized that it has become an embarrassment." Nothing especially new there; Big Tim Sullivan, Tammany leader and congressman at the turn of the century, remarked that "God and the people hate a chesty man." True enough, but showiness survived in the old time and survives, in a changed skin, in the new one. Posing has replaced exploit. The satire that killed the old showiness has itself become the new.

The Theory of
the Leisure Class

*J*ohn *Kenneth Galbraith* has written that Veblen is "the nearest thing in the United States to an academic legend, equivalent to that of Scott Fitzgerald in fiction or the Barrymores in the theatre." Galbraith calls *The Theory of the Leisure Class* "a tract on snobbery and social pretense" that is "wonderfully relevant to modern affluence." As this book must make clear, I agree with the latter statement, but believe that Galbraith does not go far enough. To be fully relevant to our times, Veblen's theory needs some revising.

On some small but not insignificant matters, Veblen as a prophet has been proved dead wrong. For example, he held that the custom of men wearing beards, which had fallen somewhat into disuse in the eighteen-nineties, would return on a permanent basis as soon as men came to realize that a shaved face was a pretentious affectation. In fact, in our time a bearded one is more apt to be thought of that way. (Veblen usually wore a beard.) The beard–no beard question appears to be cyclical, and, incidentally, the alternations in male facial-hair fashion appear to be an excellent demonstration of the workings of Veblen's theory of fashion (see chapter 18).

Moreover, on several much larger matters he now appears to have committed serious errors of commission or omission.

277

The automobile — a rich man's toy when he wrote, but a very visible and much-discussed one — does not seem to have appeared to him to have any particular symbolic importance. It is not even mentioned in *The Theory of the Leisure Class*. Yet within less than a generation it was to become by all odds the most Veblenian of all American artifacts. Although Veblen was obsessed with the differences between white ethnic types, he failed to grasp the coming importance of the black race in American social styles, manners, and customs. Finally, he was apparently blind to the fact that his own main theme — approval for the industrious, unambitious hand worker, ridicule and contempt for the invidious, pretentious manipulator of money — was itself as invidious as possible.

Still, Veblen was a true prophet in that he had the power to change permanently the way people thought about themselves and their society. His book has the classic quality of a work of genius — that of creating its own world. If that world is not exactly ours, it may (like Freud's) serve as a key to the understanding of ours, provided we do not accept every word as gospel, but rather allow for human error and unpredictable events, and revise the theory as seems necessary. That is my objective in this book.

Veblen's "theory of the leisure class" at first appears fragmentary and inchoate because of the author's seemingly casual way of organizing his material. However, when the parts of the theory are assembled and fitted together like the parts of a puzzle, the theory comes out remarkably logical and self-consistent. The book itself is strongly recommended to readers of this one, for its vivid descriptive passages, its apparently vague and obfuscating language that on close reading turns out to express unexpectedly precise thought, its mordant wit, and the rolling rhythms that make it utterly unlike any other work of social science.

What follows is an attempt to set forth, in drastically condensed form for the reader's ready reference, the essential parts of the theory.

Anthropological framework.

Since Veblen's time, the idea of evolutionary stages of human society has generally been discredited. But what it leads to as he used it — his theory of the dynamic of modern American social behavior — not only has stood the test of time but now in some respects looks stronger than ever. Here, then, are the essentials of Veblen's anthropology, a shaky foundation under a sound edifice.

Human societies, Veblen believed, pass through two principal stages, the second having several subsidiary stages of its own.

1. First comes *peaceable savagery*, best exemplified at the time Veblen was writing (or so he believed) by the Andamans, dwellers on islands in the Bay of Bengal, or the Todas of the Nilgiri Hills in Saharan Africa. This stage is characterized by friendly, noncompetitive relationships between people; a sedentary, unambitious manner of life; work done for its own sake more than for survival, in response to "the instinct of workmanship"; and "idle curiosity" about man and nature.

2. This is duly followed by a *predatory barbarian* period that, as Veblen saw the matter, still existed in a late stage in the United States of his time. He divides the barbarian period into the following stages:

(a) A *primitive-barbarian* stage, exemplified by the feudal societies of Europe or Japan, and marked by the primacy of warriors and priests.

(b) A *quasi-peaceable barbarian* stage, presumably exemplified — Veblen does not specify — by Europe in the centuries before and during the Industrial Revolution, and distinguished by the institution of chattel slavery.

(c) A *modern-peaceable barbarian* stage, with money payments and wage labor. This is modern society, and in particular, the United States in Veblen's time. All of the principal characteristics of the primitive-barbarian stage — in particular, ferocious competitiveness in pursuit of status — are carried over into the modern-peaceable stage. The difference is that competition in hunting and fighting has been mostly replaced by competition in such fields as sports, money manipulation, and public display of affluence. On the other hand, peaceable-savage traits also survive, and exist as a minority force. The outcome is a society marked by a constant tension between the conflicting forces of "predatory barbarism" and "peaceable savagery."

All of the stages of the barbarian period are marked by "unremitting emulation and antagonism between classes and between individuals," and a class system in which the chief qualifications for membership in the top class are "clannishness, massiveness, ferocity, unscrupulousness, and tenacity of purpose." In the primitive-barbarian stage, the idea of private property makes its first appearance by way of the "possession" of women by men. (Veblen was an early theoretical feminist.) Men in the early part of this stage are hunters, while women do the "industrial" work, mainly agriculture; in conformity with the accepted sexual hierarchy, a high value is put on men's predatory "exploits" and a much lower one on women's *"uneventful diligence,"* a peaceable-savage trait. Later on, hunting is gradually replaced, as the male activity thought most praiseworthy, by waging war. Military "exploit" then becomes the chief measure of status.

Beginning with the quasi-peaceable stage, and reaching fruition in the modern-peaceable stage, a new status-measuring system comes into being. Neither hunting nor war is any longer a major feature of life. Property, typically acquired through "force and fraud," has been extended from women to land and objects, and eventually to money. Meanwhile, the need for status not only continues but intensifies, becoming, "the dominant feature in the scheme of life." The new road to status is *invidiousness* — that is, successful competitive display, direct or indirect, of wealth or power. Such display comes to replace physical exploit (other than athletic exploit) as the predatory activity used to achieve and hold status.

Predatory invidiousness is the key to Veblen's system; it is seen as the main driving force in modern American society, tempered and to some extent balanced by the contrary tendency toward peaceable savagery. Chief among the forms that it takes, according to Veblen, are the following:

Pecuniary decency.

By no means what it sounds like: that is, being generous with money. Veblen uses the word *decency* with great precision and elegance, in its old meaning of "conventionally proper and seemly." Thus, "The substantial ground of this high requirement [of drunkenness among workmen in certain trades] is . . . a manifestation of dominance and pecuniary decency." Here *decency*, shorn of the moral connotation that we have come to give it, means the opposite of what we customarily mean by it. The "decent" thing for, say, a journeyman printer to do is to get drunk at regular intervals. It is in the fulfillment of pecuniary decency that people resort to "conspicuous consumption" and "conspicuous waste."

Emulation.

Imitating a competitor's display of wealth, and trying to surpass it; or, in a later phrase, "keeping up with the Joneses."

Vicarious consumption.

The woman is now no longer needed for "industrial" work, which is taken over successively by slaves, wage workers, and finally machines. Through elaborate and expensive clothes, a pretentious and impeccably kept home, and so on, she now comes to fill a "vicarious" or "ceremonial" role: to serve as a walking advertisement of her husband's wealth.

Industrial exemption.

Objects of conspicuous consumption should be evidence of exemption, through wealth, from the need to work with one's hands. For example, clothing must be confining and inconvenient. Proof of abstention from physical labor becomes a man's or a woman's principal basis for esteem, in his or her own eyes and those of others. Leisure itself becomes "beautiful and ennobling in all civilized men's eyes." Because leisure serves as the product and evidence of successful predation, the idea of leisure and the idea of predation become closely associated. To maintain status, new invidious displays of waste and abstention from labor must constantly be devised. The way to stay on top is by putting on at intervals displays of consumption, waste, and abstention from labor more mind-boggling than anyone else's. The "leisure class," as Veblen means the term, consists of those constantly and successfully engaged in this endeavor.

Veblen's theory is now in place; a few of its details, and some of Veblen's shadings and qualifications, must be added to round out this summary. Good manners, for example, in the modern-peaceable stage have come to have a "sacramental character" and to constitute "a voucher of a life of leisure," partly because attention to them constitutes "a substantial and patent waste of time" from the point of view of producing goods and services. (However, leisure-class manners reach their peak in the quasi-peaceable stage. In the modern-peaceable stage they have tended to deteriorate, as participation in leisure-class observances becomes more democratically disseminated and therefore less refined.) As a result of the innate conservatism of manners, social innovation of any kind comes to be looked upon by the leisure class as "bad form." Curious little eccentricities — invidious in that they serve as distinguishing marks of a leisure-class background — make their appearance: for example, "exaltation of the defective" (valuing crude handwork over smoother machine work) and "veneration for the archaic" (epitomized in a vogue for antiques). These, Veblen insists, are not the reversions to peaceable savagery that they appear to be at first blush, but are rather secondary expressions of the predatory-barbarian temperament.

The effects of conspicuous consumption and invidious emulation run through all of the major aspects of life. The very conception of God is affected: "It is felt that the divinity must be of a peculiarly serene and leisured habit of life," and that His habitation must be characterized by "the insignia of opulence and power." Science, in its effort to advance the industrial process, must constantly fight against the handicap of a leisure class need to make its teaching and research entirely theoretical — that is, useless for practical purposes. The dress of both men and women must be so impractical as to certify that the wearer is never by any mischance engaged in productive work. The perception of beauty is shaped by the same influences; it finally comes about in architecture, home decoration, and the fine arts that objects are valued aesthetically in relation to their wastefulness, uselessness, and expensiveness, resulting in a "substitution of pecuniary beauty for esthetic beauty," and thereby conforming to the accepted canon of "decency."

But all the while, a contrary tendency is at work. This is the instinct of workmanship, a survival of the peaceable-savage period. In *The Theory of the Leisure Class*, Veblen introduces the idea of the instinct of workmanship (on which he later elaborated at book length), insists that it is present in all men, and states that it "comes into conflict with the law of conspicuous waste." That is, there is a powerful influence working directly against the influences that are being described and proposed as the basis of a national style of living. But the counterinfluence is almost always the loser in the conflict. It is runner-up in the American tournament.

Nevertheless, the counterforce is strong enough to bring about certain refinements in the theory. The leisure class is affected along with everybody else by the instinct of workmanship. In spite of its characteristic "laziness with dignity," it has a sort of workmanship of its own. Sometimes its members even show a "more or less appreciable element of purposeful effort directed to some serious end" — for example, philanthropy and support of the arts. Moreover, leisure-class behavior has various permutations, some of them paradoxical. There is a subclass of the leisure class made up of *nouveaux pauvres* —"the decayed gentleman and the lady who has seen better days" — for whom exquisite adherence to and even improvement on the less expensive manifestations of "decency" is nothing less than a passion. Such persons tend to attach themselves — on the one hand, as pecuniary sycophants, but on the other, as mentors in matters of taste — to the newly rich of their time. A principal purpose of the schools and adult social groups of the leisure class is to drill the newly rich and their children in correct leisure-class deportment; thus, "a syncopated evolution of gentle birth and breeding is achieved."

Eventually, status competition within the leisure class leads, in a few cases, to a polar reversal of standards. A few of the most self-assured and long-established members of the class (here Veblen surely had in mind the Rockefellers) come to feel that adherence to its standard canons is beneath them. Their status, they believe, is so well known that for them to indulge in those observances would only lower them into the common ruck. They can best announce their unassailability by reversing the canons — by dressing and living simply, and by doing their extravagant consumption only in private. They become, categorically, *in*conspicuous consumers. They have, Veblen ingeniously explains, adopted an apparently noninvidious way of life for the quintessentially invidious purpose of showing that they are above taking part in a game played by lesser mortals.

There begins counterdisplay. It is only one more step to parody display.

Parody Display

$D_{wight \ Macdonald,}$ *in* the introduction and afterword to his book *Parodies*, gives a brilliant description of parody in its original form, as a literary genre. Distinguishing it from travesty (literally, "changing clothes") — the most primitive form of literary mockery, in which the sole intention is to make the object seem ridiculous — and burlesque, which is more advanced in that it "at least imitates the style of the original," Macdonald says that true parody requires that the parodist express for the original a subtle mixture of feelings — respect and even admiration on the one hand, and perception of ridiculous affectation or excess on the other. That is to say, the parodist must be ambivalent and the parody ambiguous. "A successful parodist," Macdonald says, "must live himself, imaginatively, into his parodee. . . . Most parodies are written [primarily] out of admiration rather than contempt."

Macdonald goes on to say that some of the best parody is self-parody, and to make a distinction between parody that is intentional and conscious and that which is unintentional and unconscious. Most self-parody, naturally enough, falls within the second category. The unconscious parodist has lost control of his material, and is taking off his own or someone else's writing style without realizing it — as, say, practically all of the American writers who try to imitate Ernest Hemingway end up doing, and as many critics believe Hemingway himself did in much of his later work. Although Macdonald does not say so, his discussion implies that there are degrees of consciousness or unconsciousness in all parody, ranging across the whole scale from one extreme to the other.

The term *parody* is used in this book in its extended meaning, as applying to acts in life rather than passages in literature. To adapt a term from the art world, we deal with Action Parody. Although the classic Veblenian kind of competitive display, containing no trace of irony, amply flourishes in modern America, a new, post-Veblenian form — parody display — has made a strong appearance and is gaining ascendancy. In parody display, a wide range of degrees of consciousness on the parodists' part will be readily discerned. However, right at the outset, we will have to rule out Macdonald's literary category of totally unintentional and unconscious parody. The overblown mansions of Veblen's robber barons or the absurd costumes and parties of their wives could be called parody, in that they can easily be seen by a detached viewer of today as laughable aberrations. The same could be said of practically everything in present-day Beverly Hills, California: the small, flimsy roadside houses that look as if they came from Levittown and sell for a small fortune each; the tiny backyards entirely occupied, apart from the narrow walkway and the postage-stamp patio, by the swimming pool; the Gucci shop at a Beverly Hills hotel that only the privileged possessors of a key to it can so much as enter; the Norwegian blue fox automobile blanket, with sixteen tails, that can be bought by a key-holder for a small fortune. Or take another familiar phenomenon of Veblen's time — the architectural vogue, particularly in the West, for fronting modest, inexpensive buildings with large, pretentious, Greek-Revival facades like those of antebellum southern mansions. Parodies, apparently, of leisure-class architectural pretension.

But these past and present manifestations of display are not really parody. The displayers were or are in deadly earnest;

the farthest thing from their minds was to laugh, or even smile, admiringly or otherwise, at either themselves or others. They were and are engaged undeviatingly in the unhumorous act of pecuniary emulation. In other words, it could perhaps equally well be argued that *all* competitive display, to the detached eye, is unintentional or unconscious parody — or that none is.

For our purposes, Action Parody must be to one degree or another conscious. The perpetrator must have at least an inkling of what in the law is called *scienter* — knowledge of what he is doing. There must be a gleam of irony in his intention. Indeed, it is the rise of this sense of irony — fostered by increased education, progressive disillusion with all blind social faiths, promotion by the entertainment-mad media, and even, perhaps, the recent decline of the United States in the esteem of the rest of the world — that is the chief feature of the change in the character of competitive display since Veblen's time.

"Hint and Warning Respecting the Evil of Treating to Strong Drink"

The following document, which is undated and signed with a pseudonym, was among family papers that I inherited. Its most likely author — Lucius Quintus Cincinnatus Elmer, my great-great-grandfather — was born in southern New Jersey in 1791, and was converted to abstinence (traumatically, I gather) in the eighteen-thirties. On such circumstantial evidence, I date it tentatively late in that decade. In any case, the fact that it employs the old-style "s" when the letter is doubled ("businefs," "glafs," "afsistance") strongly suggests that it was written well before 1850. For the sake of readability I have eliminated this usage in the transcription that follows.

To treat, in the language of those who tamper with ardent spirits, means to give a person liquor, by way of compliment, or reward, or bribe. The landlord or housekeeper treats his friends, by setting out the brandy bottle; the more he urges the greater is his hospitality, and by fair proportion, if he can make you drunk, his generosity is lordly. The farmer treats his laborer, by pouring him out a glass of whiskey or rum, as a reward for some special service, or after some difficult labor. The candidate for office treats his constituents by procuring at his own expense, in some suitable place, such quantities of intoxicating liquors as he may judge sufficient to buy the votes of such as are given to drink.

This may serve to explain what is meant by treating. There are various other occasions upon which the same thing takes place. It is probable however that the evils of this custom are nowhere more plainly seen than at places where numbers of people come upon business during the day, and where their custom or their assistance is desired. This custom and this assistance are purchased, or sought to be purchased, by ardent spirits. We have all seen this. At our stores, in the country, in villages, in towns, where there is a brisk retail business, or where barter and exchange are carried on, we daily take notice that after a bargain is struck, or a purchase made, the parties *step into the back-shop*. In this privacy, or in the corner where a row of hogsheads and casks is standing, the cask is turned, and a small glass of liquor is given to the customer. I have heard, but do not vouch for it, that it is often found convenient to keep a hogshead of poor whiskey or spirits for such occasions. Boys as well as men have their treat. It becomes a stated thing; there is a disappointment if it is not afforded. The custom of these persons is thus secured, and if any should not happen to have a taste for ardent spirits, this is one of the most easy things to remedy; — one or two glasses create an appetite which has been known to last through life.

In like manner, whenever any extraordinary piece of work is to be done, such as the unloading of grain, groceries, hardware, produce or any merchandise, the idlers around the doors are called in to assist, and are rewarded by a dram. There is generally attached to every establishment where the practice is in vogue a small corps of supernumeraries, who are always dodging within call, as they have no other employment, and are known to prefer a treat to anything else. When a servant brings a message, or calls to take an article to oblige you, or when a neighbour assists you . . . you pay him in the same manner.

Now, I desire the reader to say with candor whether he has not seen this. Is the picture too highly drawn? Is it not like what you have observed in your own vicinity? Is not the custom so prevalent that dealers say that they are under a sort of necessity thus to act? Give me your attention then . . . while I endeavor to show the evils of this practice. . . .

[*There follows a routine hellfire sermon on the evils of drink, into which the following comments pertinent to our investigation are interspersed.*]

. . . This practice [of treating] furnishes temptations to those who are not drunkards to become such. The boy or youth or man who drinks once is likely to drink again. It is of course harder to refuse the second time. It is difficult to refuse what you offer in kindness. I believe firmly that thousands of intemperate men owe their ruin to this custom of treating. . . . No harm is suspected when the lad is asked to "drink a little." It is manly, and when it flies into his head he feels doubly like a man. The shame-faced youth may be afraid to decline, and when he has tasted he is pleased to find that his sheepish bashfulness is removed. . . .

The evil is alarming at the present time, because it occurs so often. Every hour of every day, some heedless person is undergoing the temptation by means of a treat, and some unhappy youth is falling into the snare. . . . "But I do not *force* my customers to drink," may be the apology. Neither does Satan force the assassin to commit his crime; he only presents strong temptations. . . . Men are known to love opium; will you therefore give it to such men, at the hazard of their lives? Will you furnish the suicide with the means of self-murder because he is bent upon it, and because if you do not afford him the rope, another will? . . .

In conclusion, what is to be done? The course of duty is so plain that one moment suffices to point it out. Let every dealer in the article desist at once. It is time to begin, and someone must take the lead. Let that one be yourself. . . . This is a favorable opportunity, and the decrease in the sale of ardent spirits is every day more apparent. The retrospect will be delightful, from the decline of life, of many years of business in which you have done nothing to produce vice, poverty and sin among your fellow men.

Aquarius

Notes on Sources

1. Fighting with Property

Thorstein Veblen, *The Theory of the Leisure Class* (New York, 1899). Available (1980) in the following editions: New American Library (Mentor Book), paperback; Penguin Books, paperback.

Joseph Dorfman, *Thorstein Veblen and His America* (New York, 1934. Reprint, Clifton, New Jersey 1961, 1966, 1972).

Stewart H. Holbrook, *The Age of the Moguls* (New York, 1953).

Russell Lynes, *Snobs* (New York, 1950).

Vance Packard, *The Status Seekers* (New York, 1959).

2. Showing Off with Style

Dwight Macdonald, *Parodies* (New York, 1960).

Enrique Hank Lopez, *The Harvard Mystique* (New York, 1979).

Joan Kron and Suzanne Slesin, *High-Tech: The Industrial Style and Source Book for the Home* (New York, 1978).

3. Playing Games

Christopher Lasch, *The Culture of Narcissism* (New York, 1978).

Valerie Andrews, *The Psychic Power of Running* (New York, 1978), and Joel Henning, *Holistic Running* (New York, 1978):

quoted by Patti Hagan, *The New York Times Book Review,* December 24, 1978.

Patti Hagan with Joe Cody, *The Road Runner's Guide to New York City* (New York, 1980).

Roger Angell, "Sharing the Beat," *The New Yorker,* April 9, 1979.

5. *Getting Down with the Joneses*

Elliot Liebow, *Tally's Corner* (Boston, 1967).

Russell Baker in *The New York Times,* February 6, 1979.

6. *Veblen's Cow*

H. L. Mencken, *Prejudices: First Series* (New York, 1919).

Frances Trollope, *Domestic Manners of the Americans* (originally published 1832; paperback edition, New York, 1949).

7. *Getting Drunk*

J. C. Furnas, *The Americans* (New York, 1969).

Daniel J. Boorstin, *The Americans: The National Experience* (New York, 1965).

Liebow, *Tally's Corner.*

Trollope, *Domestic Manners of the Americans.*

8. *Eating and Starving*

Hilde Bruch, *The Golden Cage* (Cambridge, Mass., 1978).

Stanley Schachter, *Emotion, Obesity, and Crime* (New York, 1971).

———, "Obese Humans and Rats," *American Psychologist,* Vol. 26, No. 2, February, 1971.

Rosemary Dinnage, "The Starved Self," *The New York Review,* February 22, 1979.

9. *Telephoning*

Michael Korda, *Power!* (New York, 1975).

———, *Success!* (New York, 1977).

Letitia Baldridge, *The Amy Vanderbilt Complete Book of Etiquette* (New York, 1978).

Minna Allman, *Corporate Etiquette* (New York, 1970).

Lillian Hellman, *Pentimento* (Boston, 1973).

10. Talking

E. Digby Baltzell, *Philadelphia Gentleman* (Glencoe, Ill., 1958).

Packard, *The Status Seekers*.

Newsweek, April 30, 1979.

Richard P. Coleman and Lee Rainwater, *Social Standing in America* (New York, 1978).

11. Praying

Alexander Leitch, *A Princeton Companion* (Princeton, N.J., 1978).

Paul Seabury, "Trendier Than Thou," *Harper's*, October, 1978.

Sermon delivered at Grace Cathedral, San Francisco by Canon Richard N. Wilmington, October 8, 1978 (mimeograph).

Donald J. Kirchhoff, "Church Cliques Attack Democratic Capitalism," *Financier*, October, 1978.

Robert G. Kaiser and Jon Lowell, "High Above Las Vegas, a Christian Nightclub!" *The New York Times*, June 21, 1979.

12. Giving

David Heaps, "The Leisure of the Theory Class," *The New York Times*, March 13, 1979.

13. Vending Wisdom

The Consultant's Library (pamphlet: Bermont Books, Inc., Washington, D.C., 1980).

14. Male Bonding

Lionel Tiger, *Men in Groups* (New York, 1969).

15. Counter-Manners

John Bainbridge, "The Diamond-Studded Saxaphone," *The New Yorker*, April 2, 1979.

Liebow, *Tally's Corner*.

Elijah Anderson, *A Place on the Corner* (Chicago, 1978).

Calvin Trillin and Edward Koren, "Low and Slow, Mean and Clean," *The New Yorker*, July 10, 1978.

16. Nesting

Jane Davison, *The Fall of a Doll's House* (New York, 1980).
Vance Packard, *The Status Seekers*.
Richard Reeves, "Boom," *The New Yorker*, December 24, 1979.
Paul Goldberger, "Design Notebook," *The New York Times*, March 22, 1979.
Anthony Bailey, "Letter from Prague," *The New Yorker*, July 23, 1979.
Landon Y. Jones, *Great Expectations* (New York, 1980).

17. Working

Korda, *Power!*
Michael B. McCaskey, "The Hidden Messages Managers Send," *Harvard Business Review*, November–December, 1979.
Lincoln Steffens, *The Autobiography of Lincoln Steffens* (New York, 1931).
John Brooks, *Telephone* (New York, 1976).
"The Ten Toughest Bosses," *Fortune*, April 21, 1980.
The New York Times and *The New York Daily News*, September 27, 1980.

18. Dressing Up

Quentin Bell, *On Human Finery* (reissue New York, 1976).
Anne Hollander, *Seeing Through Clothes* (New York, 1978).
James Laver, *Taste and Fashion* (London, 1948).
Eve Merriam, *Figleaf* (New York, 1960).
Kennedy Fraser, "Feminine Fashions," *The New Yorker*, May 5, 1980.

19. Dressing Down

John Brooks, "A Friendly Product," *The New Yorker*, November 12, 1979.
The New York Times, May 26, 1980.
Charles Reich, *The Greening of America* (New York, 1970).
Marshall McLuhan, *Understanding Media* (New York, 1964).
Newsweek, August 21, 1972.

20. Life Parodies

Bert Cantor, *The Bernie Cornfeld Story* (New York, 1970).

Godfrey Hodgson, Bruce Page, and Charles Raw, *Do You Sincerely Want to Be Rich? The Full Story of Bernard Cornfeld and the I.O.S.* (New York, 1971).

Orville Schell, *Brown* (New York, 1978).

Richard Reeves, "How Does the Governor of California Differ from a Shoemaker?" *The New York Times Magazine*, August 24, 1975.

David Harris, "Whatever Happened to Jerry Brown?" *The New York Times Magazine*, March 8, 1980.

21. The Prophet

Dorfman, *Thorstein Veblen and His America*.

Mencken, *Prejudices: First Series*.

John Dos Passos, *The Big Money* (New York, 1937).

Max Lerner, ed., *The Portable Veblen* (New York, 1950).

David Riesman, *Thorstein Veblen, A Critical Interpretation* (New York, 1953).

Robert Heilbroner, *The Worldly Philosophers* (New York, 1953).

Leonard S. Silk, *Veblen: A Play in Three Acts* (New York, 1966).

Veblen, *The Theory of the Leisure Class*, new edition with introduction by John Kenneth Galbraith (Boston, 1973).

John P. Diggins, *The Bard of Savagery* (New York, 1978).